A Toronto Album 2

For Yarmila, who has washed my clothes, cooked my meals, been my friend, and made me look good in print.

Thanks

University Avenue and Dundas Street West, circa 1941.

Real horse power, man-made horsepower, and electric power meet at this busy downtown corner. The city's original Chinatown was to be found along streets such as Centre, Chestnut, and Elizabeth in behind the houses and shops in the background of the photo. The hulking building to the extreme left is one of the T. Eaton Company factories located close to Eaton's original main store at the northwest corner of Yonge and Queen. Note the small Simpson delivery van to the extreme right of the photograph.

A TORONTO ALBUM 2

More Glimpses of the City That Was

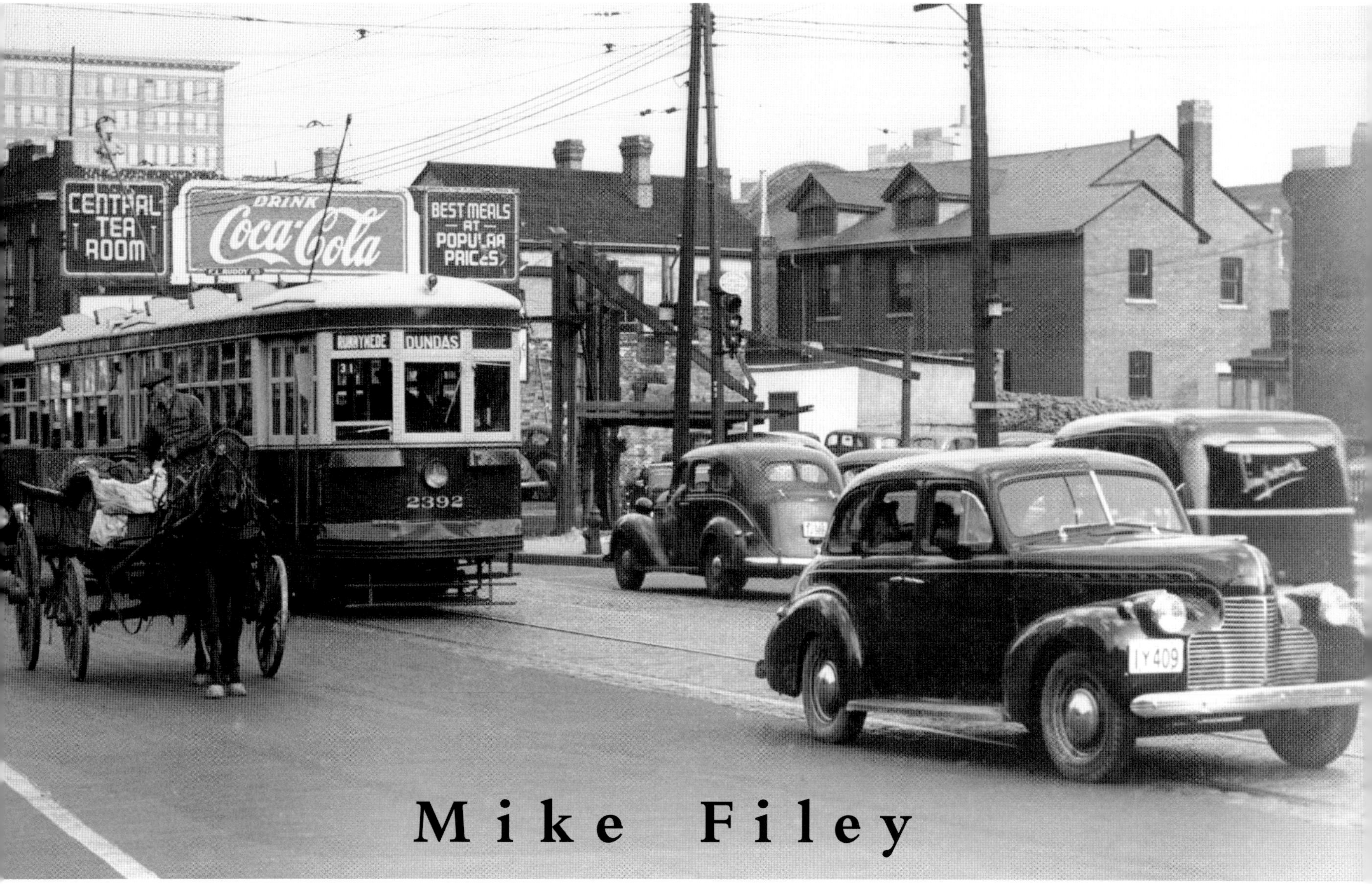

Mike Filey

THE DUNDURN GROUP
TORONTO • OXFORD

Publisher: Anthony Hawke
Copy-Editor: Andrea Pruss
Interior design and typesetting: Daniel Crack, Kinetics Design
Printer: Friesens

National Library of Canada Cataloguing in Publication Data

Filey, Mike, 1941–
A Toronto album 2 : more glimpses of the city that was/Mike Filey.

ISBN 1-55002-393-4

1. Toronto (Ont.)—History—Pictorial works. I. Title.

FC3097.37.F512 2002 971.3'54103'0222 C2002-902285-1 F1059.5.T6843F5 2002

1 2 3 4 5 06 05 04 03 02

The Canada Council for the Arts since 1957 | Le Conseil des Arts du Canada depuis 1957

Canada

ONTARIO ARTS COUNCIL
CONSEIL DES ARTS DE L'ONTARIO

We acknowledge the support of the **Canada Council for the Arts** and the **Ontario Arts Council** for our publishing program. We also acknowledge the financial support of the **Government of Canada** through the **Book Publishing Industry Development Program** and **The Association for the Export of Canadian Books**, and the **Government of Ontario** through the **Ontario Book Publishers Tax Credit** program.

Care has been taken to trace the ownership of copyright material used in this book. The author and the publisher welcome any information enabling them to rectify any references or credit in subsequent editions.

J. Kirk Howard, President

Printed and bound in Canada
Printed on recycled paper.
www.dundurn.com

Dundurn Press
8 Market Street
Suite 200
Toronto, Ontario, Canada
M5E 1M6

Dundurn Press
73 Lime Walk
Headington, Oxford,
England
OX3 7AD

Dundurn Press
2250 Military Road
Tonawanda NY
U.S.A. 14150

Introduction

When the original *A Toronto Album* was published in 1970 it consisted of 109 black-and-white photographs, each of which was accompanied by a few lines of descriptive text. There were also a few nice words from the mayor of the day, William Dennison.

The photos in the book were laid out in a sort of chronological sequence starting soon after the introduction of photography to Torontonians in the 1860s and following through to the 1940s and the years of the Second World War; the final view in the book showed preliminary work underway on the new Yonge Street subway. The opening of the subway in March 1954 was unquestionably the defining event in the city's maturation process.

Other subjects included in the book were a few old buildings, some quaint street scenes, the harbour, and lots of "ancient" streetcars. Each view was selected from old photographs I had started collecting in 1967, Canada's Centennial Year. I well remember John Fisher, the Centennial Commission's spokesman, suggesting that citizens could get in on the spirit of the year-long party by involving themselves in some aspect of Canada's past. I chose to collect old photos that portrayed my hometown's remarkable growth, and in 1970, 109 of them appeared in my first book.

Since then I've written a dozen or more books, including a reprint of my first. Like the first edition, this reprint sold remarkably well, especially for a book that's both Canadian and of local interest. In fact, the popularity of the first *A Toronto Album* prompted Hounslow Press, an imprint of Dundurn Press, which has published many of my books, to give it another try with *A Toronto Album 2, More Glimpses of the City That Was.*

In this book the subject matter is just as diverse as in the first, although with the popularity of the automobile soaring after the conclusion of the Great War and climbing steadily through the '30s, '40s, and '50s, photos of cars and trucks slowly choking Toronto streets are, of necessity, a major ingredient. In addition, some seventy-five years of changes to Toronto's skyline are highlighted, as is the unfortunate harm the city has suffered with the loss of many of its fine old buildings.

MIKE FILEY

A special thanks to Julie Kirsh and the ladies of the Toronto Sun News Research Centre.

In some cases there are only brief captions for photos. In others, captions are followed by more descriptive text about the subject in the photo.

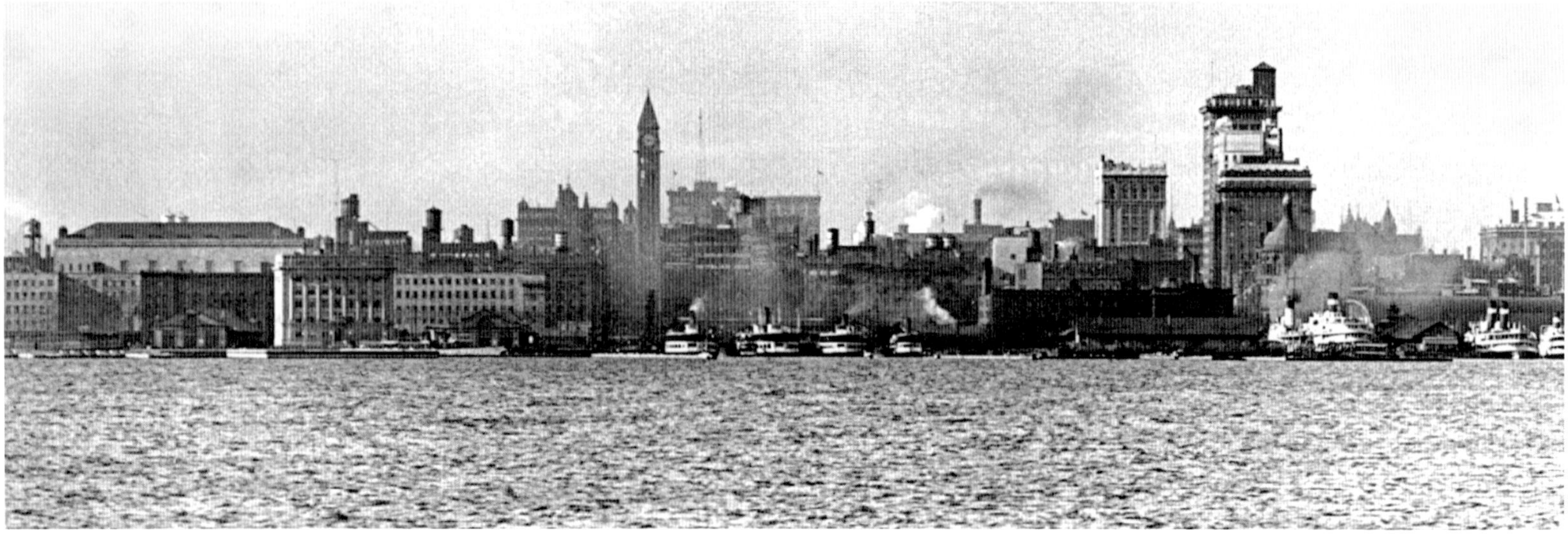

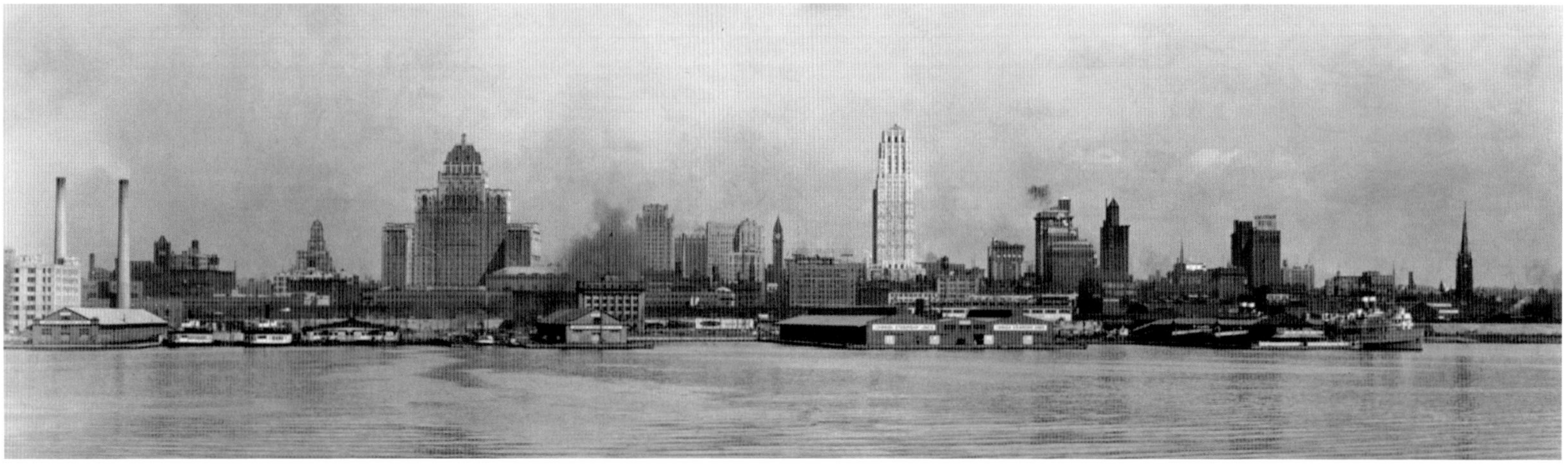

1 Circa 1925 (top)

From left to right: Union Station (ready for trains but still two years away from opening), the Toronto Harbour Commission Building (on the water's edge), the Temple Building (Toronto's first true skyscraper), the clock and bell tower of City Hall (now referred to as Old City Hall), the ferry docks, the Dominion and Royal Bank buildings and the Canadian Pacific Railway Building (all at King and Yonge intersection and all still standing), the Traders Bank Building (still standing at Yonge and Colborne street; at one time, it was the British Empire's tallest building), wharves for the lake boats, and the King Edward Hotel (celebrating its centennial in 2003).

2 1932 (bottom)

From left to right: the new Yardley Building (demolished), smoke stacks at the heating plant for the Royal York Hotel and Union Station (demolished), old Union Station, ferry boat docks, Canada Life Building, Royal York Hotel, Toronto Harbour Commission Building (no longer on the waterfront), Toronto Star Building (on King Street West, now demolished), City Hall clock and bell tower, Bank of Commerce Building (for many years the tallest building in the British Commonwealth), the trio of "ancient" skyscrapers at the Yonge and King intersection, the Metropolitan Building, King Edward Hotel and its 1920 addition, lake boat wharves, and St. James Cathedral.

Toronto's skyline and waterfront over seven decades.

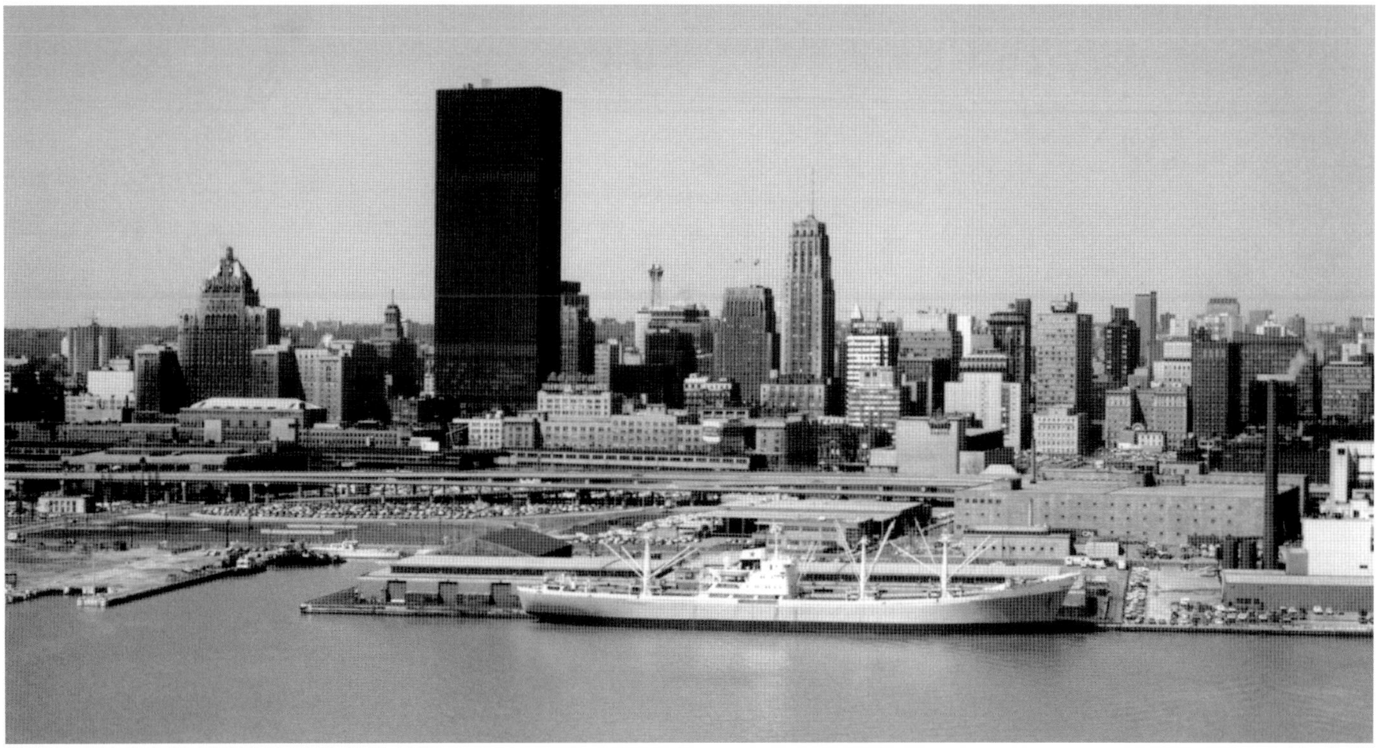

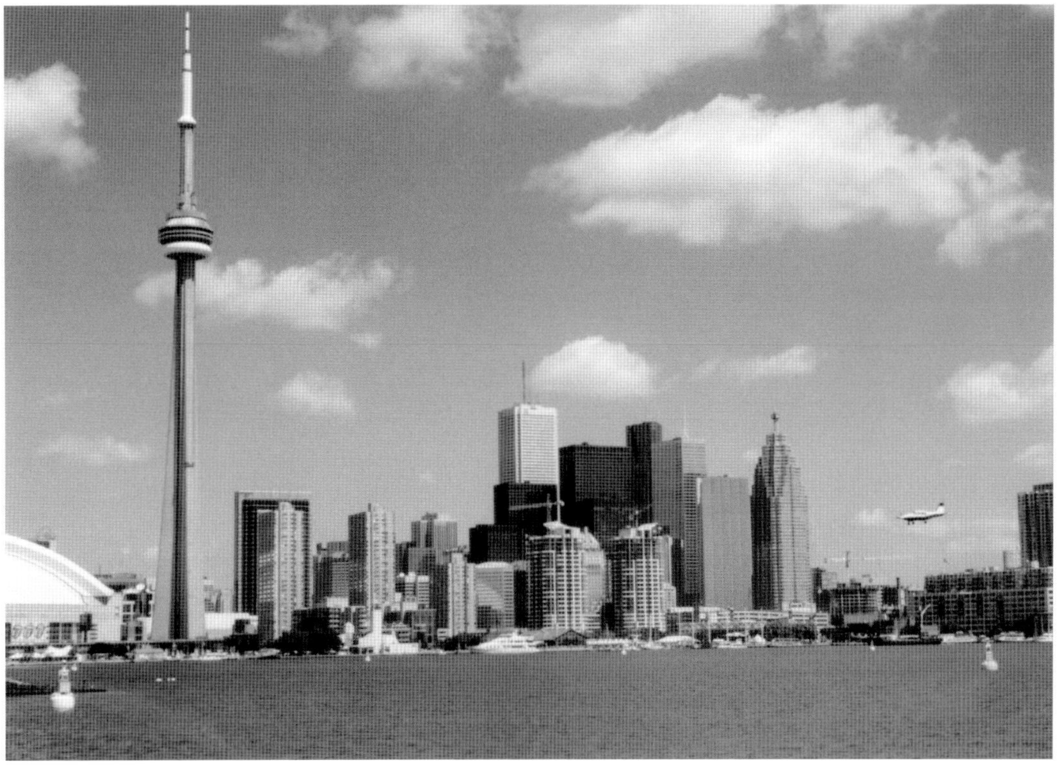

3 1970

From left to right: Royal York Hotel, Canada Life Building, T-D Centre, Toronto Star Building (peering out from behind T-D Centre), Bank of Montreal Building, Bank of Commerce, Mackenzie Building (recently converted to condominiums and offices), and, on the water's edge, the Redpath Sugar refinery.

4 2002

From left to right on skyline: SkyDome, CN Tower, First Canadian Place, Scotia Plaza, Commerce Court, Royal Bank Plaza, BCE Place, Queen's Quay Terminal, One York Quay.

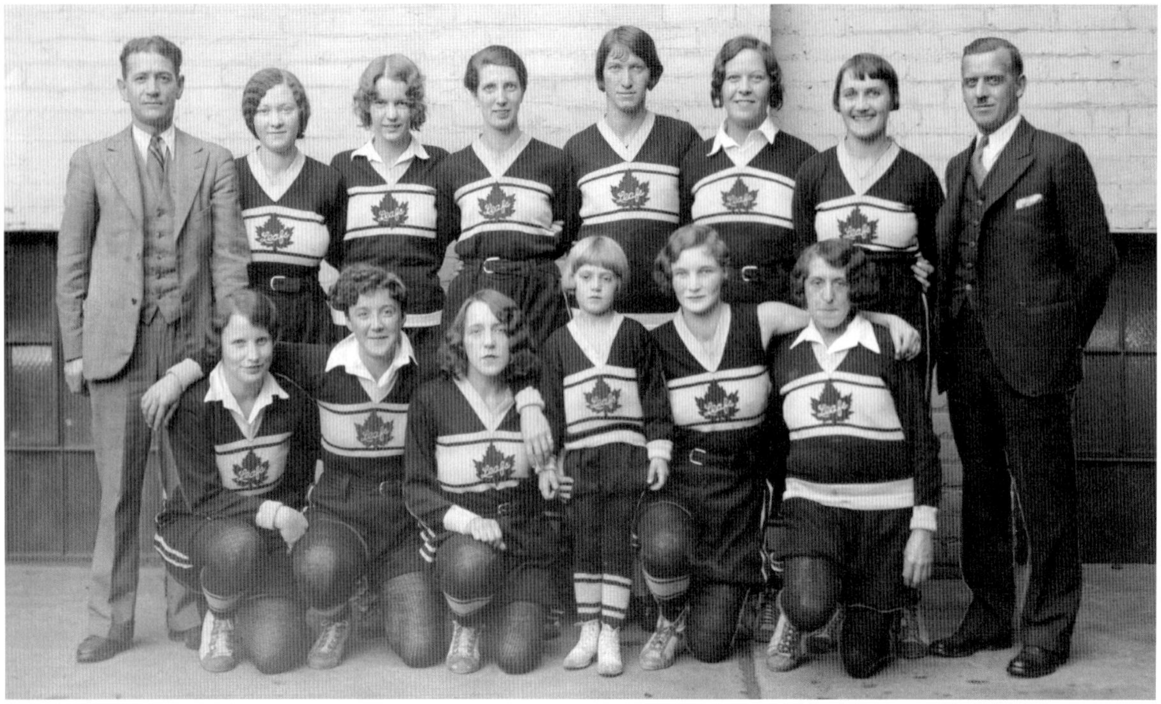

Presenting some Toronto ladies...

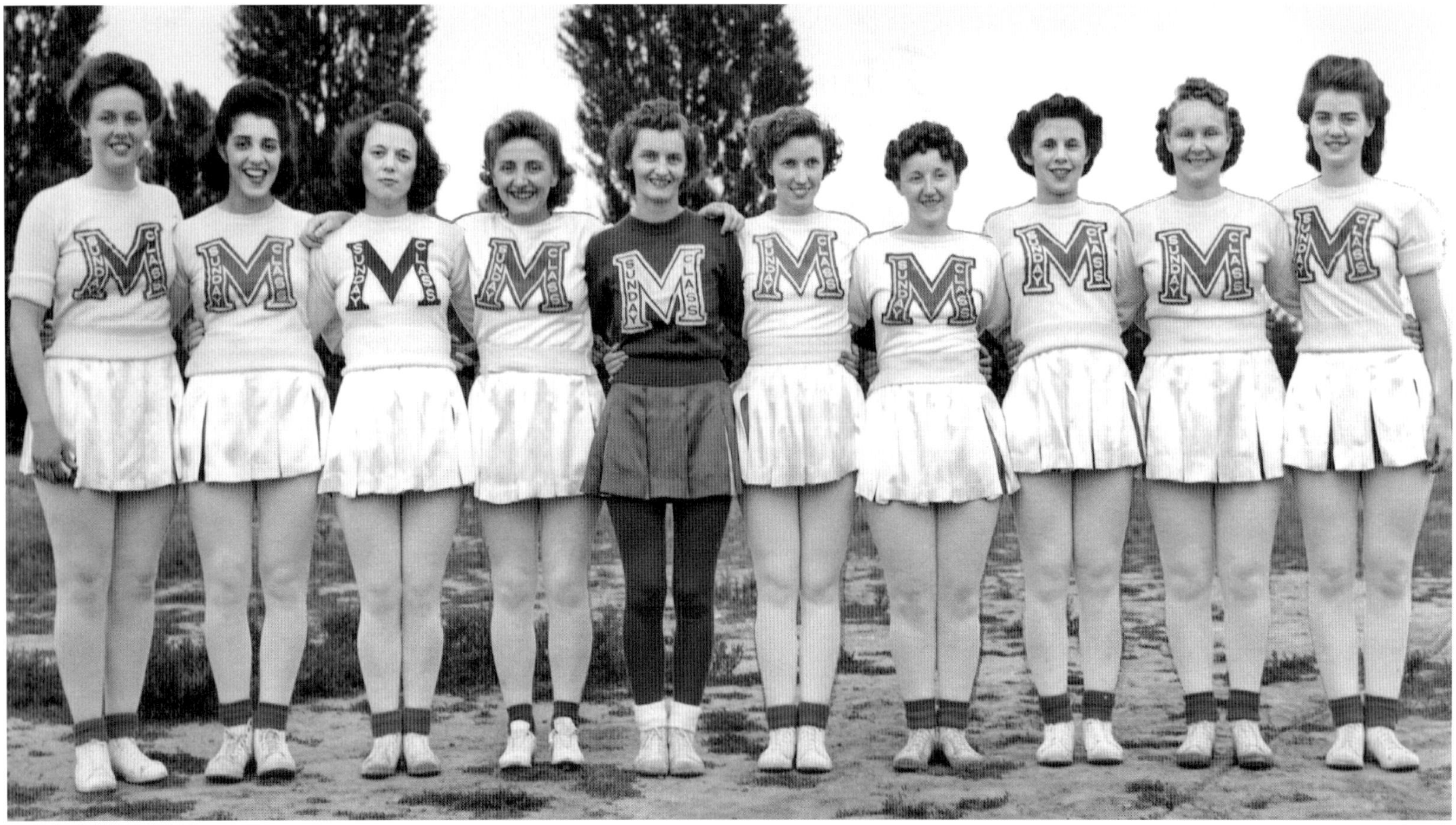

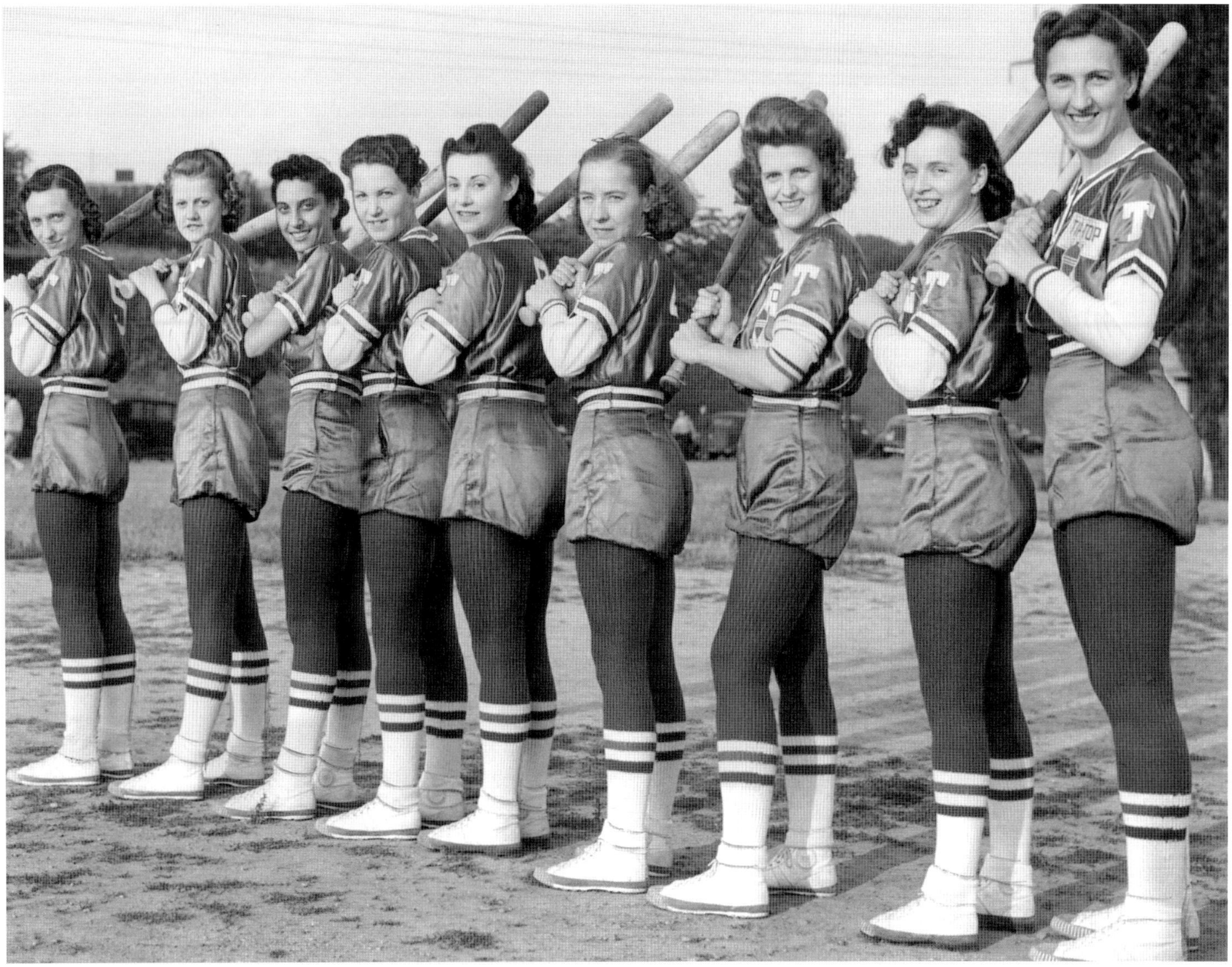

5 Sunnyside Senior Ladies Softball champions for 1930.
(facing top)

The Maple Leaf team defeated the Parksides, champions for the previous two years, at the old Sunnyside Baseball Stadium, which was located just east of the Parkdale Canoe Club (now Boulevard Club). Members of the Maple Leaf team were: (back row, left to right) Leo Goldsmith, coach; Sylvia Katzman, right field; Doris Moffatt, second base; Margaret Devere, pitcher; Bobby Rosenfeld, manager and first base; "Babs" Lopponen, right field; Audrey Dufton, third base; Al Haake, assistant coach; (front row, left to right) Jo Haake, left field; Eva Hickey, centre field; Thelma Lamb, catcher; Lily Hardy, pitcher; and Annie Miller, shortstop.

6 Sunday Morning Class Ladies Softball team, 1943.
(facing bottom)

From left to right: Verne McCormick, third base; Theresa Capalbo, pitcher; Marie Genereux, left field; Shirley Smith, second base; Isobel Denault, pitcher; Thelma McRae, short stop; Eva Burkitt, centre field; Kay Doughty, catcher; Bea Sanderson, right field; Evelyn Enright, first base and pitcher.

7 The Tip Tops Ladies Softball Team, 1941. (above)

Recognize any of these ladies?

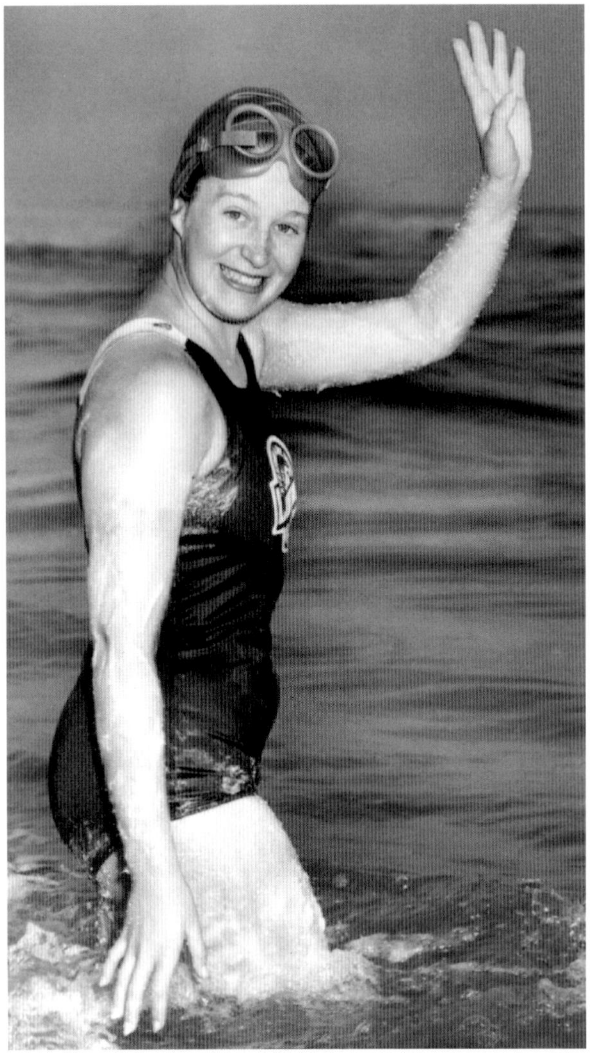

8 Marilyn Bell, the first person to swim Lake Ontario.

Many remember with great fondness and pride the exploits of a sixteen-year-old, Toronto-born schoolgirl whose unexpected triumph over Lake Ontario back in September 1954 turned the entire nation on its ear. Loretta College student Marilyn Bell was an unwelcome participant in a CNE-sponsored cross-lake solo swim offering American distance swimmer Florence Chadwick $10,000 if she was able to complete the gruelling thirty-two-mile challenge, and nothing if she was not. Chadwick was full of confidence as she entered the water at the Coast Guard Station not far from the pretty little community of Youngstown, New York, her goggle-covered eyes firmly set on the finish line miles away at the CNE waterfront. Without question, this swim would be tough — probably the toughest the American had ever faced. Nevertheless, just about everyone, including Florence, was convinced the prize-winning distance swimmer could do it. And when she did, Florence would become the first person ever to swim Lake Ontario. As for the CNE management, $10,000 was little enough to pay for the incredible exposure the Exhibition would get. And there was no doubt that the huge chunk of prize money would be quickly replaced by the thousands who would hand over the fifty-cent admission (a dime for kids) to witness Florence's historic arrival at the Ex's waterfront. Well, as they say, the best laid plans... About seven hours into the swim Chadwick was forced out of the water, complaining of nausea and cramps. The highly touted swim was over — or was it? There in the distance, well behind where Florence's handlers were busy hauling the very sick American swimmer from the lake, young Marilyn Bell was being encouraged by her coach, Gus Ryder, to keep swimming.

Actually, Marilyn's appearance in the lake was a surprise to just about everybody. There was nothing in it for her except the chance to conquer the lake "for Canada and for the kids at Ryder's Lakeshore Swimming Club." For more than twenty hours the youngster fought with the lake. In fact, in the later stages of the swim, that fight was carried on with Marilyn virtually out of it. Then, at precisely 8:04 P.M. on the evening of September 9, nearly twenty-one hours after she started, the exhausted youngster finally touched the breakwall in front of the Boulevard Club, her course altered by the high winds and unpredictable currents. Nevertheless, Marilyn Bell had done it; she had become the first person to swim Lake Ontario. And in doing so, she had actually covered a distance of sixty-four kilometres (forty miles), not the anticipated fifty-one kilometres (thirty-two miles). The management sheepishly acknowledged the youngster, and the prize money was hers, along with a huge assortment of gifts given to Marilyn by adoring Canadians from coast to coast. Her hometown awarded both Marilyn and her coach the first of the newly established Civic Awards of Merit. And as the fiftieth anniversary of this momentous event approaches, we still await decisions by the senior levels of government as to whether Marilyn Bell Dilascio deserves the Order of Ontario and Order of Canada.

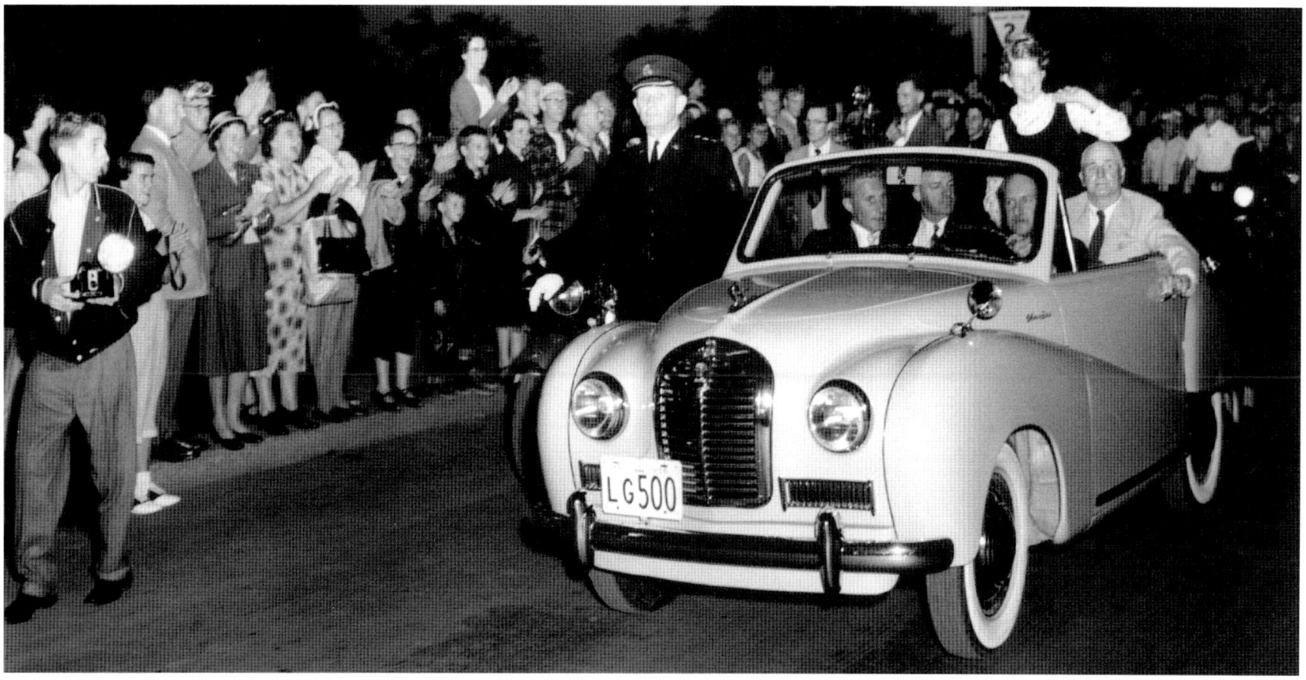

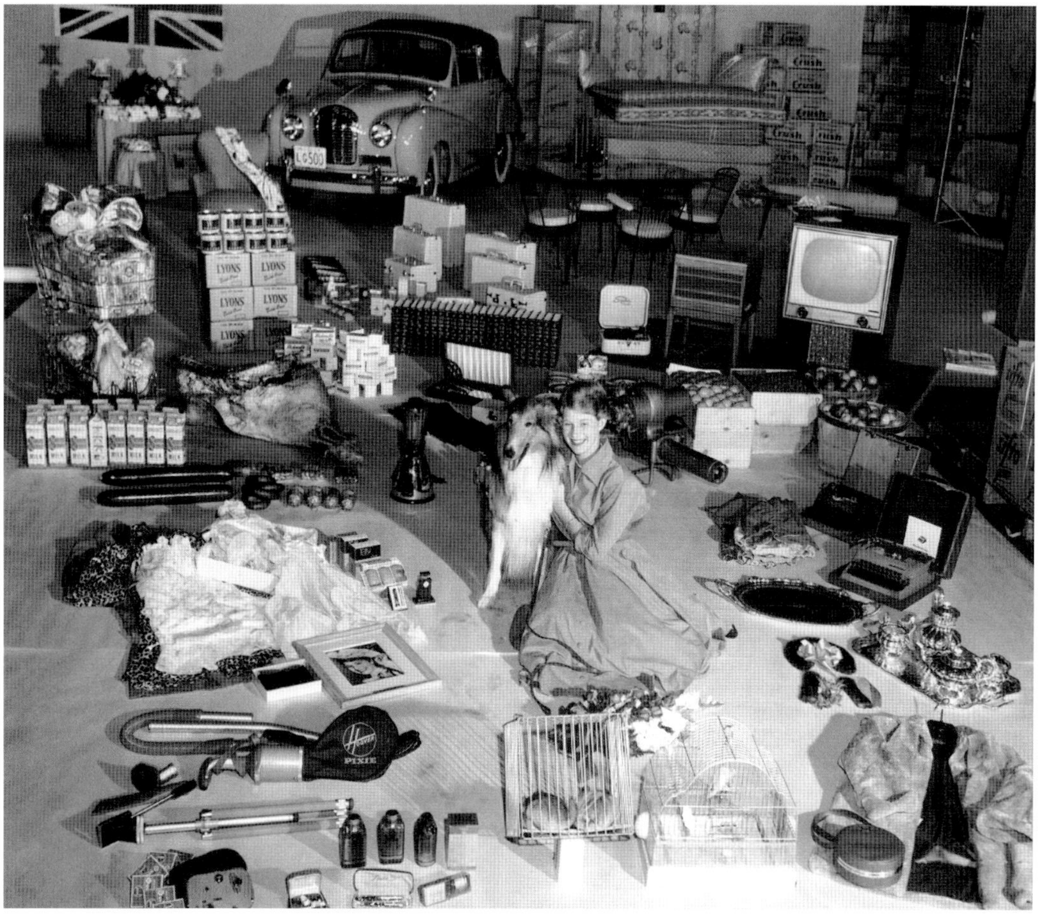

9 Sixteen-year-old Marilyn Bell waves to her fans from one of her many gifts, a brand new baby blue Austin A-40 convertible.

This car was donated by the Austin Motor Company, whose Canadian office was at the corner of Yonge and Church streets. The car was a spontaneous gift, which subsequent research reveals was worth almost $2,200.

10 Marilyn Bell, surrounded by some of the many gifts she received from admirers.

Among the presents were a two-week, all-expenses-paid vacation at any summer resort she chose, a set of the Encyclopedia Britannica, a year's supply of nylons, two steak dinners in a Toronto restaurant, a five-dollar box of chocolates and one hundred dollars cash from the Laura Secord company, a twenty-one-inch television (black and white, of course), and an assortment of pets.

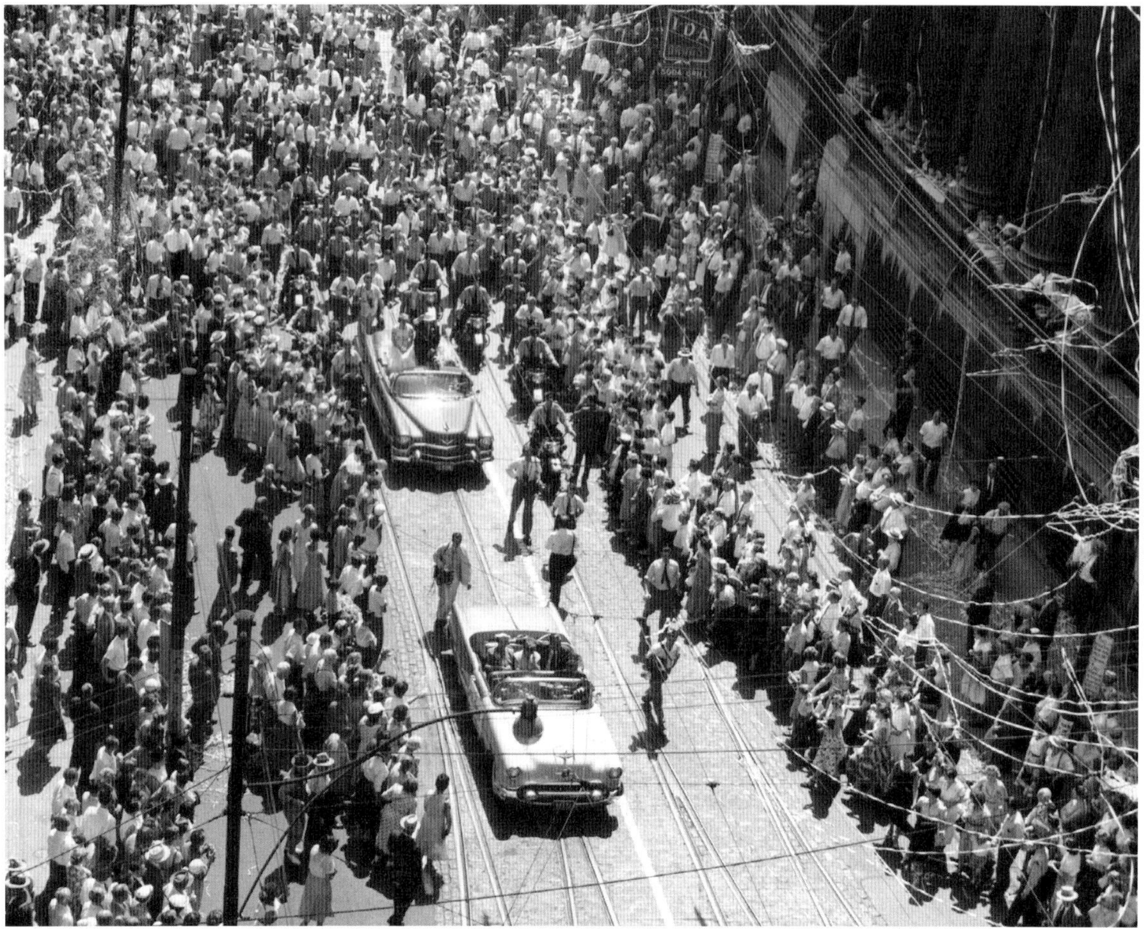

11 Marilyn Bell and her coach, Gus Ryder, acknowledge the cheering crowds during her second motorcade up Bay Street, August 19, 1955.

In this photograph, Marilyn, now seventeen years old, had just conquered the English Channel. The following year she would add a third victory with the successful crossing of the treacherous Strait of Juan de Fuca, which connects Washington State with British Columbia. This parade was done in brilliant sunshine, while the first parade, saluting her Lake Ontario swim, was done in the pouring rain.

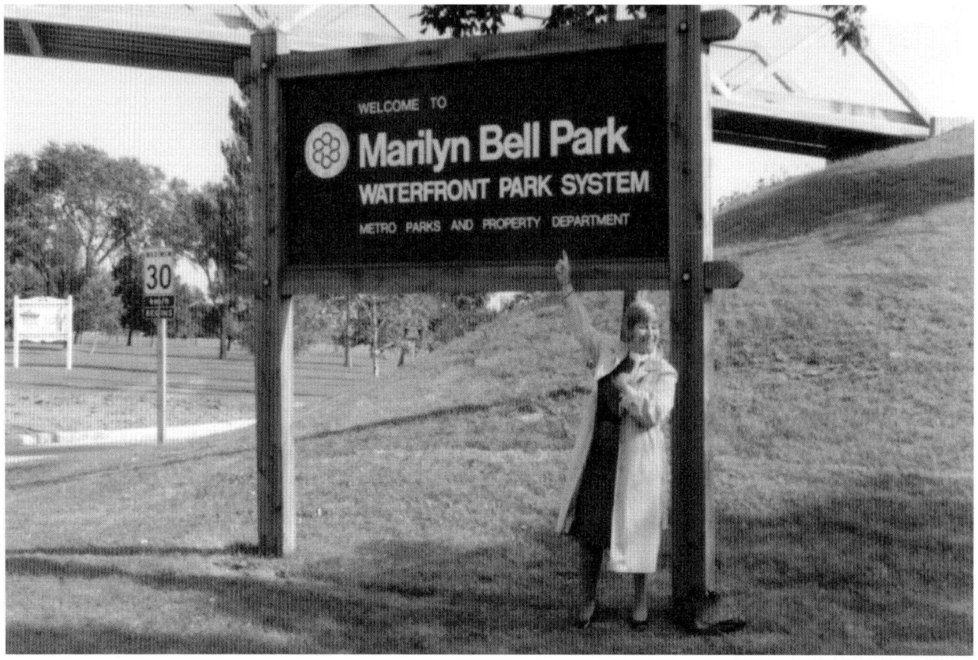

12 Marilyn Bell Dilascio, now a resident of New Jersey, visits Marilyn Bell Park during one of her frequent trips to Toronto.

Marilyn Bell Park, which was formerly known as Aquatic Park, is located due south of the Exhibition Grounds and was renamed in her honour in 1984. Earlier, Marilyn had officially opened the annual CNE — a fitting tribute, as 1984 was both the 30th anniversary of her Lake Ontario swim and the 150th year of Toronto's incorporation as a city.

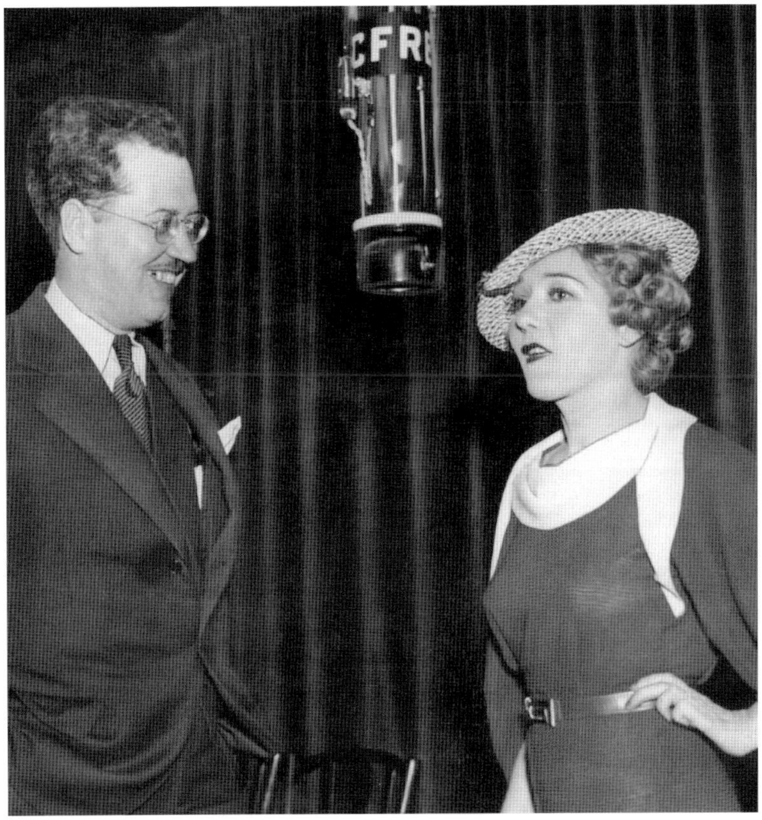

13 "America's Sweetheart," Toronto-born Mary Pickford, meets famed CFRB newscaster Jim Hunter during the actress's visit to her hometown in the city's centennial year, 1934.

Now a street lined with towering office buildings and sprawling hospitals, Toronto's University Avenue was much different when Gladys Marie Smith first saw the light of day in the tiny bedroom of number 211 on April 8, 1893. Gladys's father died when the youngster was a mere four years old, as a result of an accident on board the S.S. *Corona*, one of the many passenger steamers that operated out of the port of Toronto. Without the social safety nets we take for granted today, the Smith family was destitute. Gladys's mother, Charlotte, decided to take advantage of the acting abilities often demonstrated by her daughter, who eagerly performed in plays put on by the various stock companies that frequently visited Toronto.

Charlotte believed that by working as a child actress, Gladys could help supplement the family's meagre income. The two made the long trip to New York City, where, after much coaxing, the youngster was finally allowed to audition before the great David Belasco, one of the most influential stage producers of his day. While Belasco was impressed with Gladys's abilities, he was convinced that her real name should be changed to something "catchier." The youngster much preferred Mary to Marie. And to it she added her grandfather Hennessey's middle name, Pickford. And so it was that Gladys Marie Smith became Mary Pickford. During her career, spanning the years 1909–1933, Mary appeared in more than two hundred silent motion pictures. During that time, she was often described as the "most popular woman in the world." Mary Pickford died in 1979 at the age of eighty-seven.

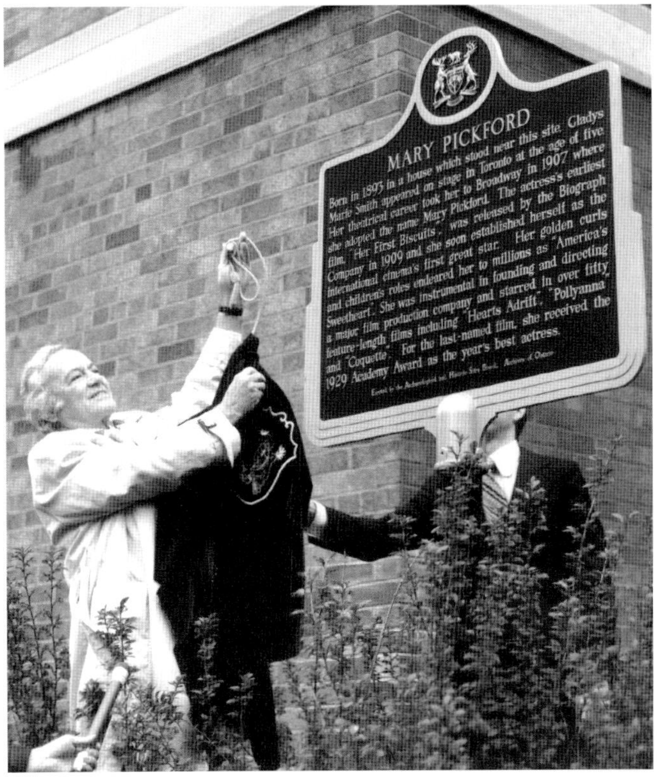

14 Mary Pickford's husband, Charles "Buddy" Rogers, unveils an Ontario Heritage Foundation commemorative plaque honouring the world's first motion picture star and "America's Sweetheart," Toronto's own Mary Pickford, in 1973.

The plaque, one of more than eleven hundred OHF plaques throughout the province, is located on the lawn of the Hospital for Sick Children on University Avenue, on a site not far from Mary's birthplace. When the old house was demolished in 1943, many of its bricks were removed to Mary's residence in California, where, she remarked, they continuously reminded her of "home." While the plaque, along with almost all biographical material written by or about Mary, claims she was born in 1893, her official birth certificate reveals she was actually born one year earlier. But we all know that when it comes to age, it's not nice to correct a lady. Next to the plaque is a sculpted likeness of Mary by artist Eino Gira that was unveiled ten years after the plaque.

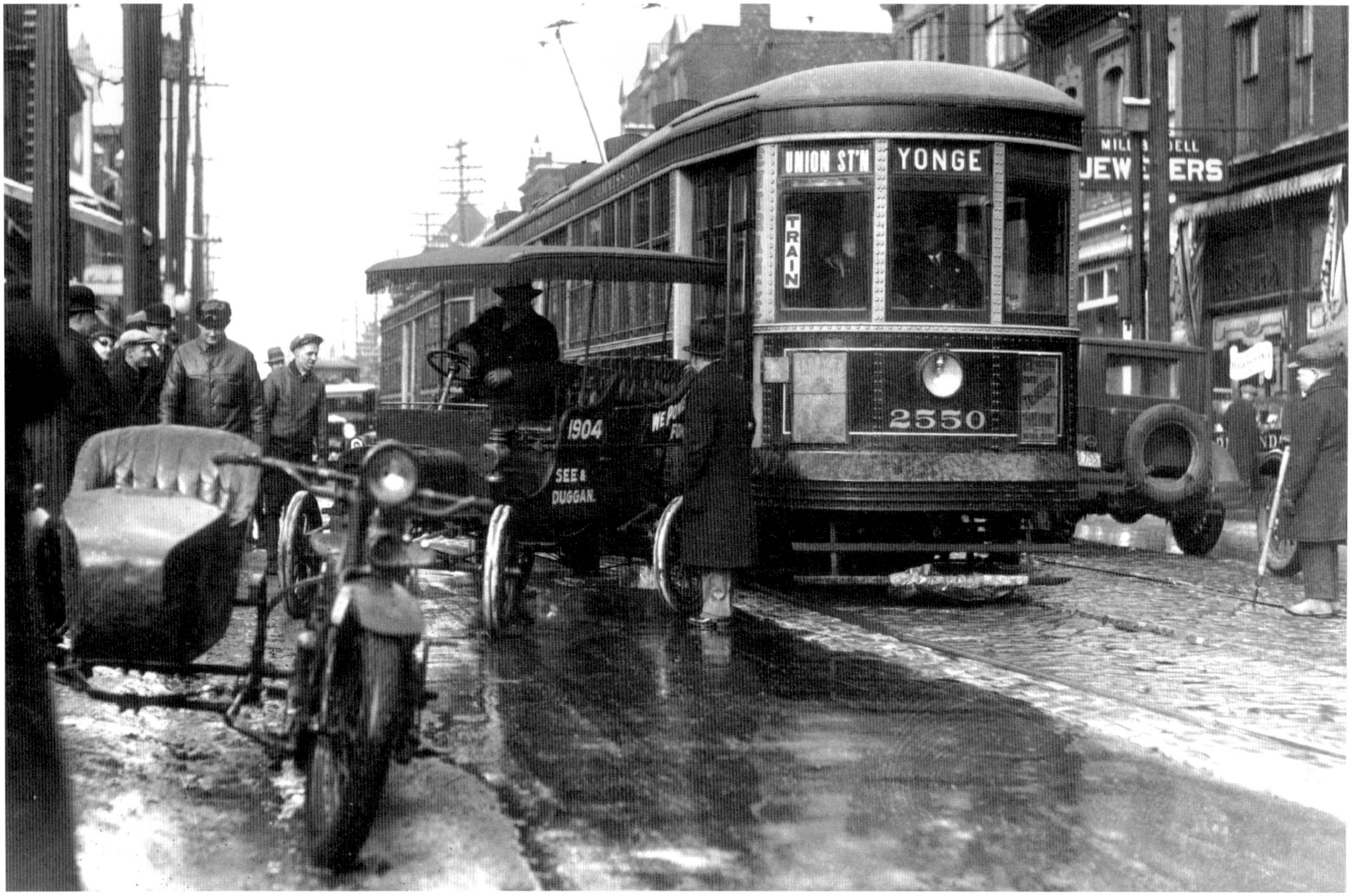

15 Yonge Street looking north towards College Street, circa 1926.

The sign in the front window of this Toronto Transportation Commission Peter Witt streetcar (named in honour of its designer, a Cleveland, Ohio transit expert) reveals that the car is headed for Union Station on Front Street. However, at the time this photo was taken that would not have been the present Union Station but rather the 1873 station located on the south side of Front Street west of York Street. While construction of the new station had been finished for several years, the final alignment of the tracks serving it had yet to be given the necessary approvals, thereby rendering the station useless. In fact, the travelling public wasn't able to use the present Union Station until late summer 1927 and even then only on a limited basis. Nothing has ever been easy down on Toronto's waterfront. The "flivver" in the view is a 1904 Ford owned by See and Duggan Motors, one of the city's pioneer car dealers, whose showroom was on the east side of Yonge Street several blocks south of the Bloor Street corner. To the left of the view is a police officer returning to his motorcycle after checking out what was holding up traffic. The buildings in the background were demolished in 1930–31 when the Yonge-College-Carlton intersection was realigned into its present configuration.

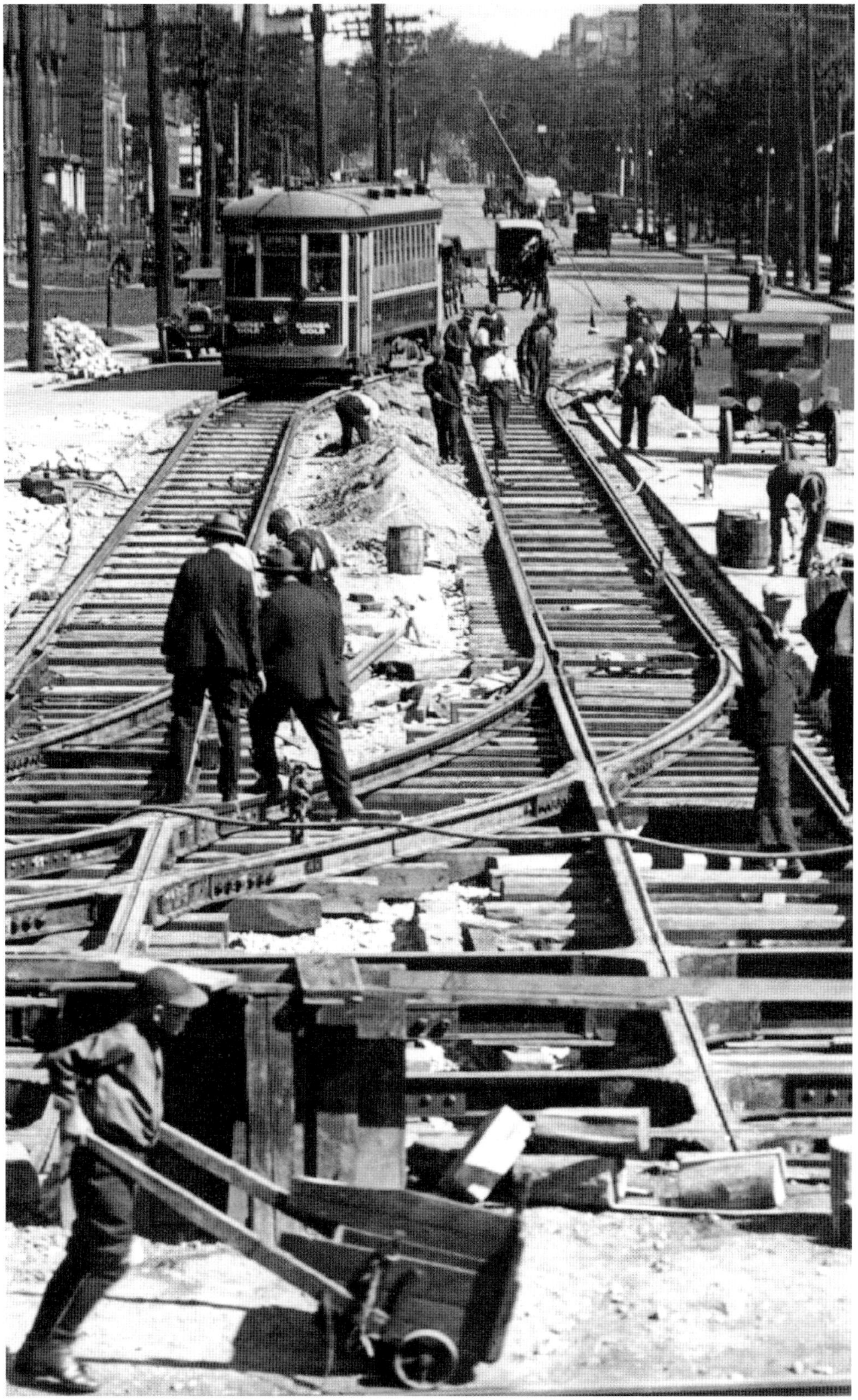

16 Looking north up Spadina Avenue from Front Street in the late summer of 1926.

Public transit first came to Spadina Avenue in the form of horse-drawn streetcars in 1878. In 1891 the street became the western leg of the new streetcar "Belt Line" route that also included Bloor, Sherbourne, and King. One year later electrically operated vehicles began replacing those pulled by horses, and by August 31, 1894, all of the city's routes had been electrified. The Belt Line vanished in 1923, and Spadina once again got a route in its own name, with double-end cars operating in a traffic-free centre boulevard from Front Street on the south end to a northern terminus at Bloor Street. In 1927 the south end was extended via a new bridge over the myriad of steam railway tracks south of Front Street to a thoroughfare called Fleet Street, which was renamed Lake Shore Boulevard West in 1960. Following the end of the Second World War most Ontario communities were faced with a severe shortage of electricity. In an effort to lessen the impact on power-hungry Toronto, the TTC converted two of its electric routes, the North Yonge radial line to Richmond Hill and the entire Spadina line, to gas buses. Then on July 27, 1997, the new Spadina LRT (Light Rail Transit, a fanciful name for streetcars in a traffic-free corridor) line opened, the city's first new major streetcar line in almost seventy years. In this photograph TTC crews extend the tracks over the new Spadina bridge, which was built over the railway tracks south of Front, to the route's new southern terminus at Fleet. Note one of the special "double-ended" streetcars approaching Front Street. Further north and somewhat hidden by the trees at the top right of the photo is Clarence Square, a planner's interesting dream to break up the city's monotonous street grid pattern — which, with the construction of Rennie's hulking seed warehouse nearby, didn't quite make it.

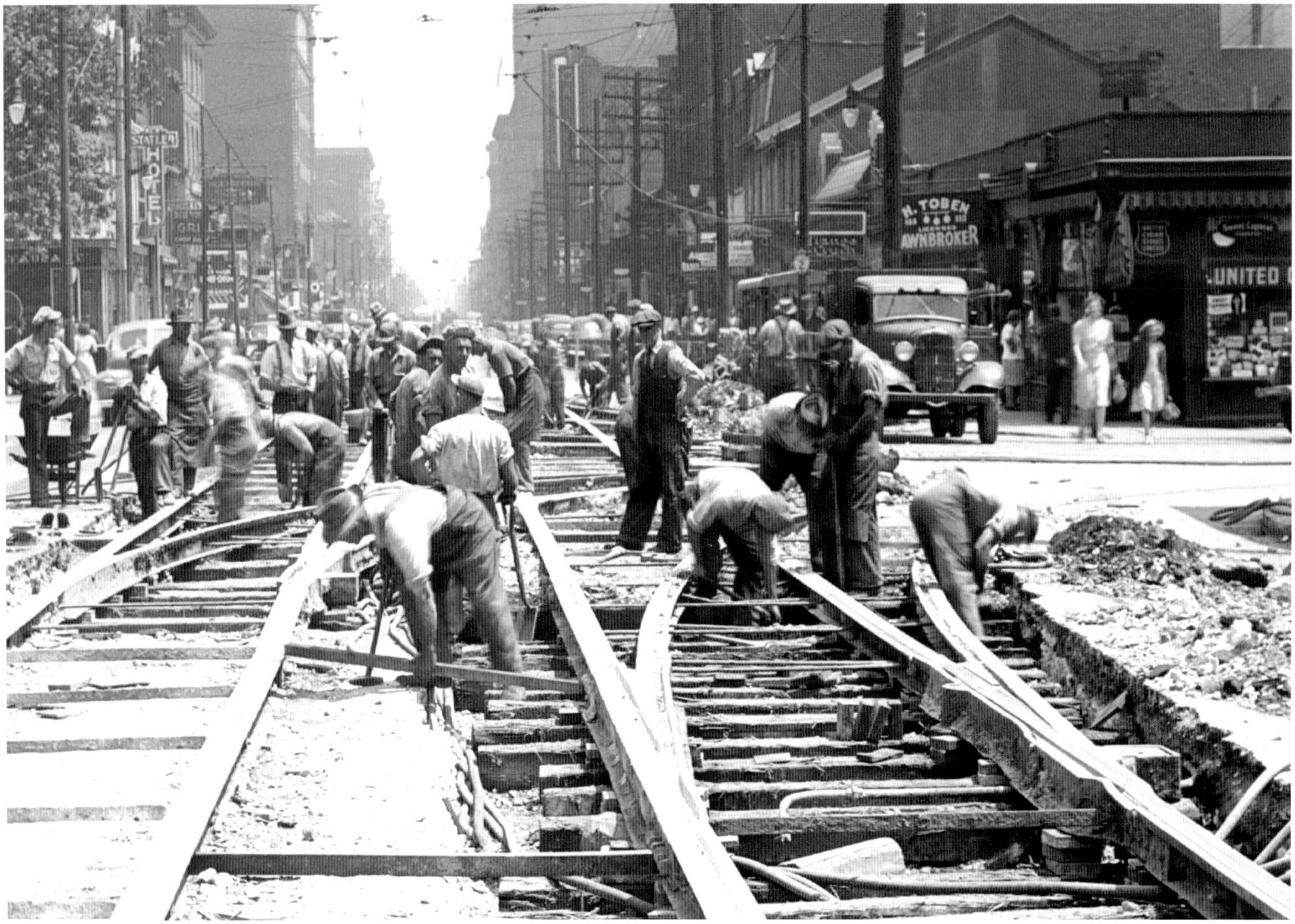

17 Looking east on Queen Street at York Street, 1946.

Ongoing maintenance of streetcar tracks has always been (and continues to be) a major concern of the TTC as well as a major component of its annual budget. In the background at left we can see the Casino Theatre, which started out as a burlesque house in 1936. Its chorus lines bounced their way across the theatre's stage until 1951, when the place changed its policy and began featuring up-and-coming recording stars such as Patti Page, Rosemary Clooney, Tony Bennett, Kay Starr, Julius LaRosa, Johnnie Ray (the most popular individual to ever appear at the theatre), and Toronto's own Four Lads, to name just a few. Every once in a while long-time motion picture personalities like Mickey Rooney, Gordon McRae, the Three Stooges, Van Johnson, and Huntz Hall and Gabe Dell of Bowery Boys fame would come to town in an effort to supplement their dwindling incomes. One young comic from Denmark, who also happened to play the piano, made his Canadian debut at the Casino. His name was Victor Borge. The Casino, along with all the other businesses on the south side of Queen, was displaced by today's mammoth Sheraton Centre Hotel. One such enterprise, an ancient pawnbroker's shop known as Henry's, lives on today as the highly successful Henry's photography emporium. On the north side of Queen Street, the Statler Hotel is now the Rex, and Toronto's two city halls, new and old, occupy property in the left background.

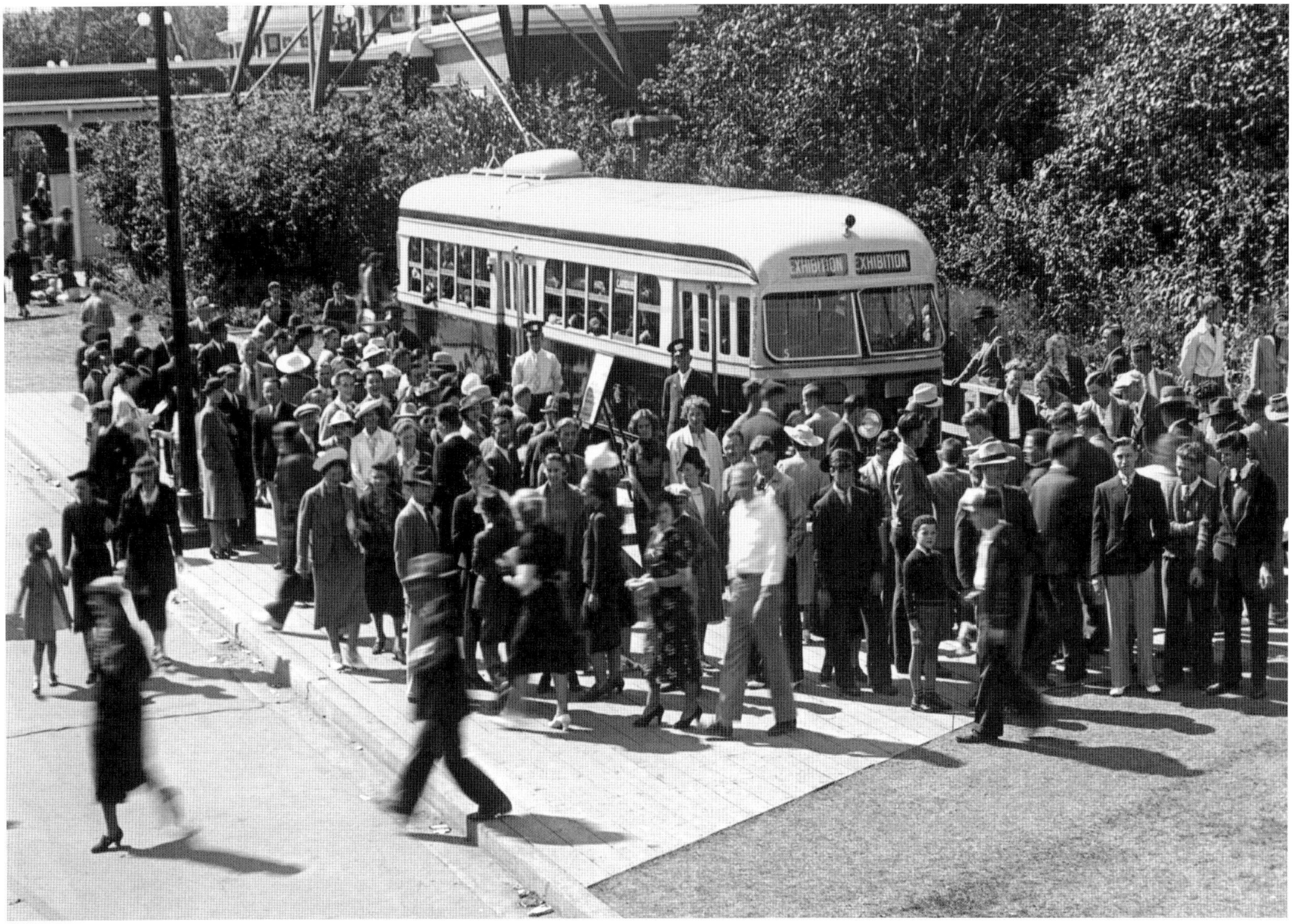

18 Toronto's new streetcars on display at the Dufferin Street Entrance to the Canadian National Exhibition, 1938.

One of the feature attractions at the annual CNE in 1938 was the TTC's newest model streetcar. It was known as the Presidents' Conference Committee (PCC) Streamliner, and two cars were featured that year: #4001, shown here just inside the Dufferin Gate, and #4002, on display outside the Coliseum near the East Streetcar Loop, on a site now occupied by the National Trade Centre's Heritage Court. At that time, the PCC car, having been developed with input from representatives of public transit companies in both the United States and Canada, was considered state of the art in public transit vehicles. For various reasons, initial sales of the new model weren't as high as expected. However, the TTC's first order for 140 vehicles helped ensure the eventual success of the PCC, and by the time manufacturing of this model ended, more than 5,000 PCCs had been built, with many more variants of the car manufactured overseas. Over the years, the TTC operated a total of 745 PCC cars, and while most were purchased new, more than 200 were acquired as used vehicles from transit companies eager to convert from streetcars to gasoline and diesel-powered buses. The last PCCs in the commission's streetcar fleet were retired from regular service in 1995, with two of the cars, #4500 and #4549, retained for special charter service.

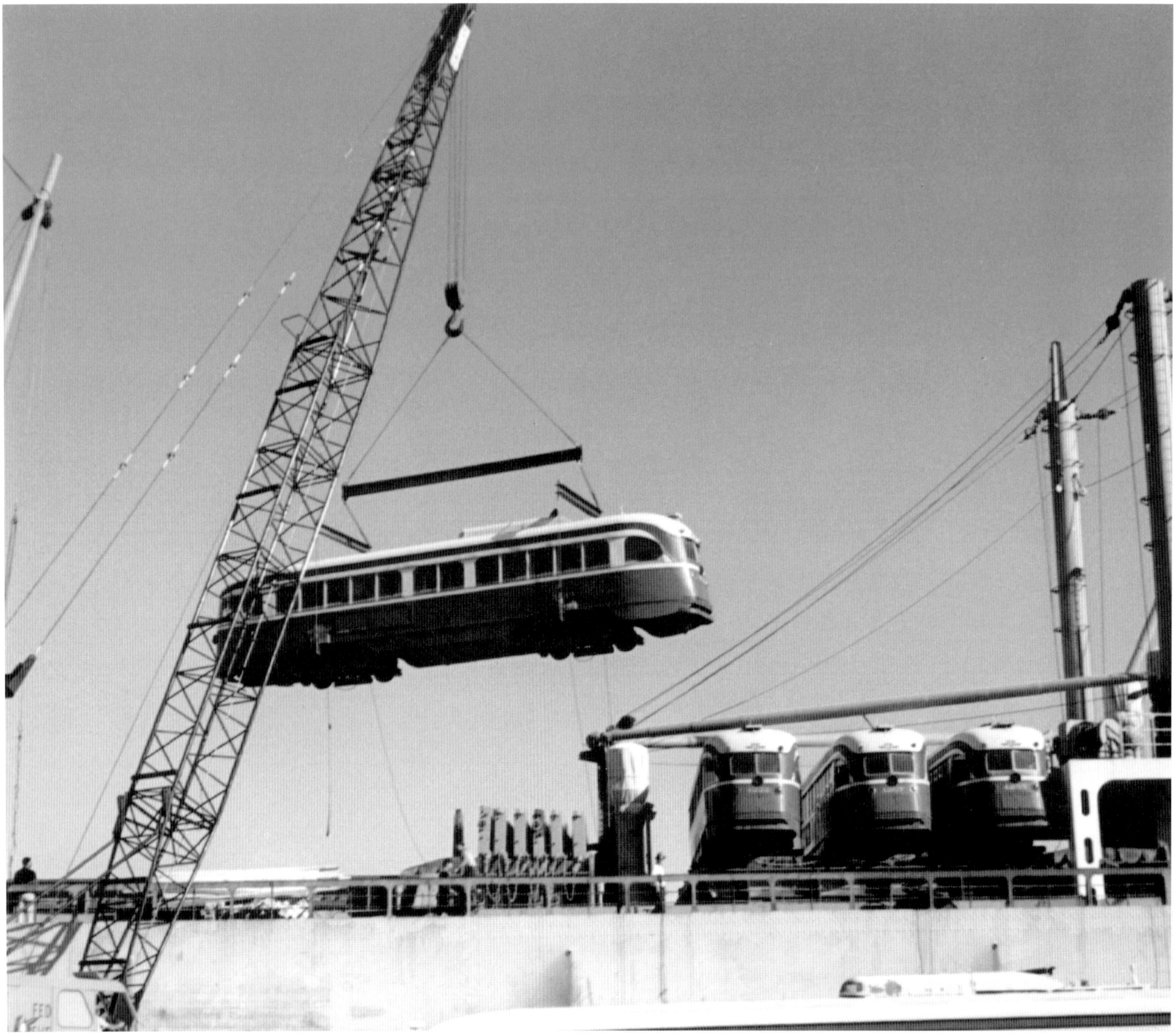

19 Toronto streetcars on their way to Egypt, July 1968.

After millions of miles on the streets of Toronto, many of the TTC's aging PCC cars were to soon see more miles of service on the streets of Alexandria, Egypt. The purchase of 140 PCC cars took place between the fall of 1966 and mid-summer 1968. In this photograph, one of the last of the 76 cars transported from Toronto to Alexandria on board the S.S. *Mare Tranquillo* is hoisted onto the deck where it sat with others perched on a hold full of corn.

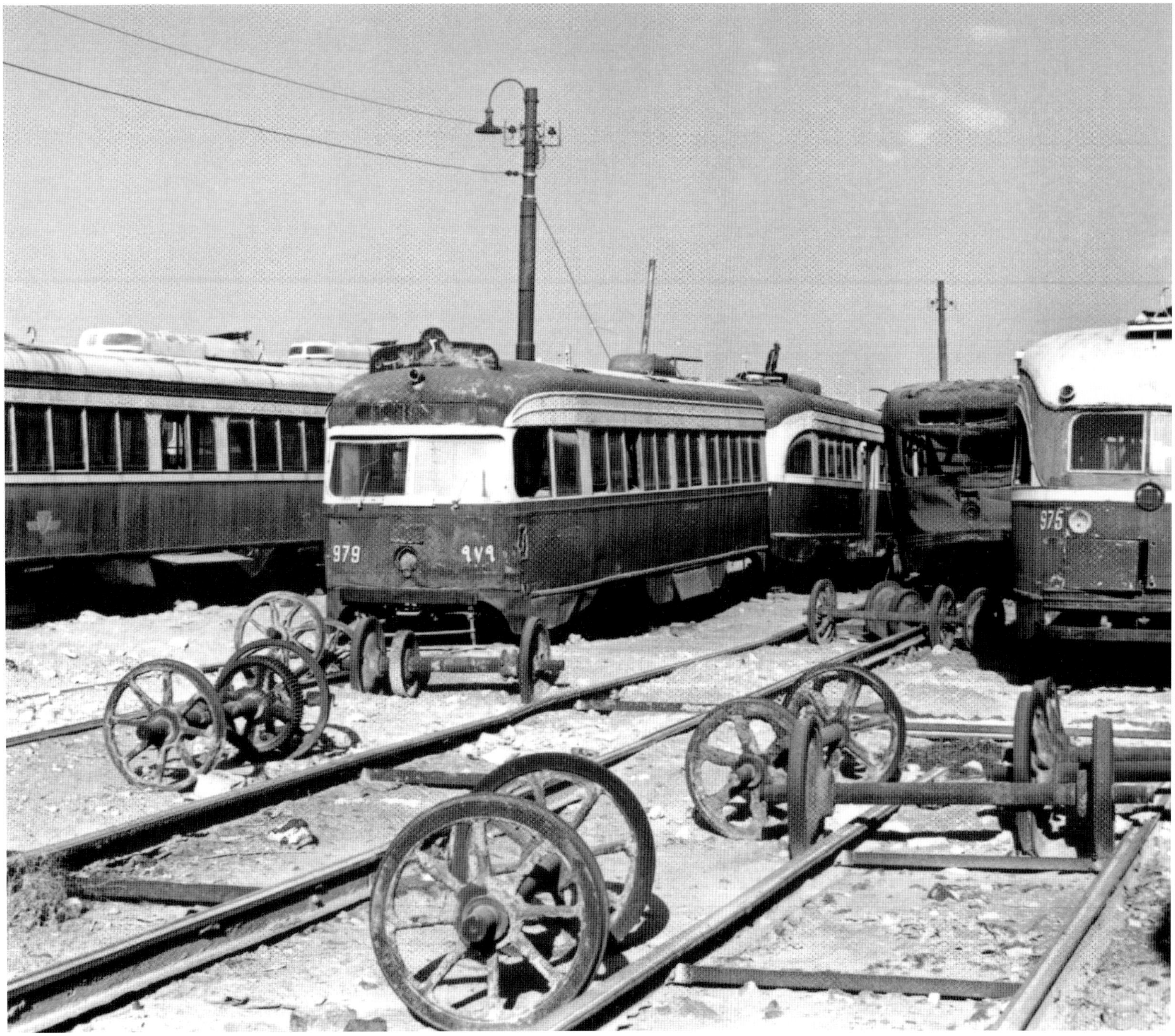

20 Streetcar "graveyard" in Alexandria, Egypt, 1968. — *Courtesy M.J. Russel*

In June 1967, several months after the arrival of the first 47 Toronto PCC cars, war broke out between Israel and the surrounding Arab countries. While it is known that many vehicles in the Alexandria streetcar fleet were damaged or destroyed during the hostilities, what is not known is whether any Toronto PCCs were among them. This view of a streetcar storage yard in Alexandria shows several damaged PCC cars. A TTC logo is evident on the car to the extreme left.

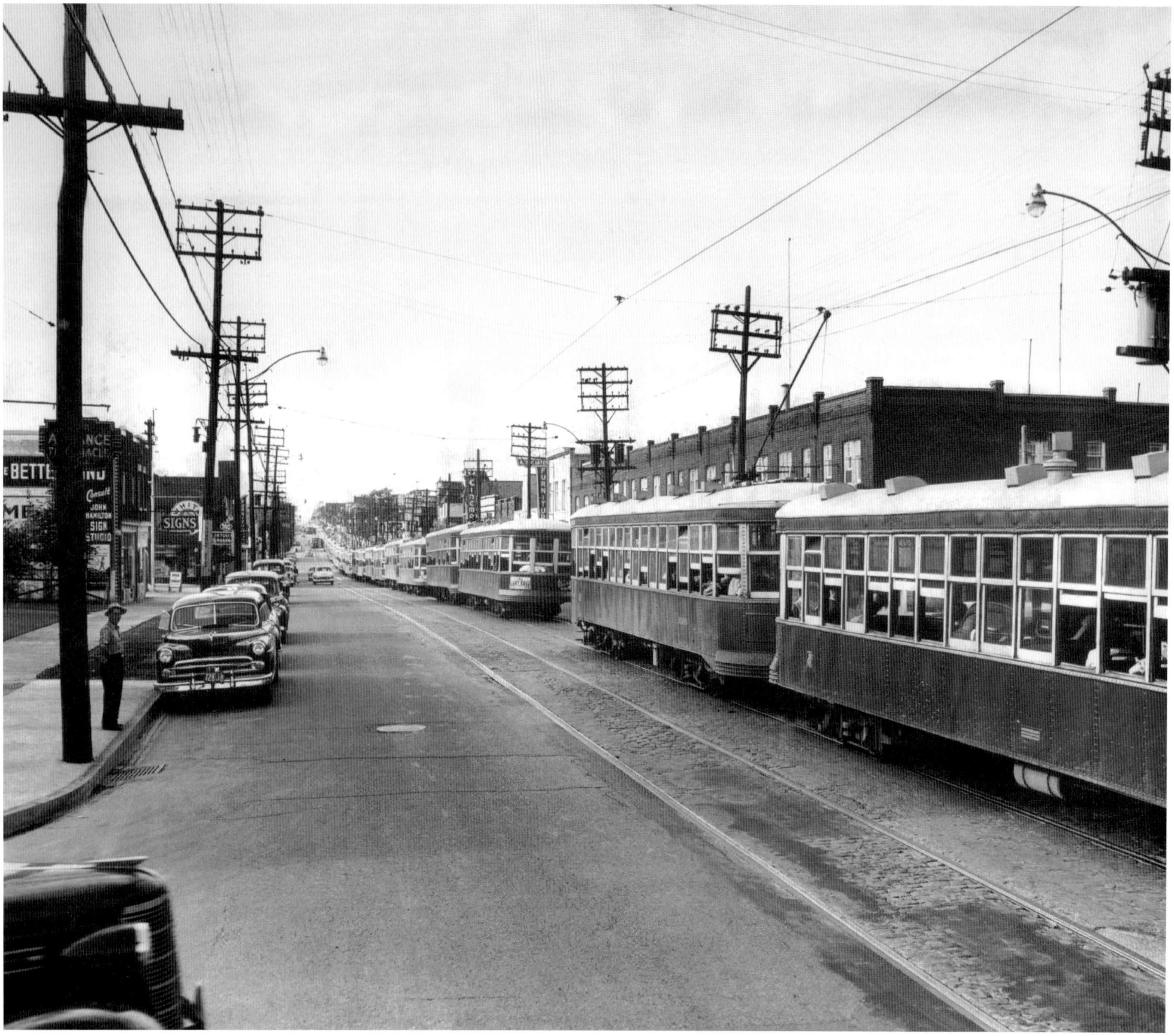

21 Yonge Street looking north at Belsize Drive, 1953.

The need for a subway under Toronto's main north-south artery as soon as possible is obvious from this photograph. Something has happened near the Eglinton intersection, resulting in a backup of Peter Witt motors and trailers as far as the eye can see. Signs of an earlier Toronto are also evident in the view; the White Rose gas station is in the distant left, while a little further north on the opposite side of the street is the International Cinema.

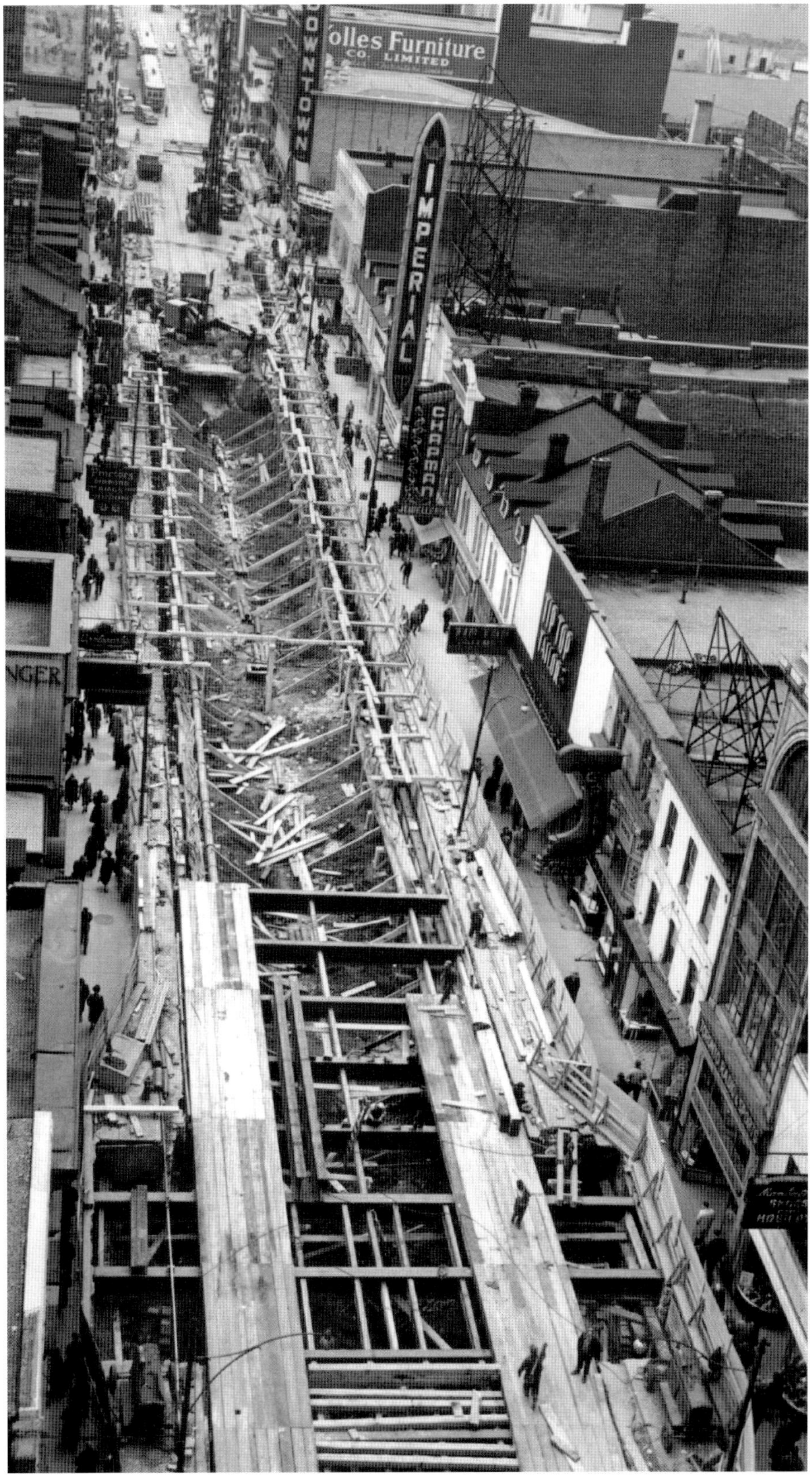

22 Yonge Street looking north to the Dundas Street intersection, April 1949.

The idea of building a "tube" or subway to serve downtown Toronto was first discussed as early as 1909, when an American consulting firm completed an in-depth study of the city's traffic problems and reported that a tube under Bay and Terauley streets from Front Street to St. Clair Avenue would be the only way to alleviate congestion in the downtown core. As a result, the suggestion that tubes be built was placed on the 1910 and 1912 municipal ballots, and while the idea was approved by the electorate both times, nothing happened.

As the years passed, the idea of a subway for Toronto was discussed several more times, including a plan put forward during the Depression to build "a big ditch" in the middle of Yonge Street in which the Yonge streetcars would operate. To ensure that as many men as possible got employment, virtually the entire project would be done using picks and shovels. Again, nothing happened. Anticipating traffic chaos in Toronto once the war was over (whenever that might be) the TTC set up a Subway Department in 1944 to begin studying the idea — what would later become the 7.4-kilometre (4.6-mile), 12-station Yonge Street subway operating from Union Station to Eglinton Avenue. In late 1946, the electorate again approved the construction of a subway, on the condition that the federal government would contribute to the estimated $35-million cost. No federal money was ever forthcoming, and the final price tag on the project ballooned to $66 million. Actual construction of the Yonge subway commenced on September 8, 1949, and 1,664 days later the new line, Canada's first, was opened with appropriate ceremonies at the new Davisville Station. In this view the "cut and cover" method of subway construction (close the roadway, cut a ditch, cover over the ditch, and reopen the road) is underway in the stretch of Yonge between Shuter and Dundas streets. Visible on the east side of Yonge Street are two Toronto theatres, the now demolished Downtown and the Imperial, which opened as the Pantages and was then successively named the Imperial, the Imperial 6, the Pantages (again), and now the Canon Theatre.

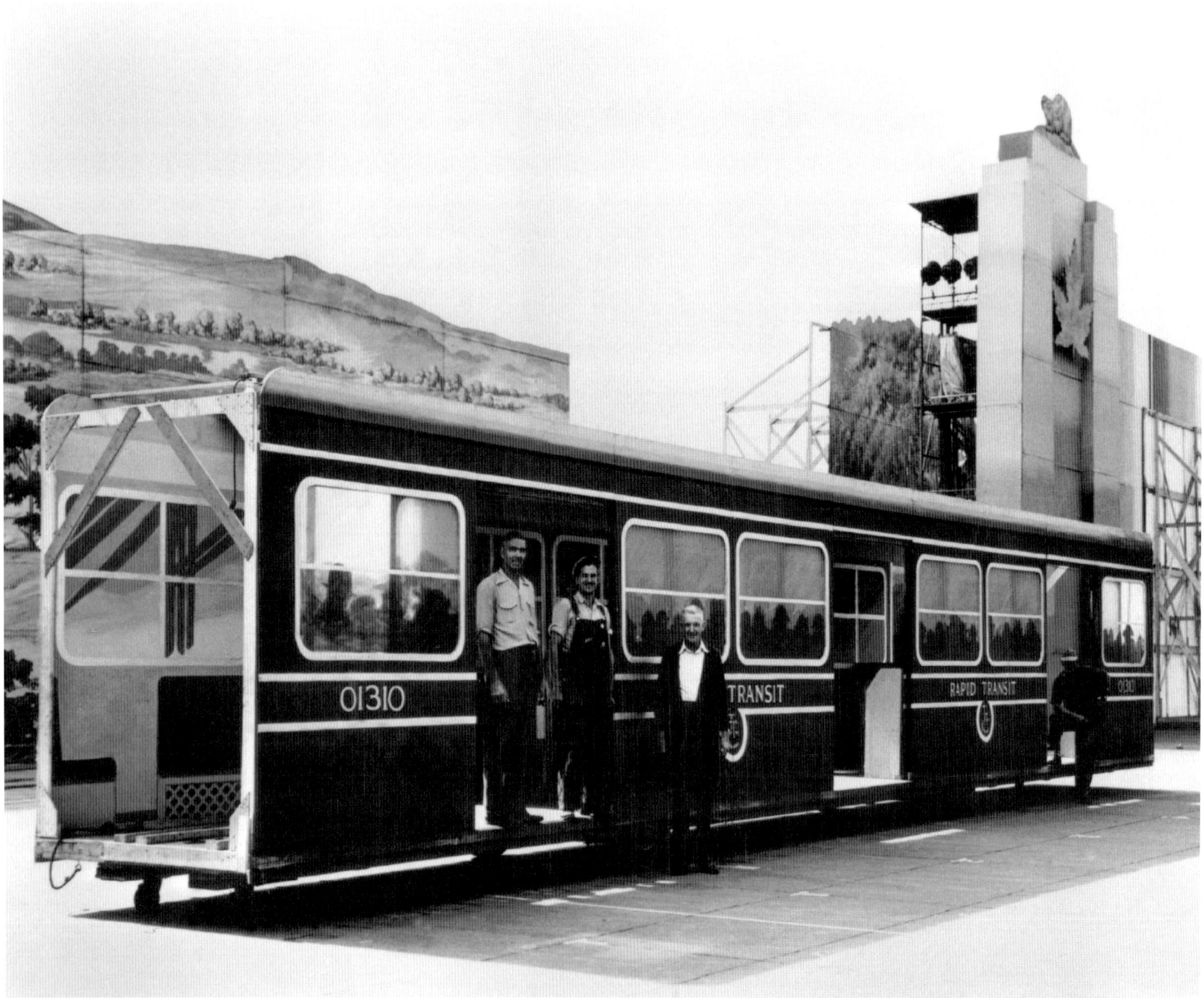

23 Mock-up of Toronto's new subway cars on display at the 1952 Canadian National Exhibition.

In 1951, as construction of the new Yonge Street subway proceeded, an $8-million order for 104 subway cars (100 cars were actually on hand when the subway opened on March 30, 1954) was placed with the Gloucester Railway Carriage and Wagon Company in England. The following year, in an effort to give its future subway riders an idea of what the new subway cars might look like, the TTC featured this wooden mock-up on the CNE Grandstand stage. Scenery for the evening Grandstand spectacular titled "Canadiana," featuring American singing star Tony Martin, can be seen behind the car. The real things appeared at the 1954 CNE, continuing the long tradition of seeing Toronto's newest transit equipment first at the annual Exhibition.

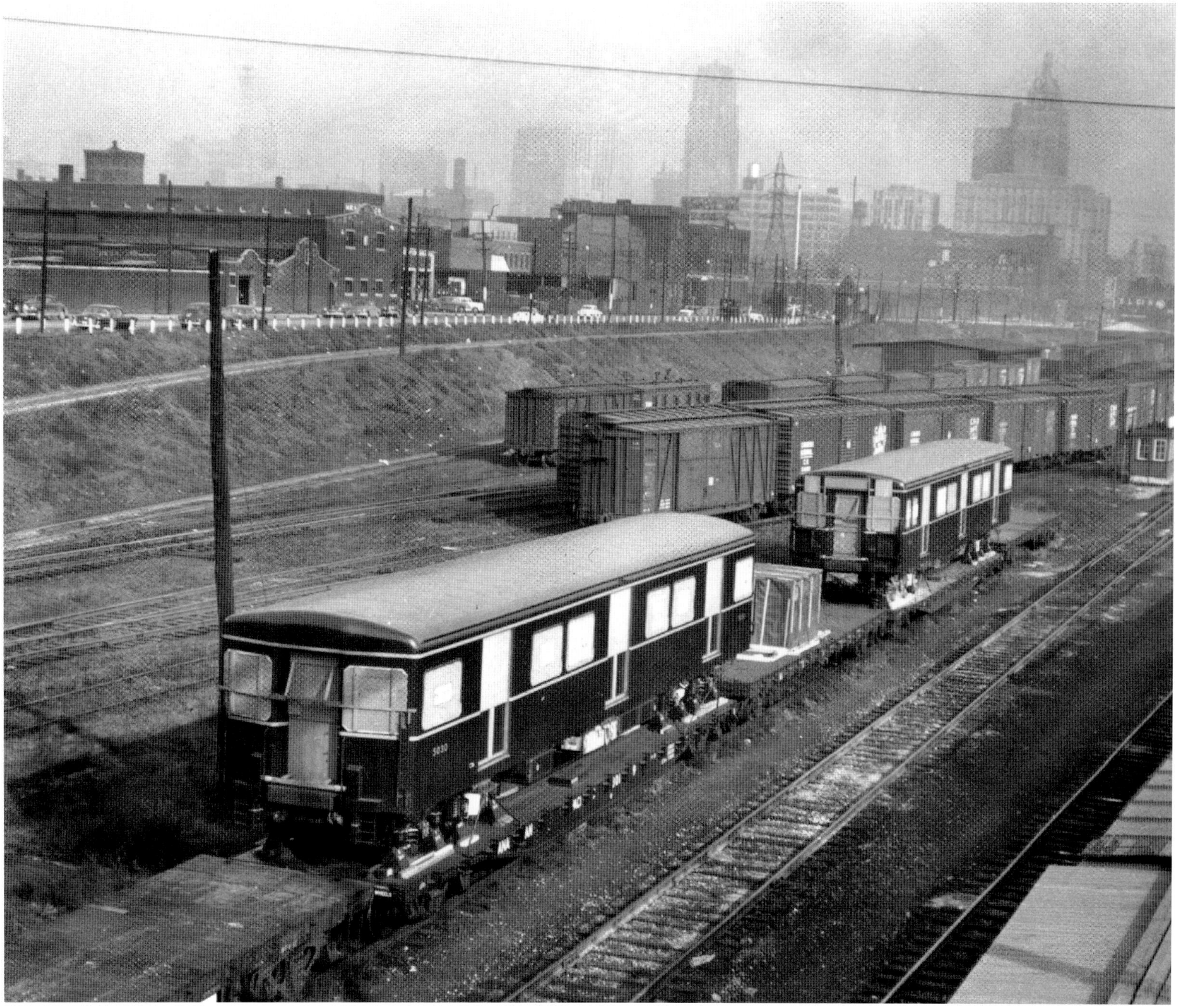

24 Two English-built "red" cars for the new Yonge Street subway arrive in Toronto, 1956.

The cars shown in this photograph, which was taken from the old Spadina bridge, are two of the last twenty-six subway cars to be built in England. All subsequent Toronto subway cars were built in Canada, the M class by the Montreal Locomotive Works, and the H class by Hawker-Siddeley. Note the Toronto skyline of 1956 with the Bank of Commerce and Royal York Hotel soaring through the somewhat smoke-blackened air. On top of the embankment to the left is Front Street, both sides of which are now lined with modern office buildings, like those of the CBC, Royal Bank, and the Toronto Convention Centre.

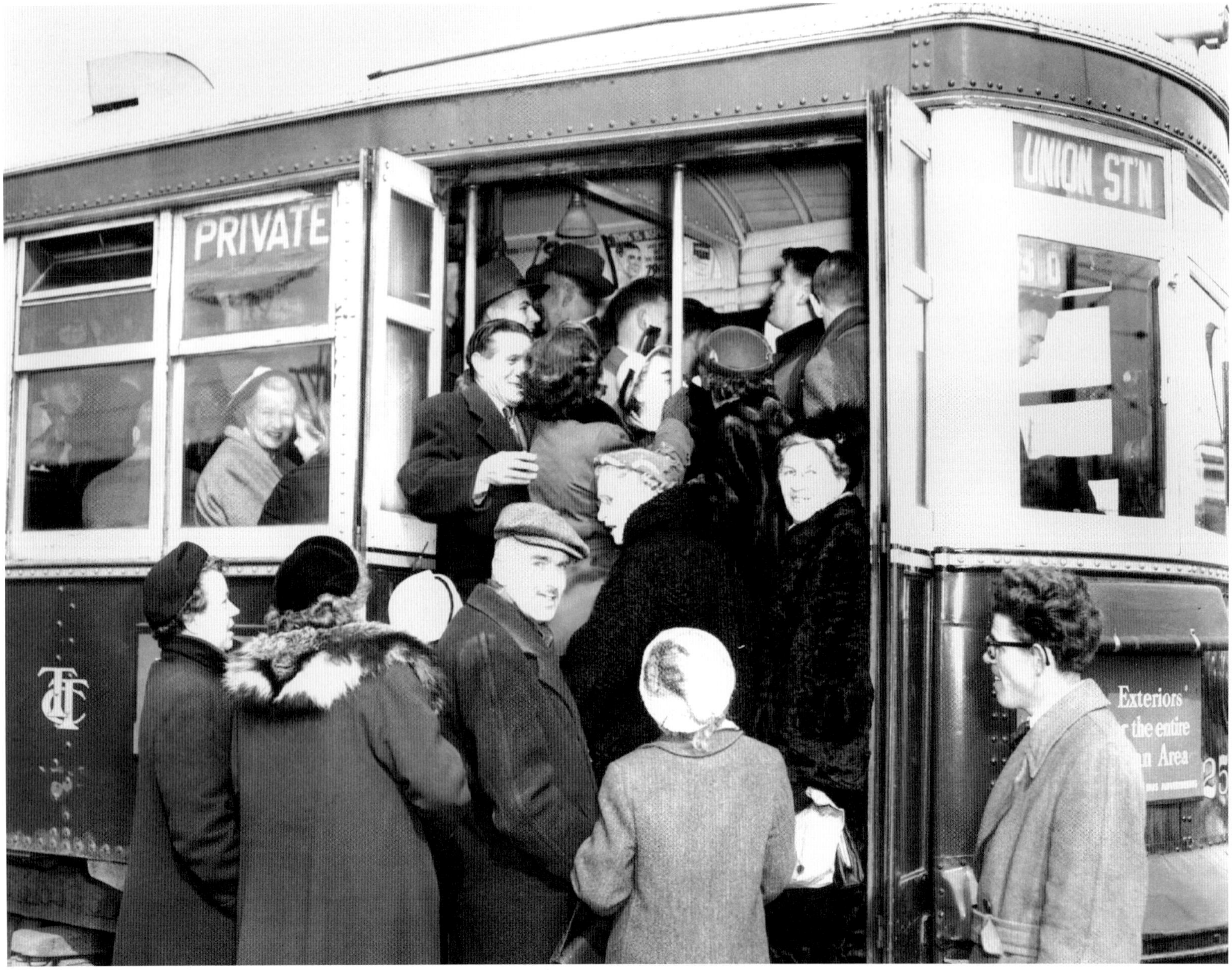

25 Enthusiastic and nostalgic passengers cram onto the last Yonge streetcar, March 30, 1954.

The day the new subway under Yonge Street opened was also the day that streetcars on Yonge Street ceased running. The Yonge streetcar route was the oldest street railway line in the country, the first horse-drawn cars having trotted up and down the street on September 11, 1861. The route connected the St. Lawrence Hall and Market with the suburban Town of Yorkville using cars operating via King Street to Yonge, then north on Yonge through the tollgate north of the Bloor Street intersection to the terminal in front of the Yorkville Town Hall (opposite today's Central Reference Library). In the fall of 1892 the line was converted to electric operation, making it the third such route in the city (after Church and King). When the Yonge streetcar line ended after ninety-three long years, the south and north terminals were, respectively, a loop at Front and Station streets (just west of Union Station) and another loop at the Toronto city limits at the south end of the steep hill into Hogg's Hollow.

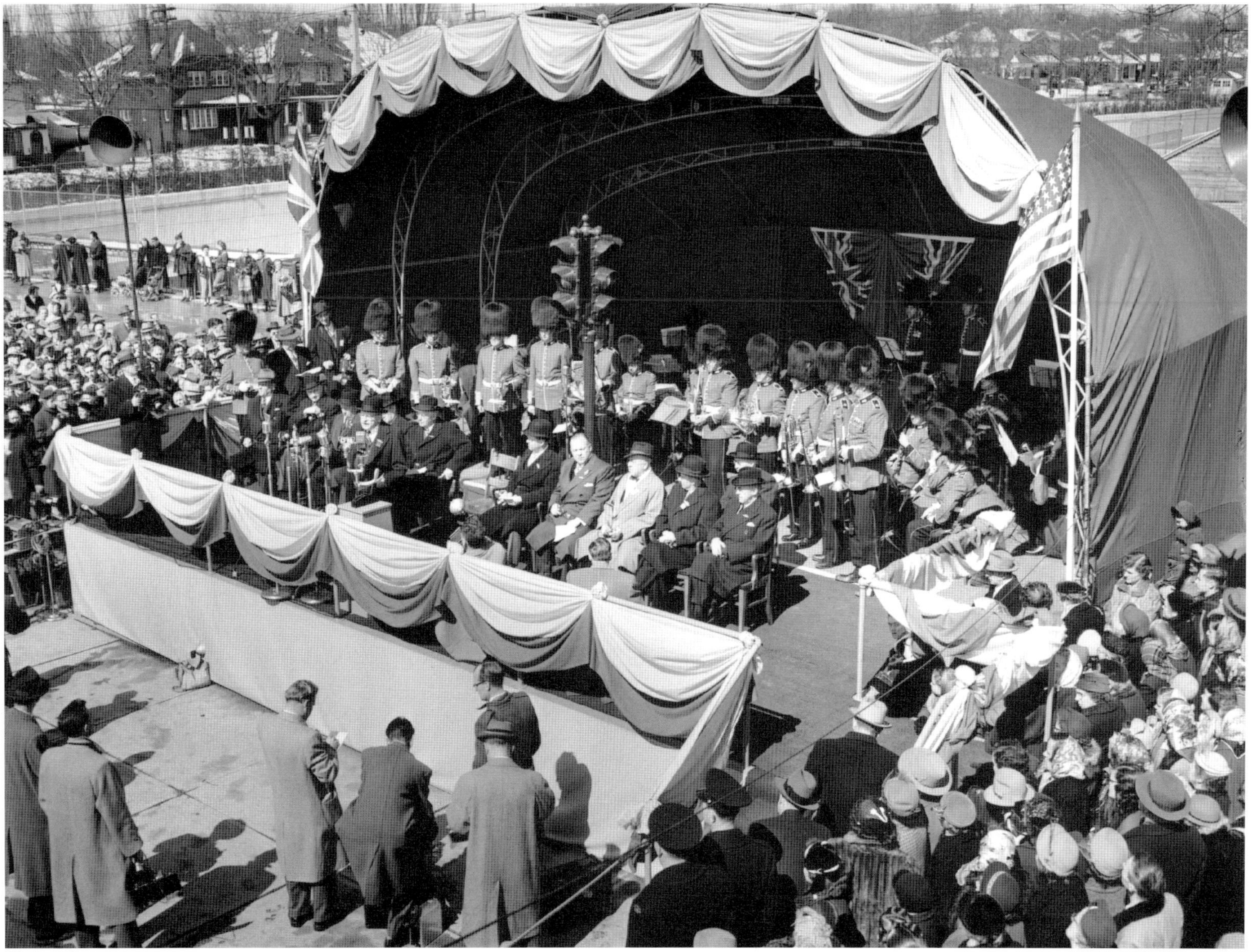

26 Crowds gather at the new Davisville Station to await the official opening of the city's new subway, March 30, 1954.

While the official duties would be performed by Mayor Allan Lamport (seated, fourth from right) and Ontario Premier Leslie Frost (seated, sixth from right) there's little doubt that the most important person at the ceremony was the TTC's respected chairman, W.C. McBrien, seen here at the microphone. McBrien, a successful Toronto businessman, was appointed a TTC commissioner in 1930 and its chairman three years later. During his tenure on the commission fares remained constant, except for a slight increase in 1951. He fought vigorously against political interference with the administration of the TTC. For years McBrien advocated the construction of a Yonge Street subway. Unfortunately, he would not live to see the subway complete its first three months of operation — he died on June 18, 1954. The Toronto Transit Commission's Head Office at the southwest corner of Yonge Street and Chaplin Crescent is named in McBrien's honour. The military band in the photograph is that of Toronto's Royal Regiment of Canada.

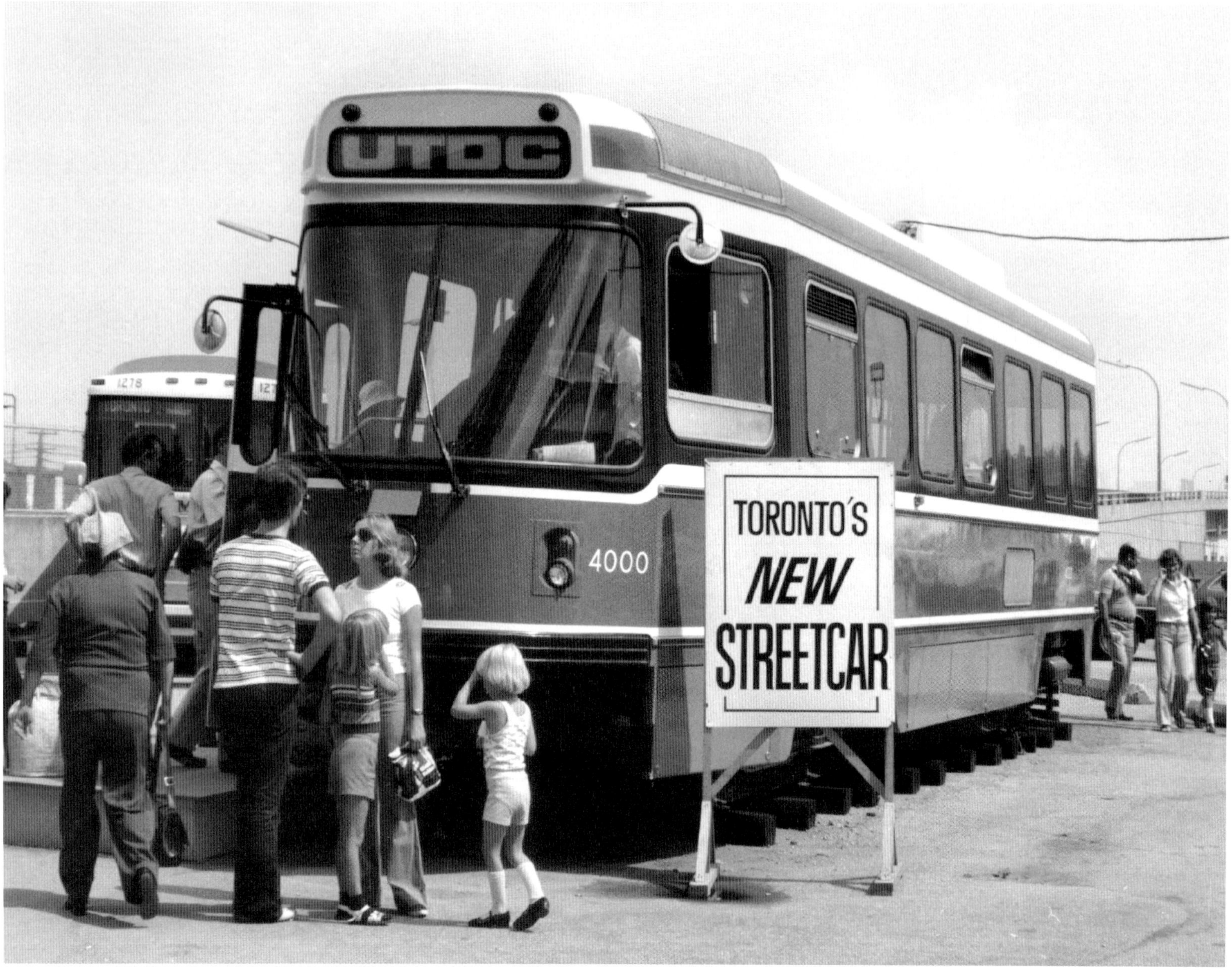

27 Visitors to the one-hundredth edition of the Canadian National Exhibition inspect the TTC's new Canadian Light Rail Vehicle, August 1978.

For many years the CNE prided itself on being "the showplace of the nation." It was at the Ex that Canadians were introduced to the latest technological advances. Things like radio, voice and musical recordings, and television were heard and seen first by visitors to the CNE. So too were public transit vehicles. The Peter Witt car, the PCC, and the Canadian Light Rail Vehicle were all introduced to the travelling public at the CNE. This trio of vehicles obtained electricity using the overhead wire and trolley pole combination that was also used successfully for the first time at the Exhibition. The vehicle in the photograph, #4000, was the first of 196 such streetcars, with the first six in the order, #4000–#4005, built in Switzerland. The remainder of the cars, #4010–#4199, were manufactured in Hawker-Siddeley Canada's Thunder Bay, Ontario factory.

Fire destroys the S.S. Noronic

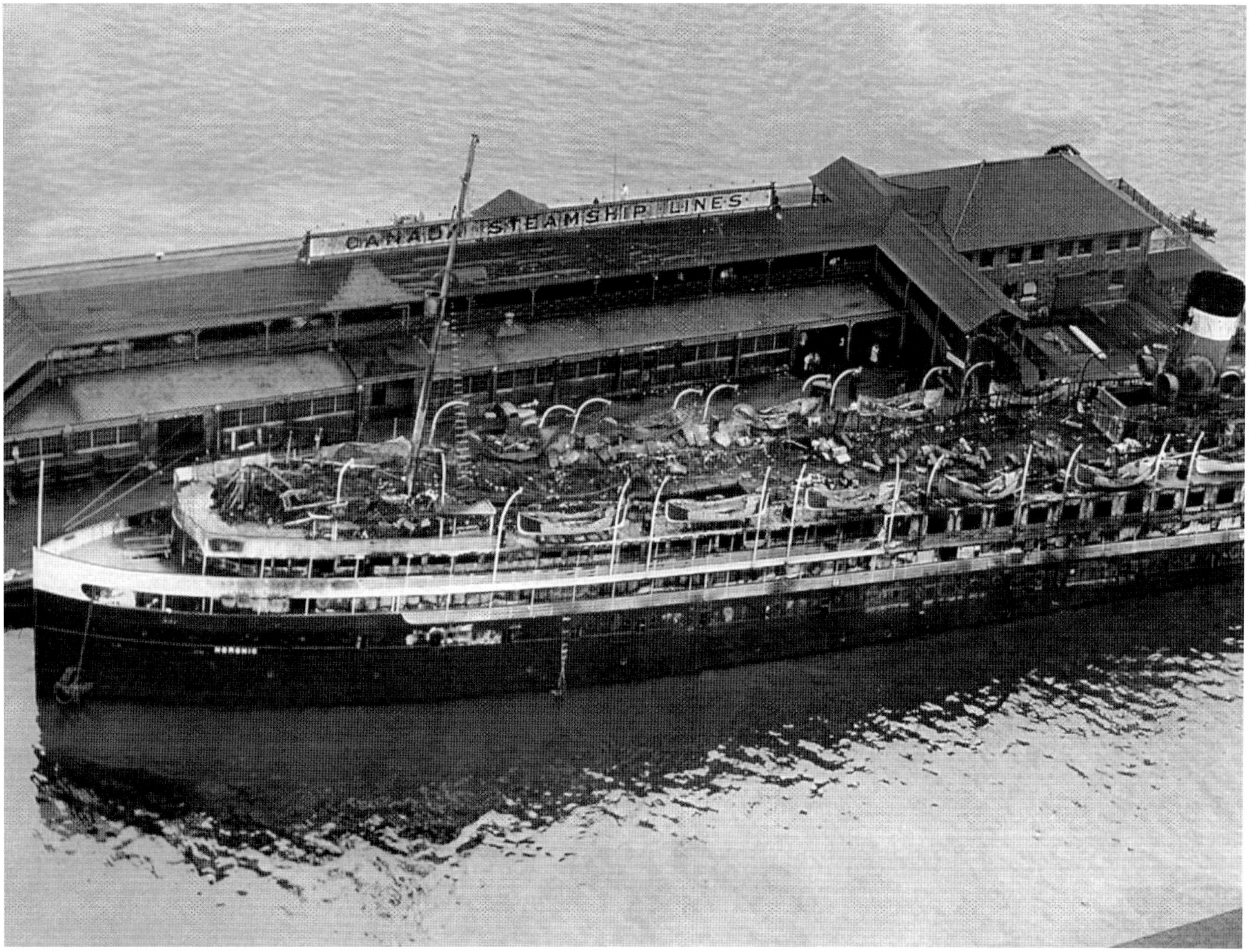

28 Canada Steamship Lines Great Lakes cruise ship S.S. Noronic *lies partially submerged at her Yonge Street berth, September 17, 1949.*

An infrequent visitor to the Port of Toronto, *Noronic* was usually to be found plying the waters of the upper Great Lakes. Her final cruise of the 1949 season, however, was a special trip from Cleveland and Detroit to the 1000 Islands with a Friday night lay-over in Toronto. Early the following morning a small fire erupted in one of the vessel's many linen closets. Efforts by crewmembers to extinguish the flames were useless and within minutes the thirty-six-year-old craft was engulfed in flames. The city's fire department was summoned, and even though its response time was mere minutes, no amount of water could extinguish what had become a raging inferno. The number of victims quickly reached 118, making this event the worst disaster in the city's history.

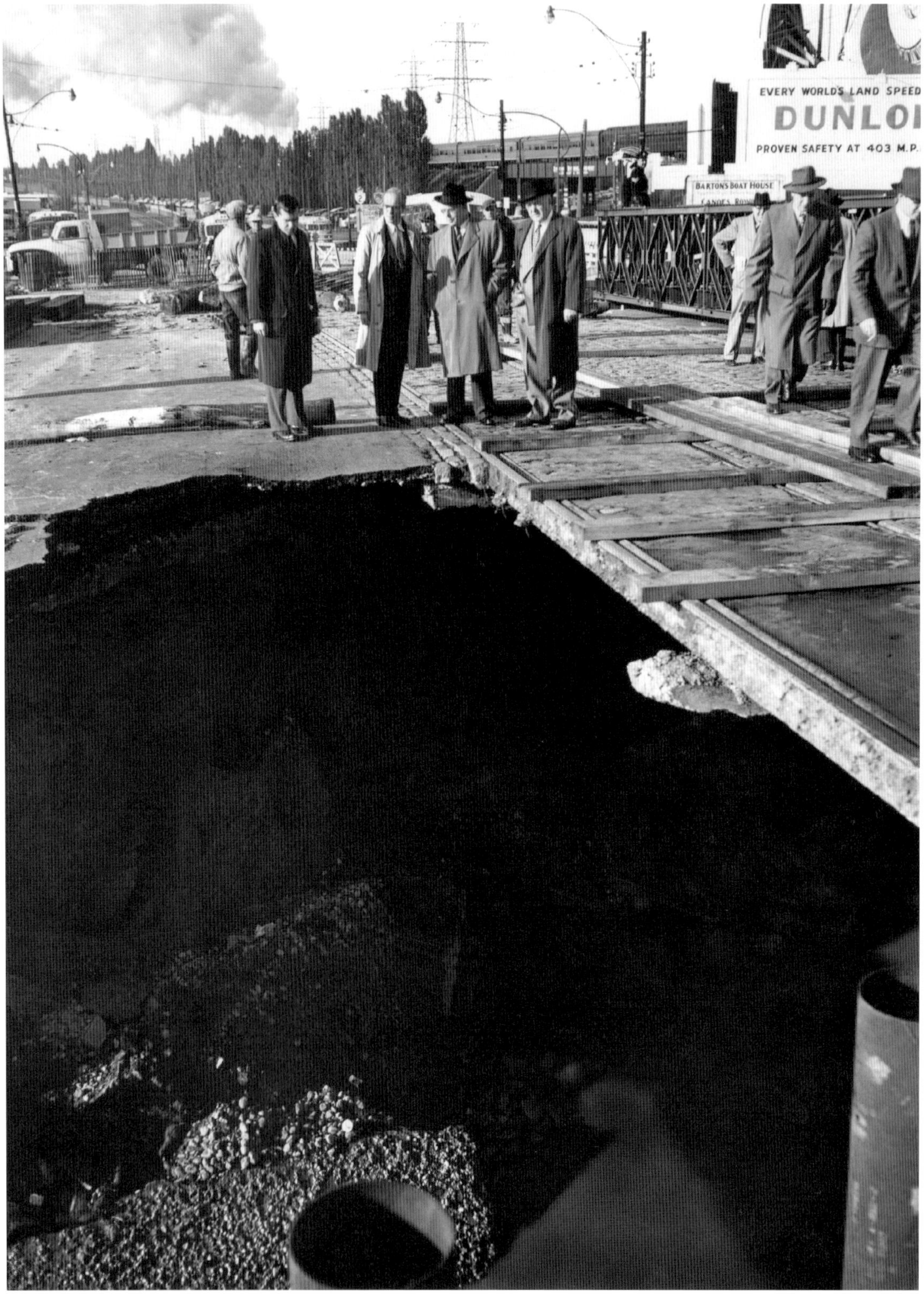

29 Ontario Premier Leslie Frost and other officials examine the damage done to the Lakeshore Road bridge over the Humber River following a surprising visit to the Toronto region by Hurricane Hazel, October 20, 1954.

The storm, which originated off the east coast of Venezuela, was not supposed to visit Southern Ontario but rather track northward up the east coast of the United States then veer easterly out into the Atlantic Ocean. This was the common trajectory for storms born in the Caribbean, but Hazel turned out to be anything but common. On the evening of October 15, 1954, the storm inflicted its might on the Toronto area, especially around the Humber River and the Mimico and Etobicoke creeks. In total, 81 people in the Toronto region lost their lives. At the height of the storm, the Humber River crested nearly twenty-three centimetres (nine inches) above normal. In doing so, the wildly flowing river swept fourteen homes on Raymore Drive, a small street adjacent to the Humber in the Weston part of the city, into the swollen watercourse. More than thirty residents of that street lost their lives.

on the evening of October 15, 1954.

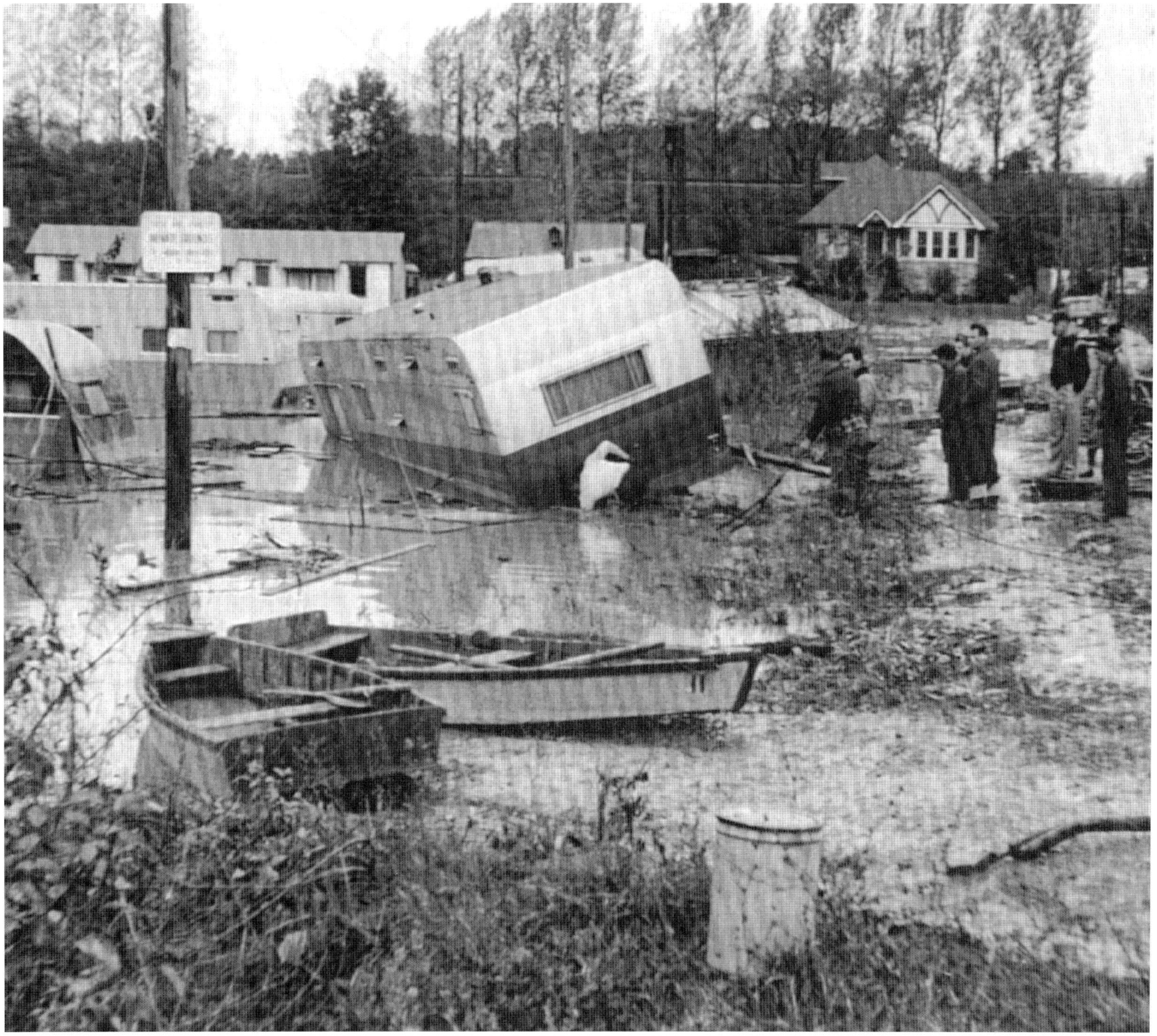

30 The waters of the normally docile Etobicoke Creek swirl around abandoned house trailers from a nearby trailer camp, October 16, 1954.

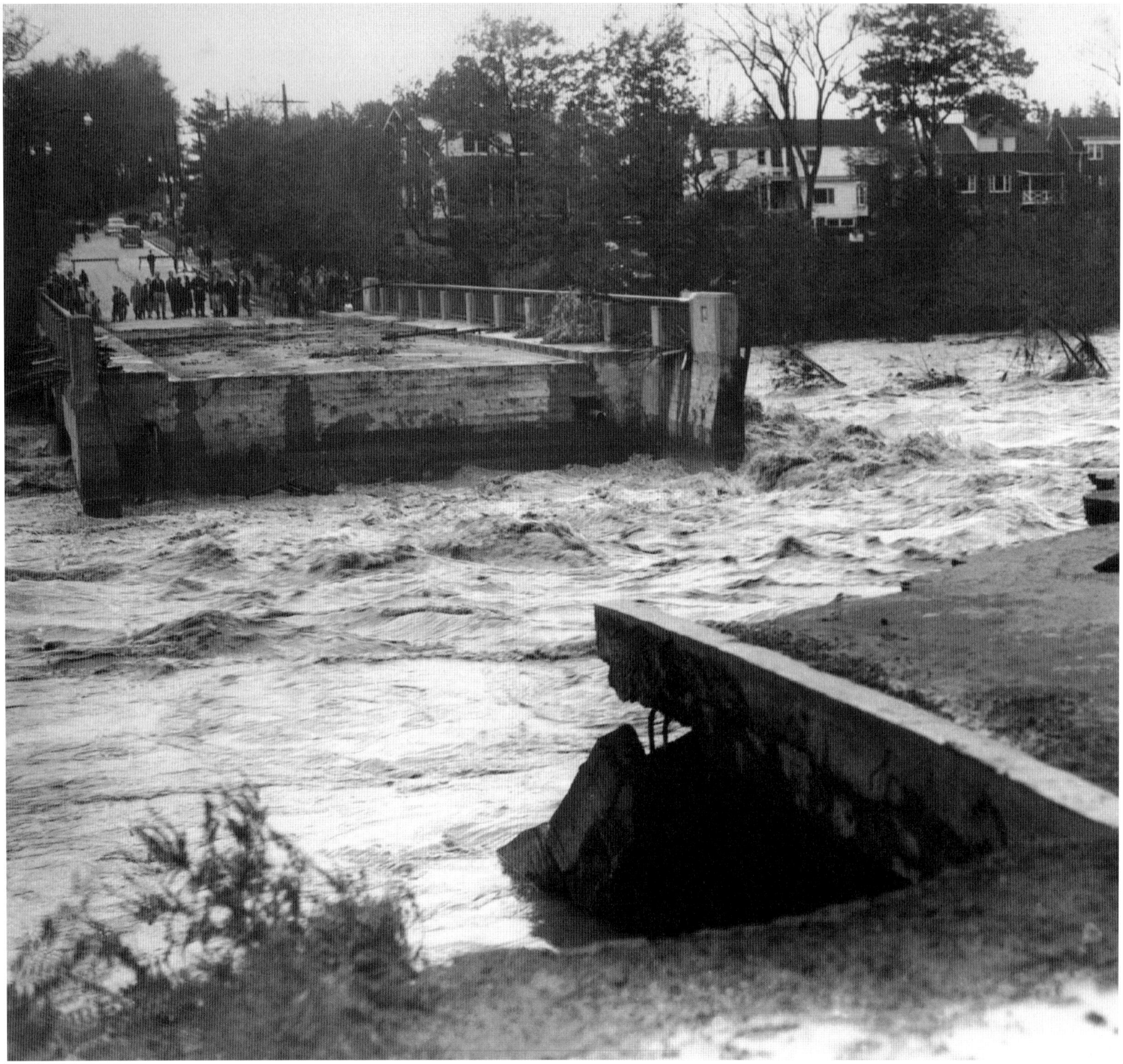

31 When a section of the busy Lawrence Avenue bridge over the Humber River was washed out, the community of Weston lost its main connection with the city to the east, October 16, 1954.

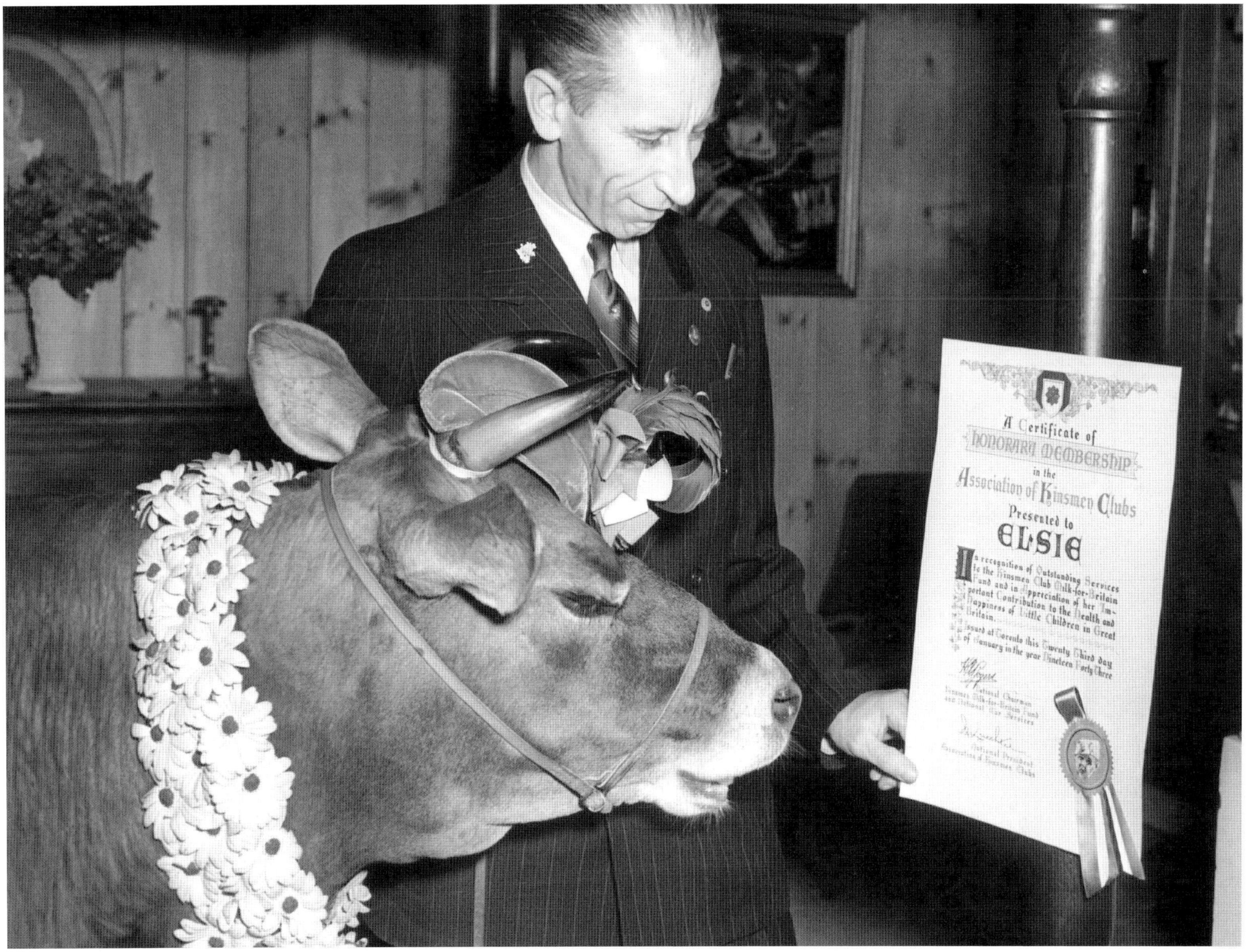

32 Elsie the Cow, during one of her many visits to Toronto, is made an Honourary Member of the Kinsmen Club, January 23, 1943.

Elsie was a creation of the marketing department of the Borden Milk Company. She first appeared in print in 1936 as a cartoon character in company advertisements. So successful were these ads that within months Elsie was heard on radio telling her mother (and the listeners) that she was so excited "That I can hardly chew! We're sending our milk to Boardinghouse — Love, Elsie." By 1939 she had become an icon, resulting in a real, live cow making a personal appearance at that year's New York World's Fair. Elsie (the first Elsie's real name was You'll Do Lobelia, and over the years there were approximately fifty different Elsies) was such a star that the company put her on tour. She raised millions of dollars for a variety of causes ranging from war bond drives to funding for children's hospitals. Many of Elsie's appearances were at the annual Canadian National Exhibition, where, in 1959, nearly 325,000 people visited her own special bungalow just inside the Dufferin Gate to see the celebrated bovine and her son Beauregard.

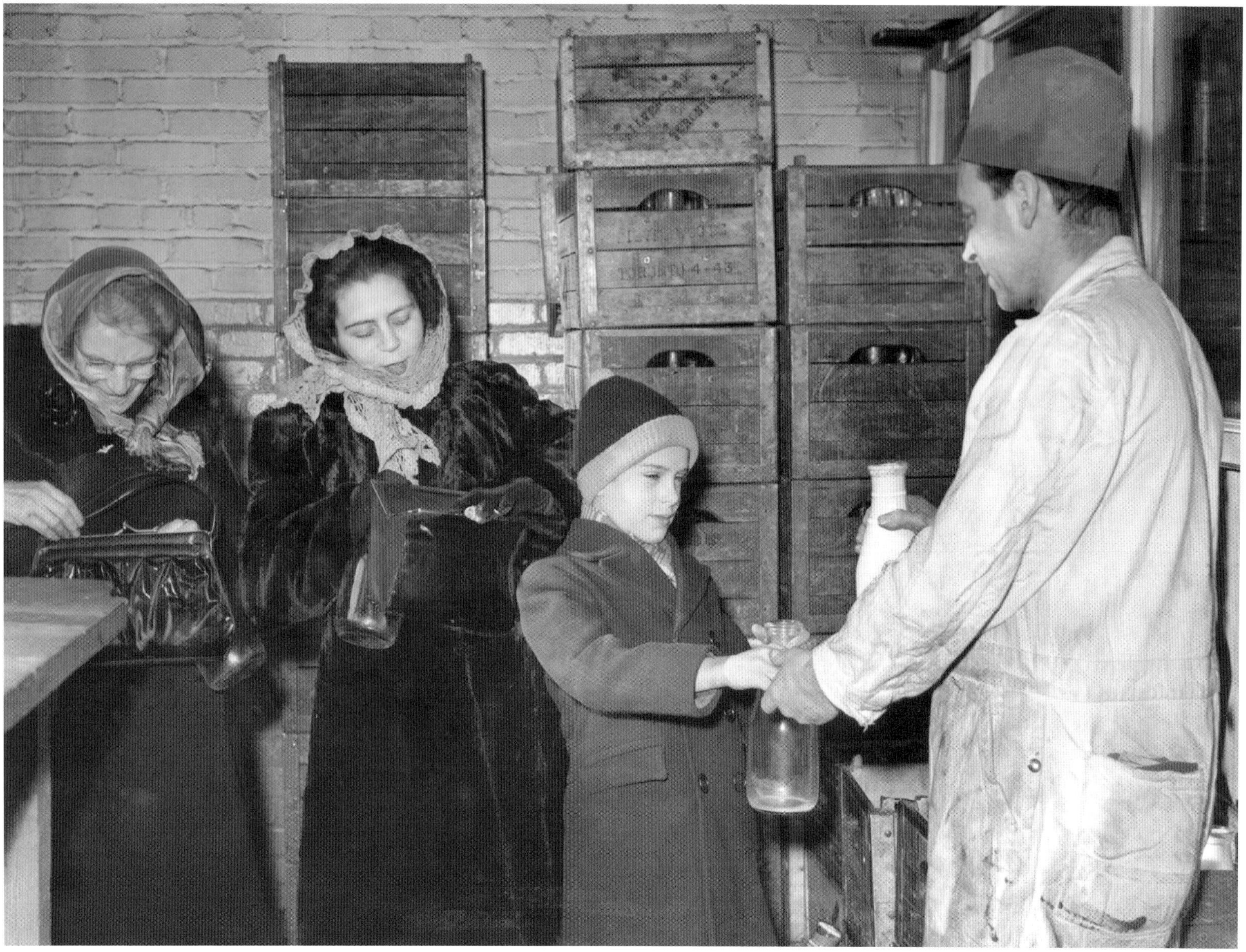

33 Milk, and the bottles it came in, was a precious commodity during Toronto's worst snowstorm, December 12, 1944.

Just as the weather officials would misfire in predicting Hurricane Hazel (just a few light showers), so too did they fumble their prediction of four to twelve inches of snow before daybreak on December 12. That prediction was off by more than ten inches — Toronto was blanketed with the greatest fall of snow in a twenty-four-hour period, a record that still stands. While traffic came to a standstill, a greater concern was the delivery of coal and milk. In the former case customers were ordered to clear a path from the street to the coal chute or the residence would be bypassed. Milk, on the other hand, was distributed to customers from local fire halls or, as shown in this photograph, from an auto body shop on Yorkville Avenue. This distribution point was pressed into service when the local milk delivery wagon got bogged down in the snow in front of the shop. The civic-minded shop owner quickly volunteered his place of business as a temporary dairy outlet.

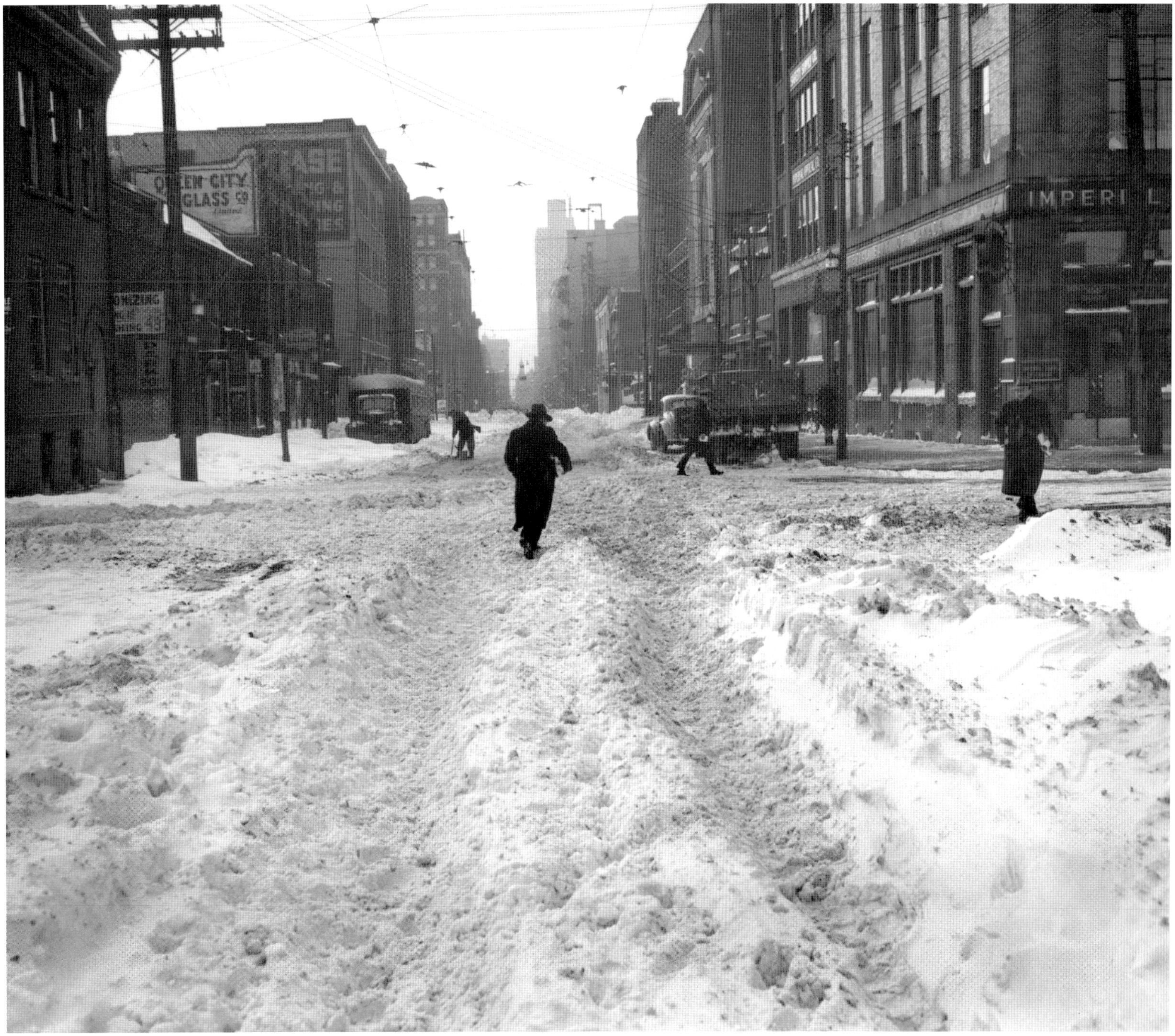

34 Things get back to normal after Toronto's big snowstorm, December 1944.

Victoria Street looking south from Dundas Street East. The Pantages (later Imperial, then Imperial 6, Pantages once again, and now Canon) Theatre is at right centre.

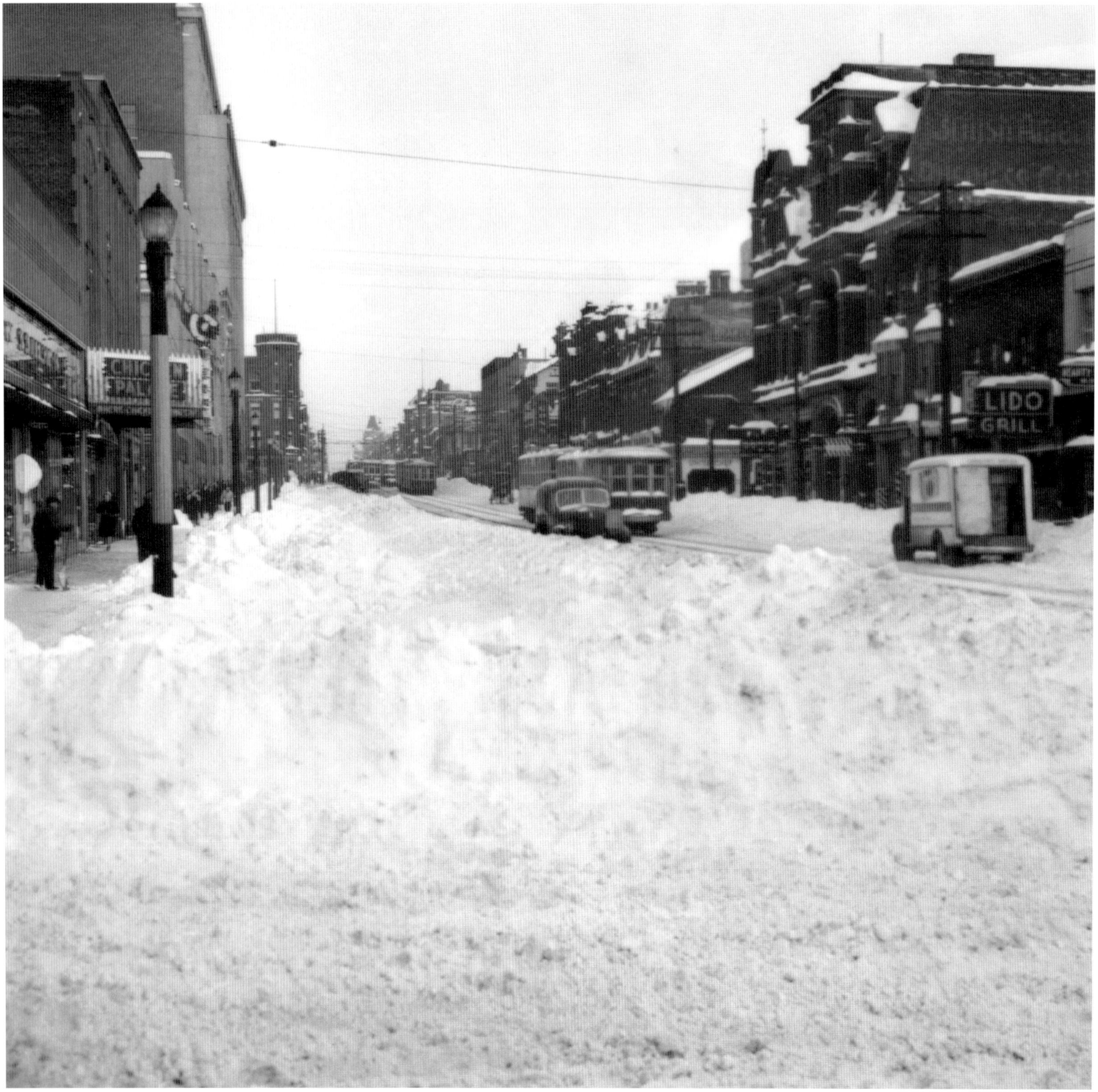

35 Yonge Street looking north from Gerrard Street, December, 1944.

The Notorious Boyd Gang

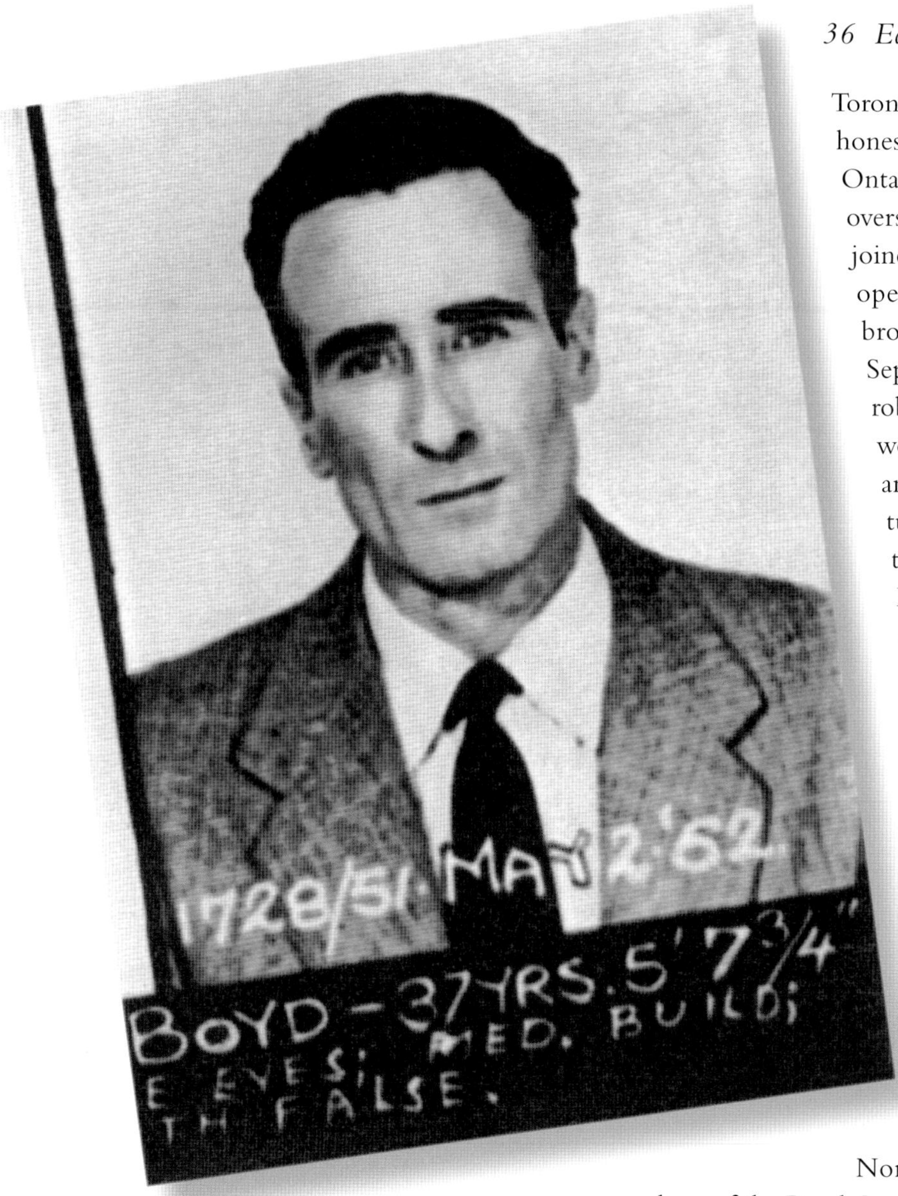

36 Edwin Alonzo Boyd. — *Courtesy Toronto Police Museum*

Toronto-born Edwin Alonzo Boyd had worked at a variety of honest jobs. He had spent time building highways in Northern Ontario before joining the Canadian Army. He served a stint overseas, and when the war concluded he returned home and joined the Toronto Transportation Commission. For a time he operated streetcars on the Yonge route, often with his two brothers as conductors on the same Peter Witt train. On September 9, 1949, Boyd thought he'd try something new. He robbed a bank in North Toronto and found that this kind of work was easier and paid more. Boyd's new career came to an end a little more than two years later when he was captured robbing another North Toronto bank. Boyd was sent to Toronto's Don Jail to await sentencing. There he met Leonard Jackson and William Jackson (no relation), two other incarcerated bank robbers. The trio stayed for only a short time, escaping from the ancient structure on November 4, 1951. They were joined by Steve Suchan, and the quartet, now dubbed the Boyd Gang by the media, quickly resumed their bank robbing ways.

On March 6, 1952, things turned ugly: Steve Suchan shot Toronto Police Sergeant Edmund Tong. The officer died of his wounds seventeen days later. Police quickly captured all four members of the gang, and once again they found themselves incarcerated in the same cell-block in the old Don Jail. On September 8, 1952, the Boyd Gang again escaped from jail. They hightailed it up the Don Valley, eluding the authorities for eight days. Toronto was in turmoil until officers of the North York Township police force finally captured all four members of the Boyd Gang in a barn not far from the present Finch Avenue East and Leslie Street intersection. The gang members were quickly returned to the Don Jail. On September 29, 1952, both Steve Suchan and Leonard Jackson (who was with Suchan when the officer was shot) were hanged for the murder of Sergeant Tong. William Jackson and Edwin Boyd were given lengthy jail sentences. The former was eventually released and vanished into obscurity. Boyd was given eight life terms, of which he served a mere fourteen years. Upon his release Boyd moved to the West Coast, where he lived out the rest of his life in virtual anonymity. Edwin Alonzo Boyd, once Canada's most dashing and notorious criminal, died of pneumonia in a British Columbia hospital on May 16, 2002.

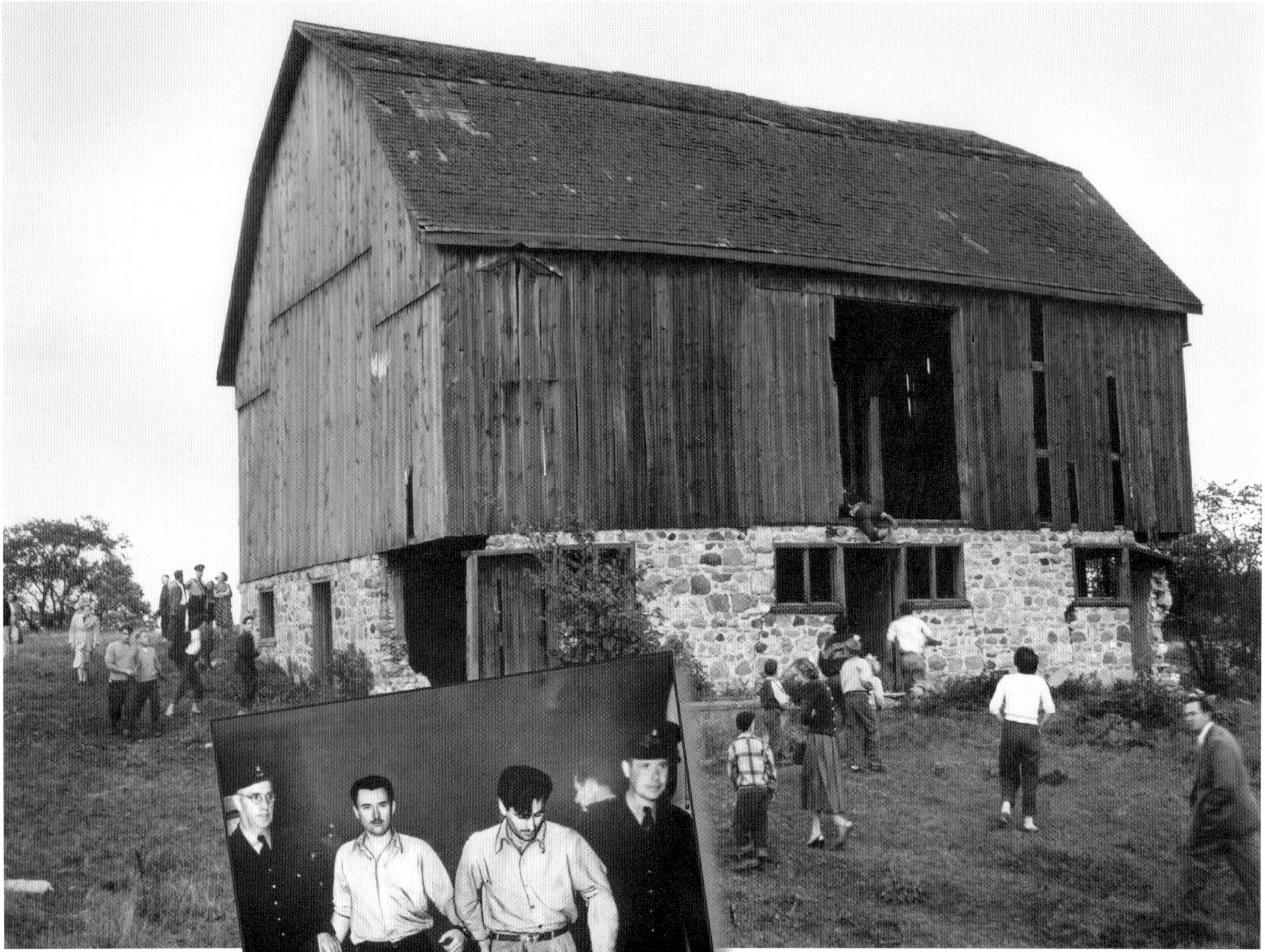

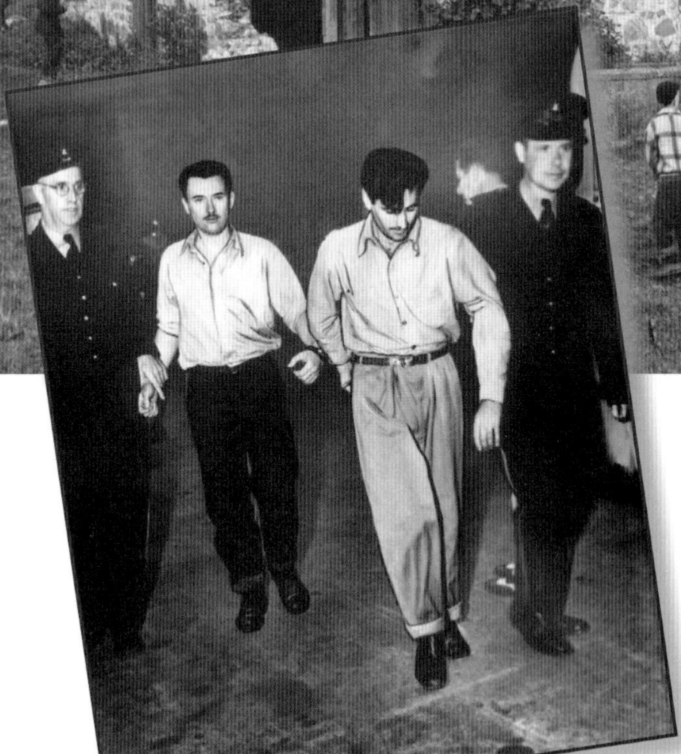

37 Old barn in North York Township, in which the notorious Boyd Gang was captured on September 16, 1952.

38 Two members of the Boyd Gang captured in the old barn were Steve Suchan and Leonard Jackson, both of whom were hanged in the Don Jail for the murder of Toronto police officer Edmund Tong.

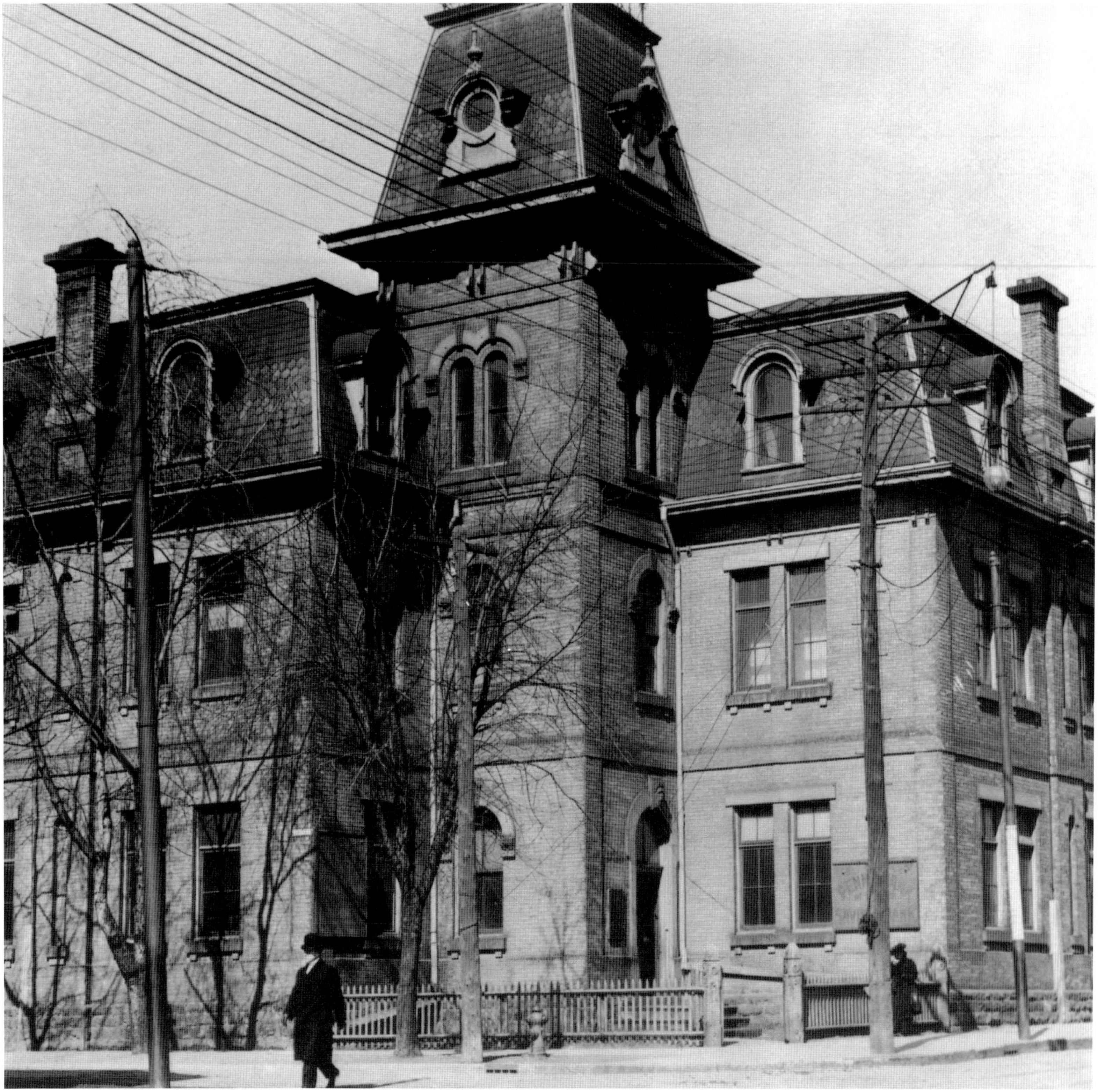

39 The Penny Bank of Ontario, northwest corner of Richmond and York streets, 1948.

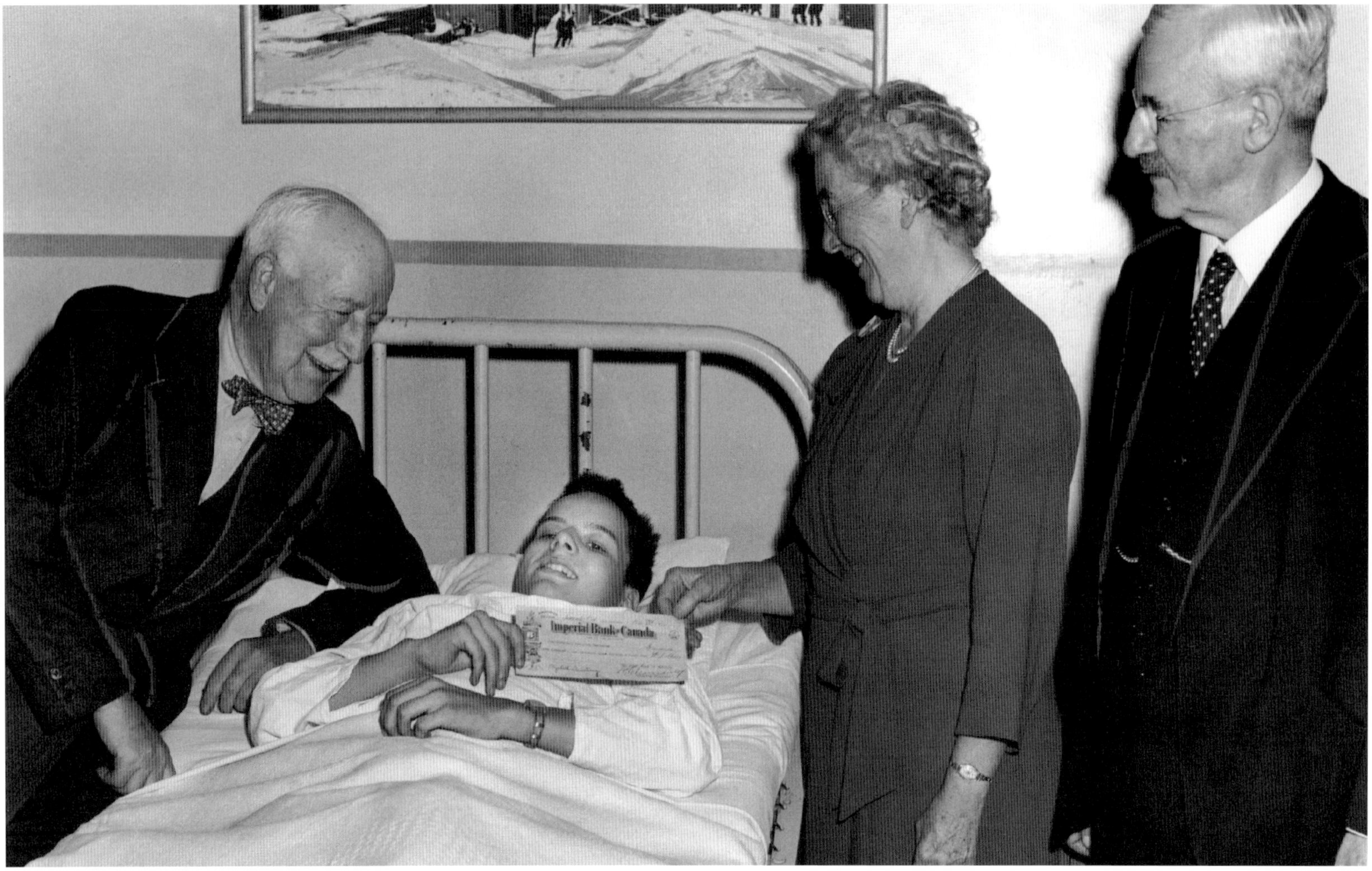

40 Penny Bank of Ontario officials Mrs. Elizabeth Armstrong and Messrs H.B. Scandrett and H.D. Lockhart Gordon turn over a cheque for more than $100,000 to Howard Foster, a polio patient in the Hospital for Sick Children, October 2, 1948.

What became known throughout the province as simply the Penny Bank was patterned on penny banks that had been established throughout Scotland in the 1800s as a place where both children and adults, hesitating to approach the big banks, could safely deposit their hard-earned pennies. Here in Toronto, the first penny bank was set up by a mission affiliated with Toronto's St. Andrew's Presbyterian Church. In 1900, a "school branch" was established in Lord Dufferin Public School. Four years later the federal government passed the Penny Bank Act, and soon the Penny Bank of Toronto operated in other city schools and, by 1922, in schools throughout the province. The pennies, nickels, dimes, and quarters collected in each school were taken to a branch of one of the major Canadian banks, where they were forwarded to the Penny Bank's main Toronto office, initially at Richmond and York streets and later at McCaul and Orde streets. The Penny Bank invested in government securities and was usually able give a higher rate of interest than the regular banks. After a period of inactivity during the Second World War (patrons were encouraged to buy war bonds instead) the idea of reopening the Penny Bank was discussed, but owing to constraints within the school timetable, it was rejected. When the Penny Bank finally closed its books at the end of August 1948, unclaimed deposits amounting to almost $7,000 were placed in post office savings accounts. In addition, surplus funds that had accrued over the bank's 44 years in business, an amount that totalled exactly $101,941.14, were turned over to Toronto's famous Hospital for Sick Children.

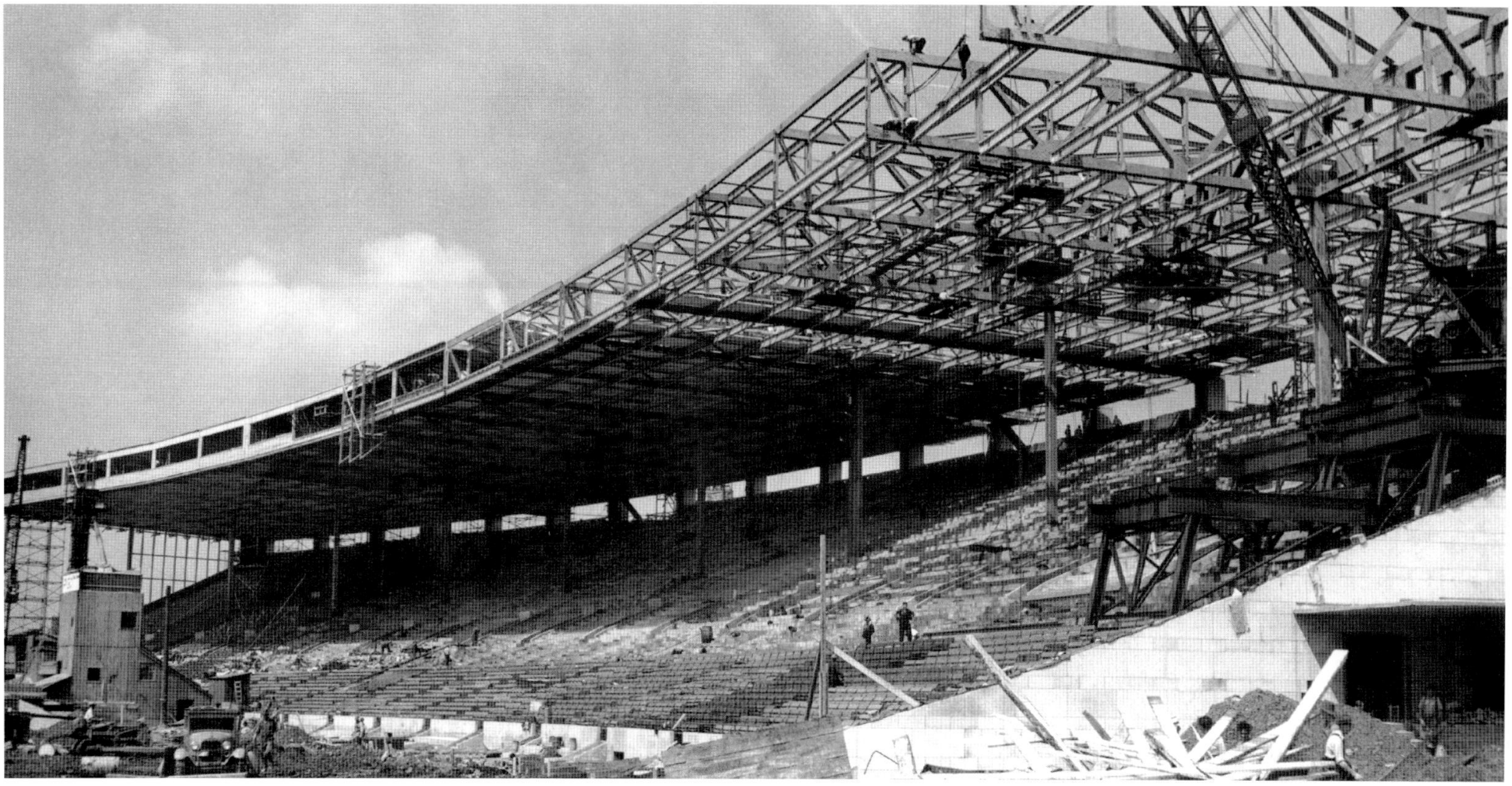

41 Workers rush to complete the Canadian National Exhibition's new Grandstand in the spring of 1948.

Over the years an interesting variety of grandstands have served the needs of the Exhibition. The first such structure was completed in time for the fair that was held in 1878. This event was simply another in the succession of provincial fairs, and it wasn't until the following year, 1879, that the city sponsored the first of the exhibitions that we now recognize as the Canadian National Exhibition. That first grandstand was in use until 1892, when it was demolished and replaced by a much larger structure, one that had seating for ten thousand, twice that of the first grandstand. In 1906 the second facility was destroyed by a fire that also wrecked the imposing Crystal Palace, the fair's main building. Another new and larger grandstand with 16,400 seats quickly replaced it, and this one survived for 39 years before it too was destroyed by fire. Work began immediately on an ultramodern, $3-million structure, but several setbacks, including a shortage of steel, resulted in this one not being ready until the opening of the 1948 Exhibition. The first performance on the stage of the new 20,663-seat structure featured the popular American comedy team of Olsen and Johnson. In the years that followed, Ex-goers were entertained by Jack and Midge Arthur's Canadettes, comedians Bob Hope, Victor Borge, Jimmy Durante, and George Gobel, singer Frank Sinatra (who first appeared at the CNE with Tommy Dorsey in the Exhibition's mammoth Dance Tent nine years earlier), cowboy star Roy Rogers, and numerous others. Jack Kotchman's Hell Drivers was a popular afternoon show that returned to the CNE many times. In the off season, the Grandstand was the site of a wide variety of events, including stock car races, Toronto Argonaut football games, public and high school track and field meets, the annual Police Games (which always included the Miss Toronto competition), Monster Truck shows, international soccer matches, and, on April 7, 1977, the first ever Toronto Blue Jays baseball game (won by the Jays 9–5 over the Chicago White Sox). The CNE Grandstand (which had been enlarged several times, eventually seating 54,264 spectators) was abandoned in 1995 and demolished four years later.

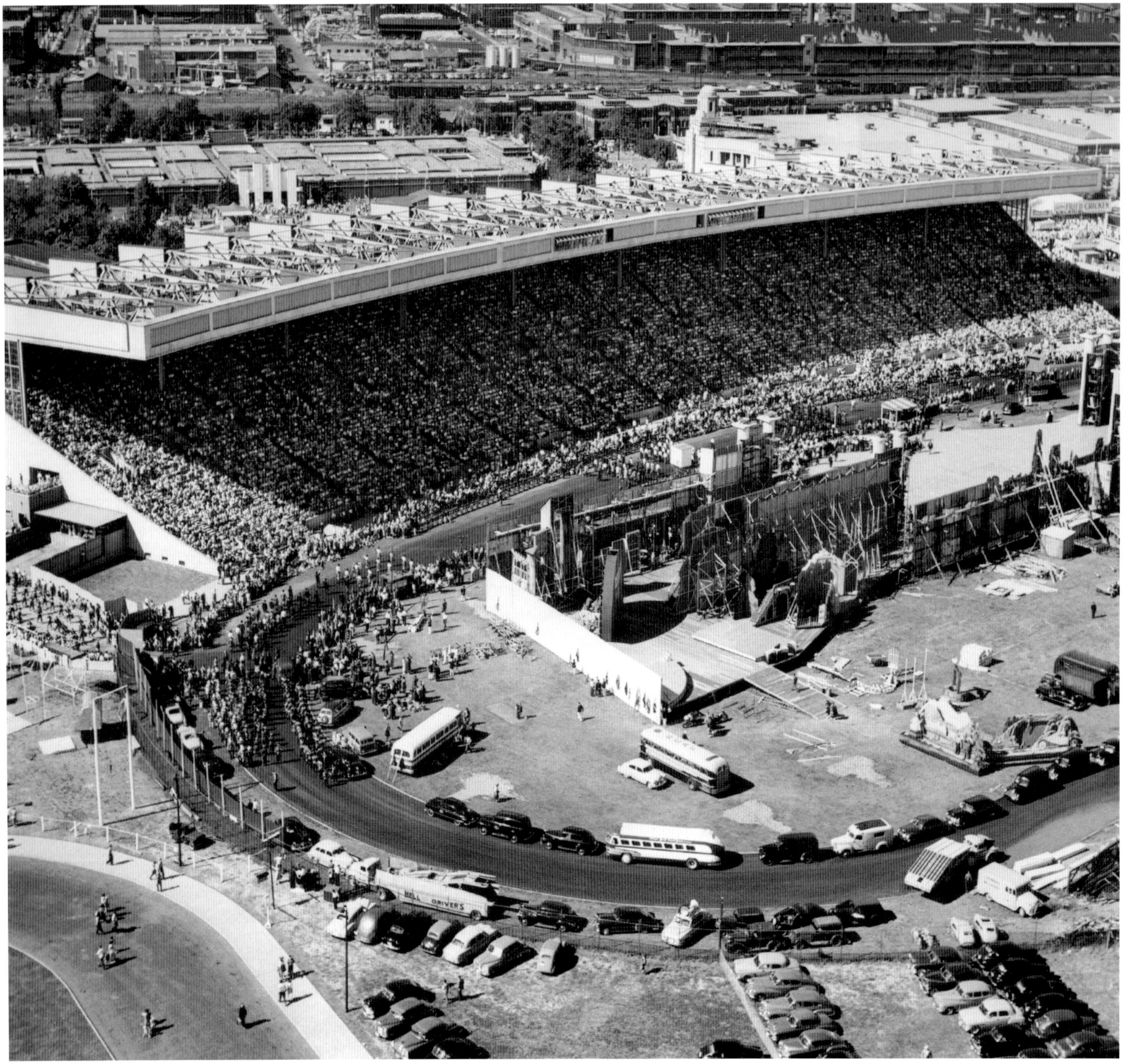

42 In addition to featuring mammoth stage shows and world-famous solo performers, the CNE Grandstand was often used as a huge "reviewing stand" for parades such as this one, the 1951 Warriors' Day Parade.

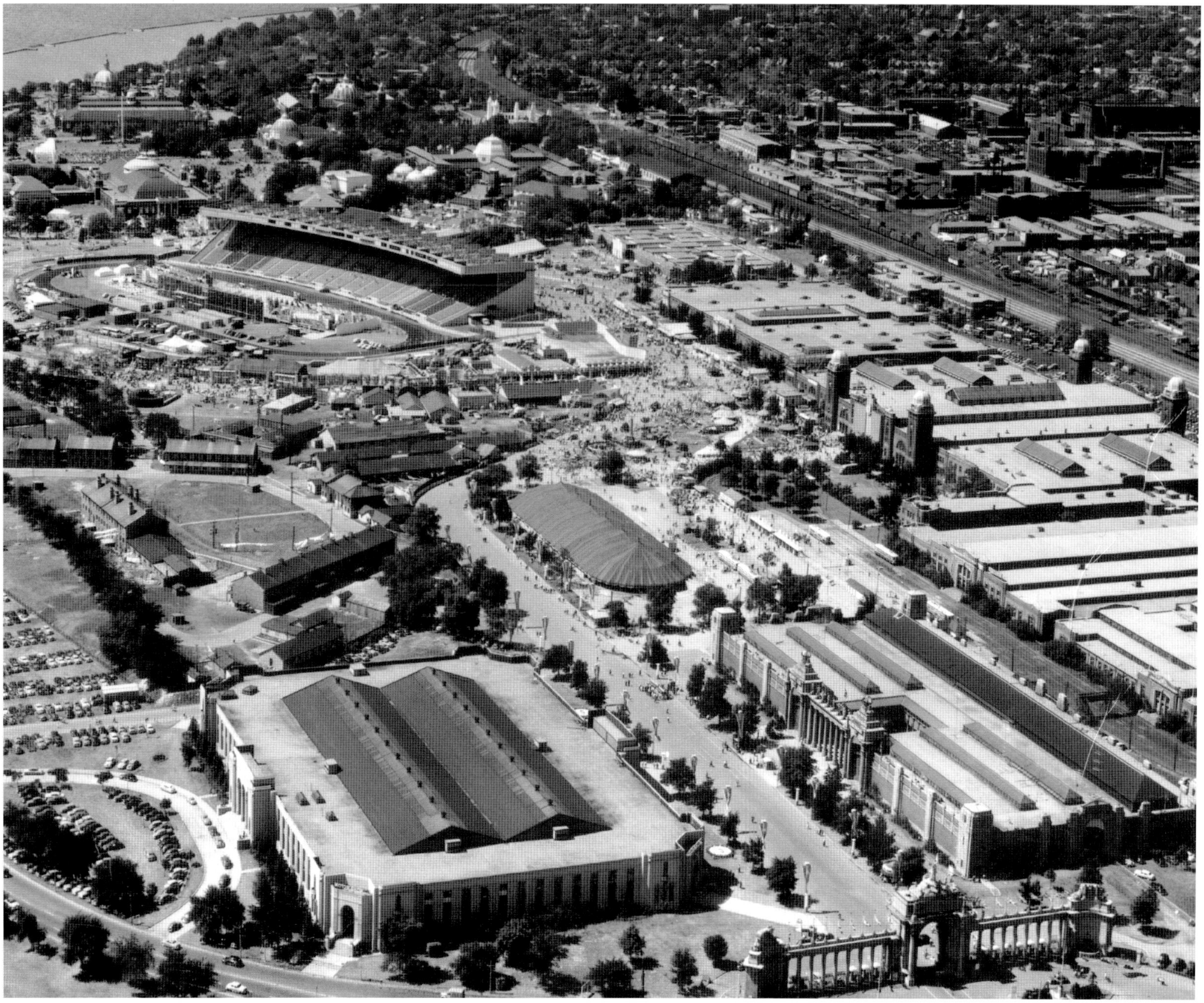

43 Aerial view of the Canadian National Exhibition grounds, 1956.

Visible in this photograph are (upper left) the CNE Grandstand, (middle left) the New Fort, also known as Stanley Barracks, (bottom left) the Automotive Building, (bottom right) Electrical and Engineering Building, and (middle right) the Royal Coliseum and Horse Palace. In the centre of the view is the huge 42.6-metre (140-foot) by 91.4-metre (300-foot) Dance Tent, which was fabricated in Chicago especially for the CNE. It was supported by more than 20,000 feet of rope and held in place by 550 tent stakes. It was in this sprawling tent that the big bands of such world-renowned performers as Artie Shaw, Benny Goodman, and Canada's own Guy Lombardo entertained hundreds of thousands of Ex-goers.

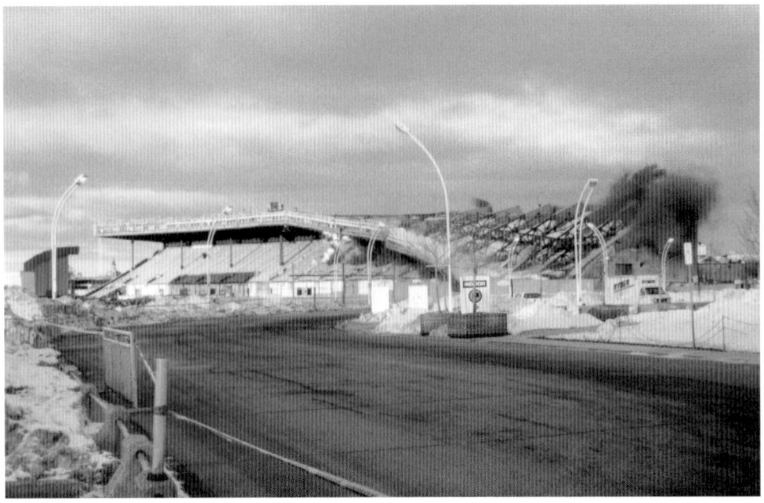

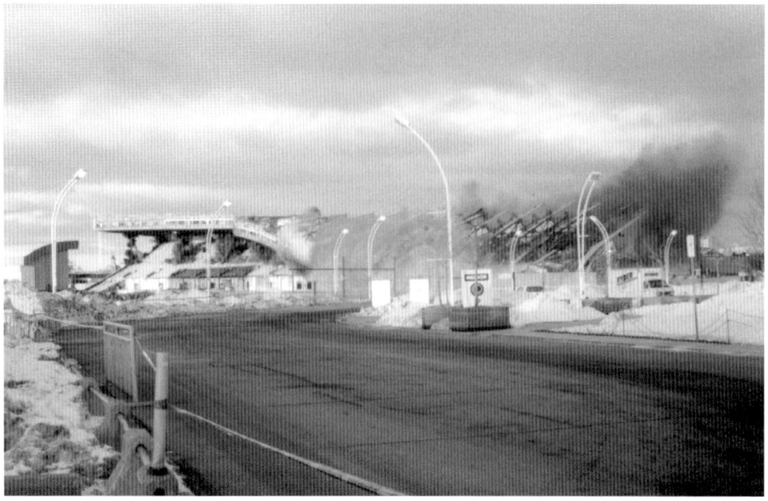

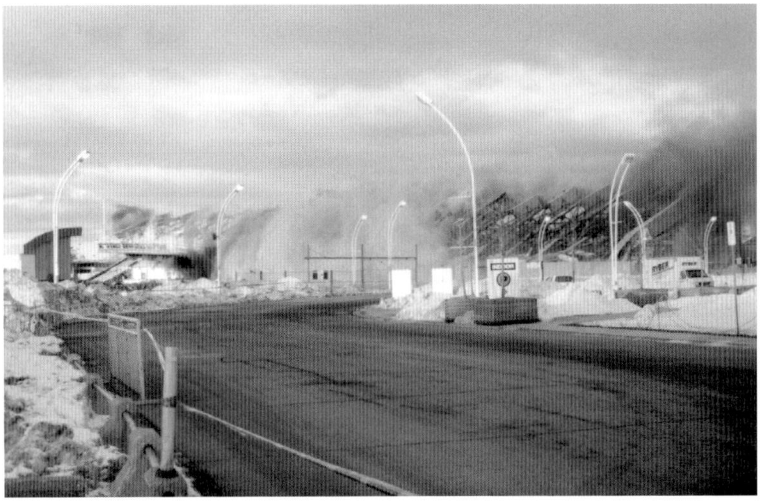

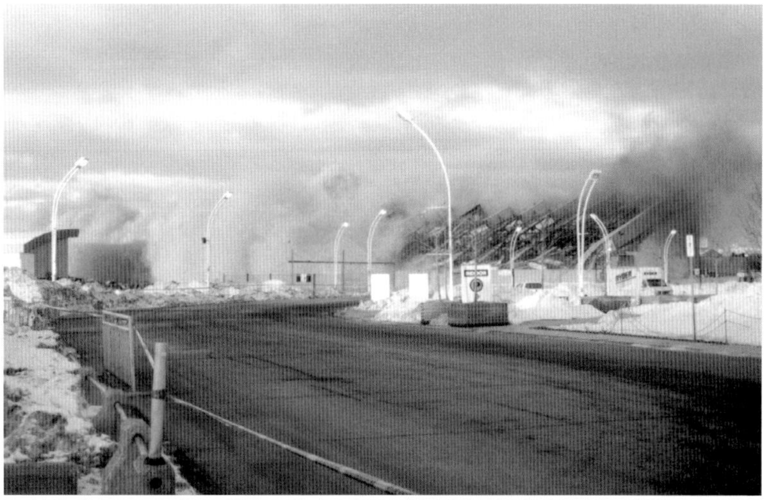

44–48 On a cold January 31, 1999, several carefully placed dynamite charges brought the once proud Grandstand crashing down.

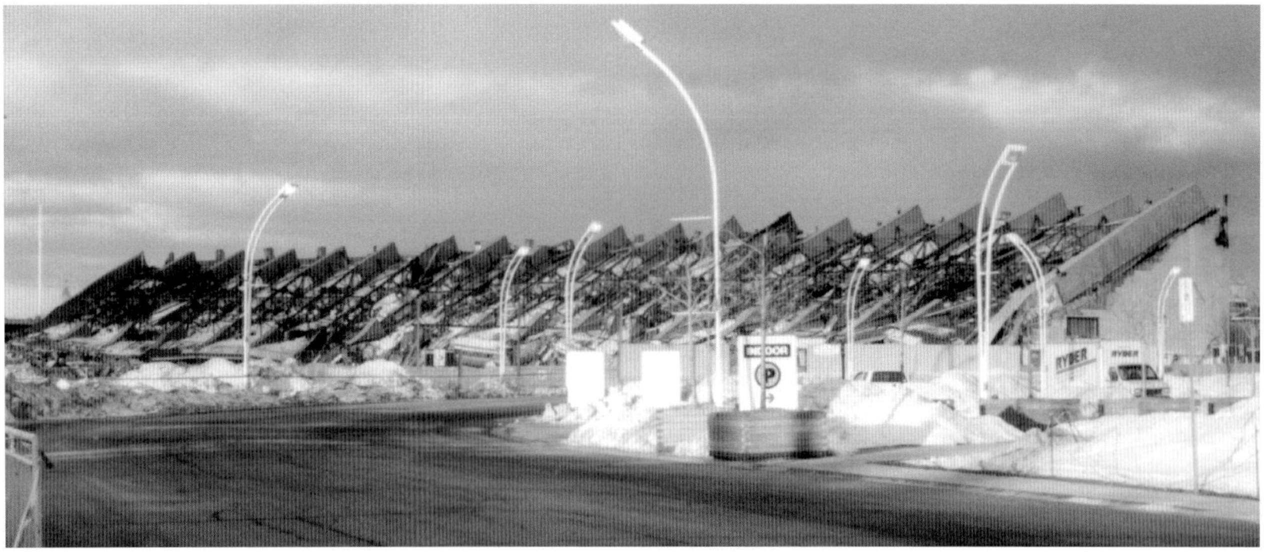

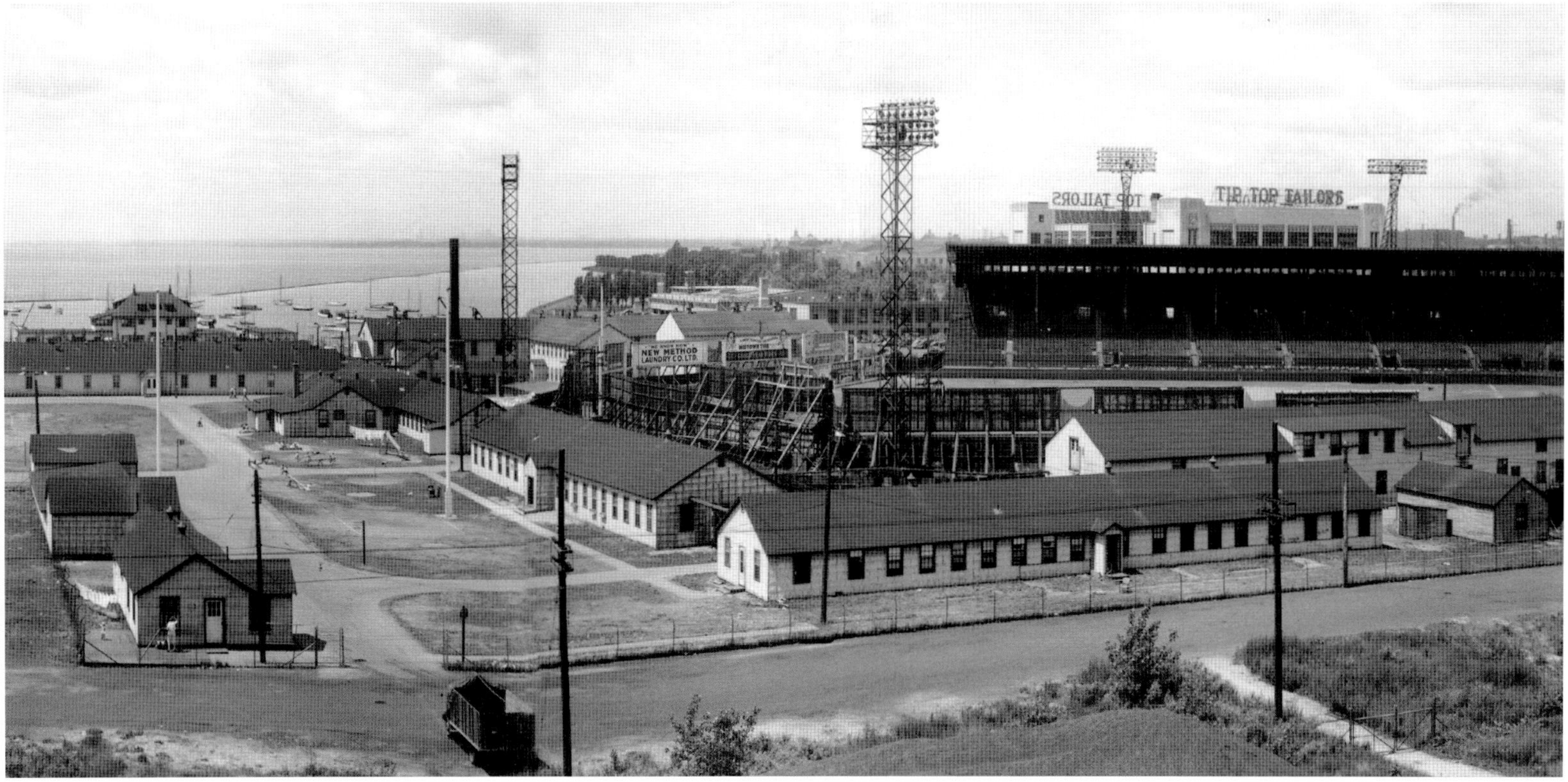

49 One of the city's wartime housing communities, the former Little Norway, and Maple Leaf Stadium flank the west side of Bathurst Street south of Lake Shore Boulevard, 1946.

The rows of small white buildings seen in this photograph were originally built as accommodation for members of the Royal Norwegian Naval Air Force and Army Air Force. When German troops invaded Norway in 1940, Canadian officials offered the government of Norway a place at the foot of Bathurst Street in Toronto, where aviators and aircraft mechanics, eager to get back into the battle, could live while training at the Island Airport just across the Western Channel. The barracks was officially dedicated on November 10, 1940, and was quickly dubbed "Little Norway." One of the dignitaries present at the opening was Toronto's own Mary Pickford. The base was used by the Norwegians until 1943, when the entire contingent moved to a new camp near Gravenhurst, Ontario. With the end of the Second World War, Toronto suffered from a severe housing shortage. City officials decided to use the structures in Little Norway for emergency housing. They were inhabited until 1958, when the badly run-down buildings were demolished and the entire area turned into parkland. In recognition of the hundreds of Norwegians who called this part of Toronto home during the dark days of the war, a special commemorative plaque, affixed to a boulder transported to the site from Norway and surrounded by flagpoles flying the flags of Toronto, Canada, and Norway, was dedicated by Crown Prince Harald of Norway during his visit to the city in September 1976.

Next door to the barracks was Maple Leaf Stadium, which was constructed in 1926 on land reclaimed from Toronto Bay by the Toronto Harbour Commission. It would serve as the new home of the Toronto Maple Leafs, the city's International League baseball team. Prior to moving into this new $750,000, 30,000-seat facility, the team had played for many years at the Hanlan's Point Stadium at the west end of Toronto Island. Then, in the early 1960s, the team's popularity began to wane. The baseball Leafs played their final game on September 4, 1967, in front of a crowd of only 802 diehard fans. The team's franchise was subsequently transferred to Louisville, Kentucky. Within a year, the once popular Maple Leaf Stadium, where crowds of more than twenty thousand fans often pushed and shoved to get in, was no more. In the back right of the photograph is the 1929 Tip Top Tailors building, which is being converted into loft-style condominiums.

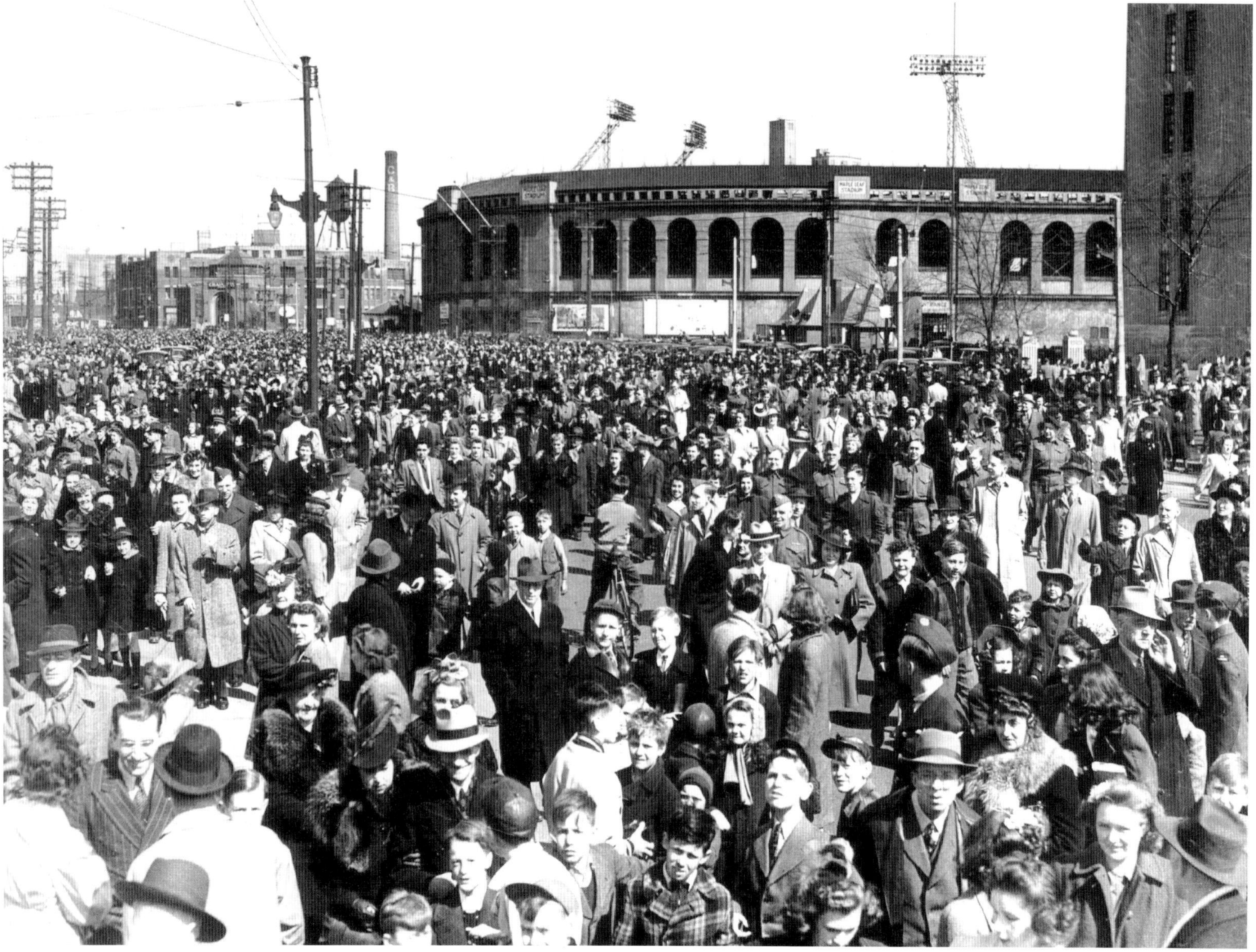

50 Crowds fill Lake Shore Boulevard in front of Maple Leaf Stadium, circa 1944.

Frequently, photographs are given to me undated and without any comments that might reveal why they were taken in the first place. This image, showing a huge crowd in front of the old Maple Leaf Stadium at the southwest corner of Bathurst Street and Lake Shore Boulevard, is one of those mysterious photos. Making it even more difficult to identify is the lack of automobiles in view — often car license plates can at least help with the date the picture was taken. A close look at the image does reveal a few armed forces personnel, leading to the assumption that this is a wartime photo. Just why such a large crowd has congregated remains a mystery. One possibility arises from the fact that most of the crowd (even the children) are dressed to the nines, which might indicate that an Easter Parade is in progress. But such parades were almost always held at Sunnyside. Therefore, the mystery continues.

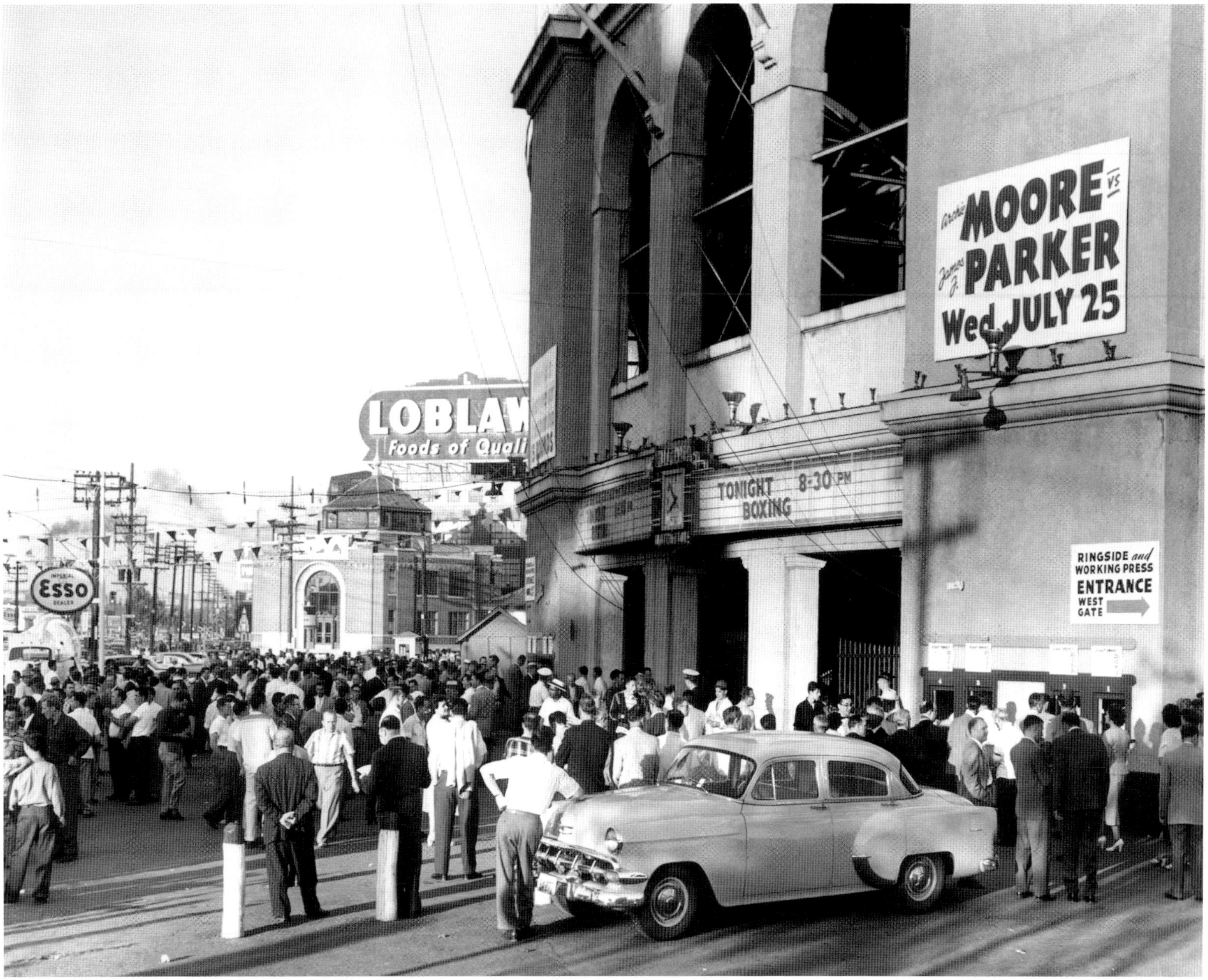

51 Fight Night in Toronto, July 25, 1956. Baseball wasn't the only sport played in Toronto's Maple Leaf Stadium.

It was also home to several National Football League games, and on several occasions it was the scene of championship boxing. In this photograph crowds await the start of the Archie Moore–James J. Parker contest. In this match, witnessed by nearly 20,000 fans who paid from $3 to $20 for a ticket, American Archie Moore scored a TKO (technical knock-out) over the Canadian and won $52,000 in the process. The loser took away $33,000 and a lot of bruises. Moore, who died in 1998 at the age of 84, has the distinction of knocking out 141 opponents, more than anyone else in professional boxing history. In the background of the photograph is the former Crosse and Blackwell building, used by Loblaws in this photo and presently the home of MTV television studios and offices. Also visible is a portion of the Esso gasoline station that, though modernized many times, has been on the corner since the early 1920s.

52 Before SkyDome ... Over the years a wide variety of new facilities have been proposed for Toronto sports fans.

This one, a $60-million idea, was created by one of the city's leading architectural firms, Parkin Associates, and was proposed for a site north and west of Downsview Airport in North York. It would be built in three phases and, in its completed form, would seat more than 65,000 people, cover nearly 15 acres (with another 66 acres nearby for parking), and have a domed roof (a moveable roof was not in the plan). In this sketch, downtown Toronto is in the distance, as is the Highway 401–W.R. Allen Road interchange, also known as "Spaghetti Junction."

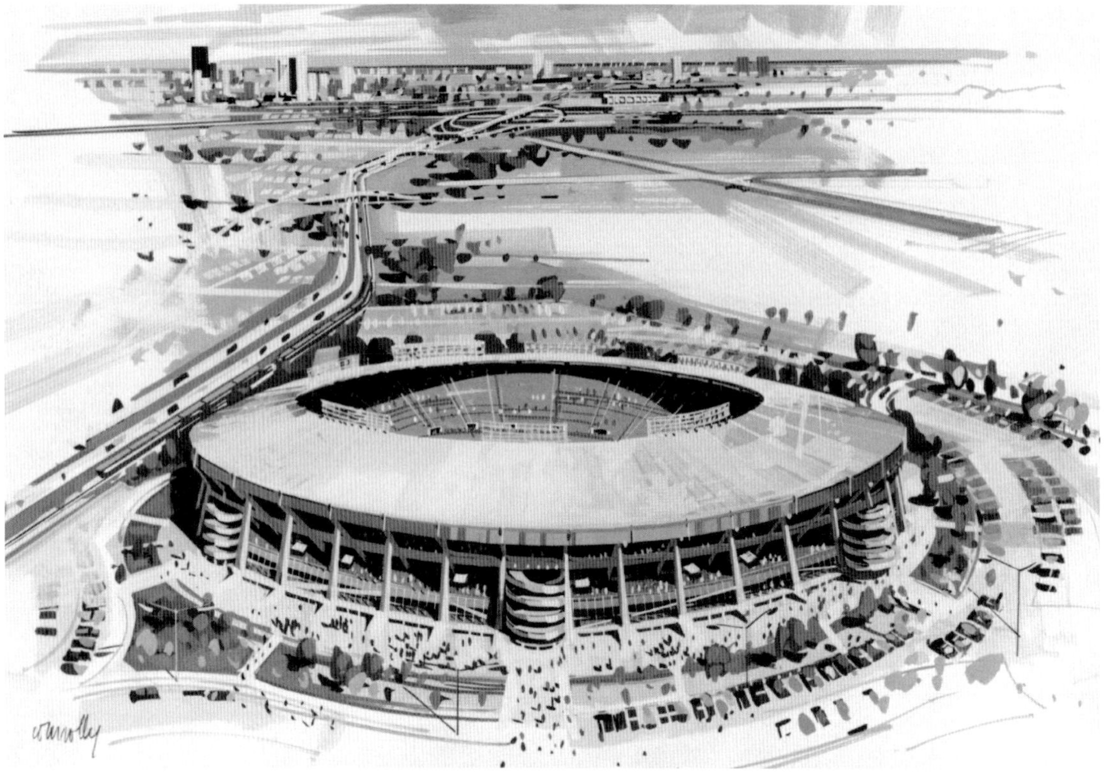

53 A second scheme, right, was presented to the city some years later by the architectural firm of Kelton and Lakka for a facility right in the heart of the city.

It was to be constructed near today's Metro Hall on King Street West at John. Obviously, neither project got very far. But, as we all know, the one called SkyDome did. It opened on June 3, 1989.

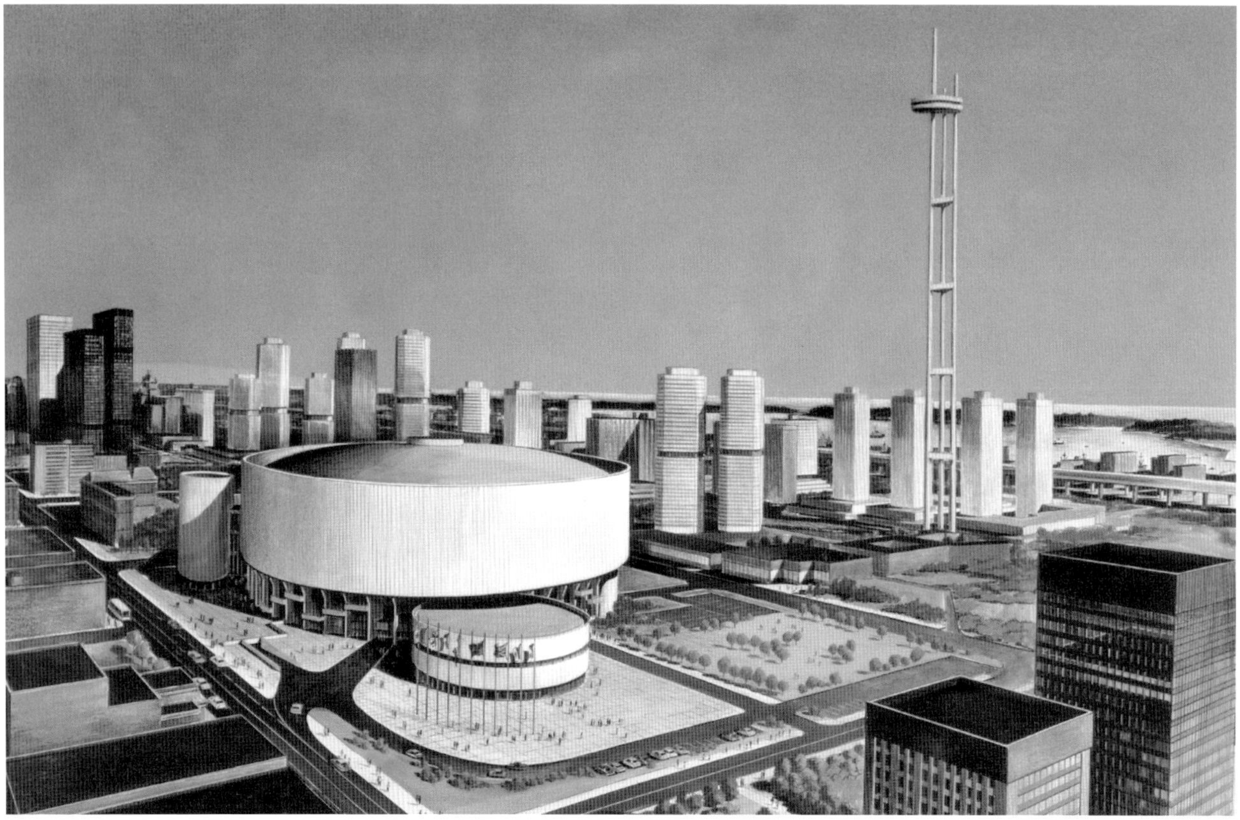

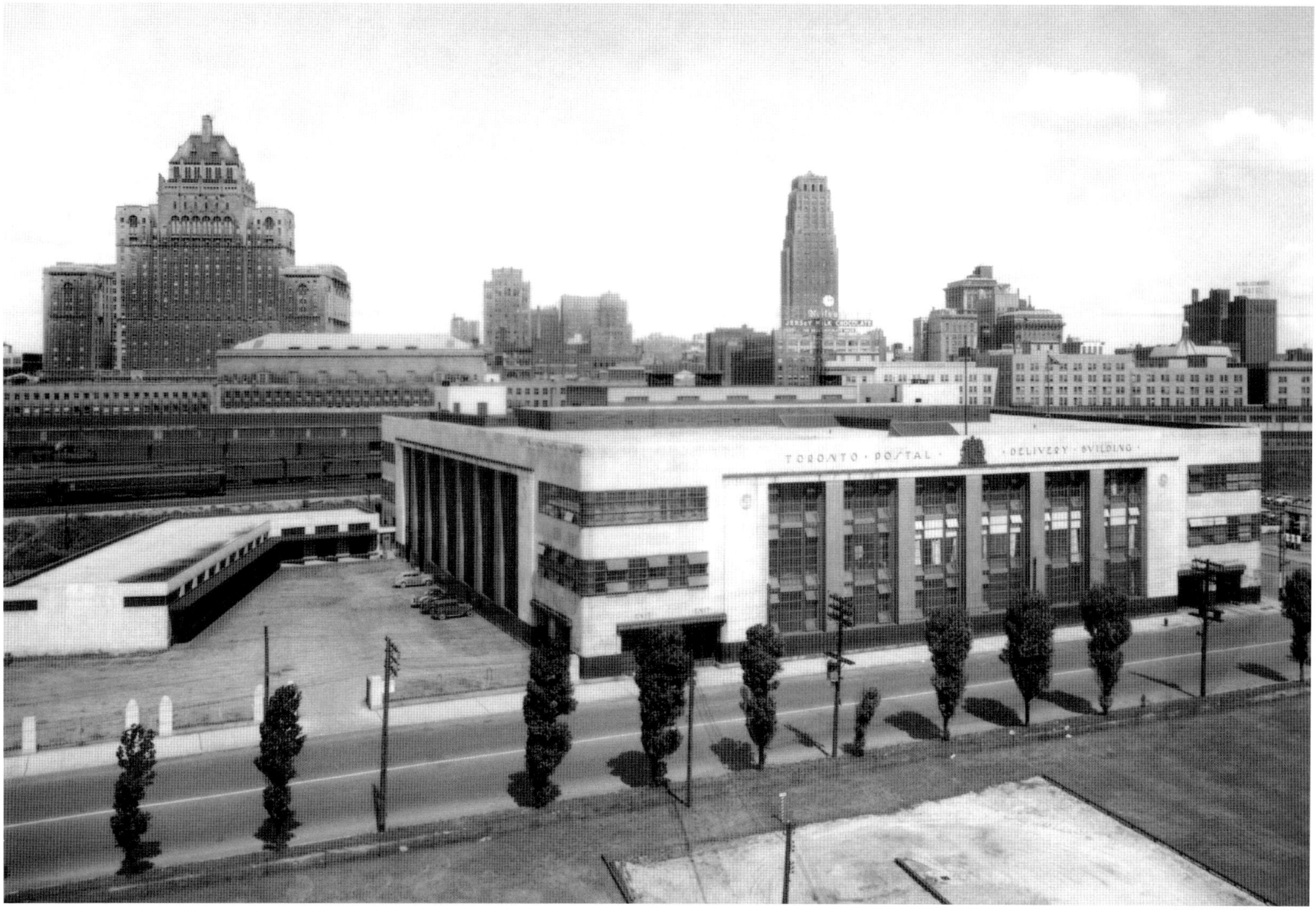

54 The Toronto Postal Delivery Building, Bay and Fleet Street (now Lake Shore Boulevard), 1944.

Toronto grew rapidly in the 1920s. However, its ability to handle the ever increasing amount of mail was severely restricted, even though a new postal handling facility had been incorporated into the east wing of the city's new Union Station. Additional facilities were badly needed, and a site for a massive new postal building was acquired at the northwest corner of Bay and Fleet streets. Construction began in the late 1930s but was interrupted by the outbreak of the Second World War. In fact, for a time the incomplete building was used for a variety of military purposes. With the war over, construction resumed, and soon the new Toronto Postal Delivery Building was ready for its intended purpose, a purpose it went on to fulfill for more than four and a half decades, until the post office moved much of its mail handling operations out of downtown Toronto. The old building then remained empty until the end of 1994, when the Toronto Raptors basketball team announced part of the building would be incorporated into its new arena, to be known as the Air Canada Centre. Construction began on March 12, 1997. Less than a year later ownership of the Maple Leaf hockey team and the Raptors came under the control of one company (Maple Leaf Gardens, Limited) resulting in the new arena having two tenants, the hockey Leafs and the basketball Raptors. The former's first game in the new arena was played on February 20, 1999, the latter's, the very next night.

55 Toronto's landmark sports facility, Maple Leaf Gardens, 1955.

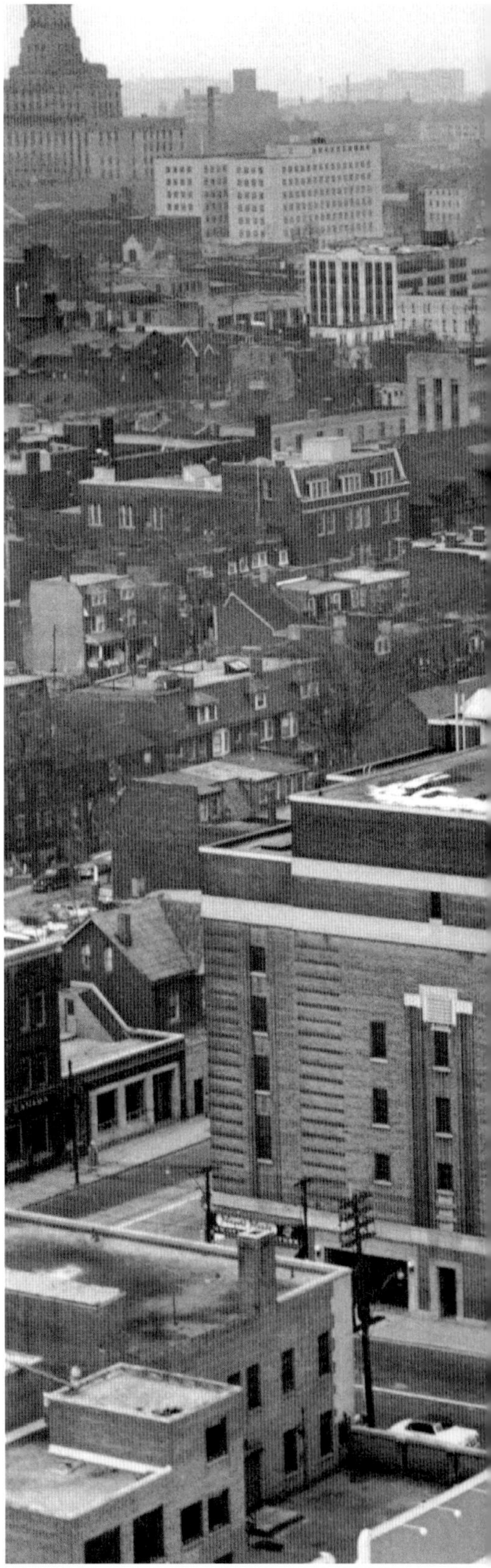

In 1919 a rumour was going around town that the so-called mystery block, a prime piece of Toronto real estate bounded by Yonge, Carlton, Church, and Alexander streets, on which Maple Leaf Gardens would eventually be built, had been secretly acquired by the Canadian Pacific Railway as the site of an enormous new hotel. This structure would be connected by a one-hundred-foot-wide, mile-long tunnel to the recently opened CPR North Toronto Station that straddled CPR's main line into and out of the city. The reason given for the CPR abandoning the almost completed Union Station on Front Street and moving uptown was their determination not to get involved with paying any portion of the $40-million price tag for the construction of a new elevated railway viaduct planned for the city's waterfront. The rumour of a hotel was eventually squashed, and the site remained undeveloped until years later, when Conn Smythe, owner of the Maple Leaf hockey team, raised the necessary money to erect a new ice palace for his team on part of the "mystery block."

With the money in the bank, demolition of the dozens of small structures that stood where the new Maple Leaf Gardens was to rise began on April 1, 1931, with actual construction of the new building commencing exactly one month later. With the Great Depression gripping the country, the thirteen hundred men on the mammoth project were glad to get the work — so much so that when money to meet the payroll was almost exhausted, many workers, as well as most contractors and suppliers, were satisfied to get 20 percent of the money they were owed, not in cash, but in common and preferred stock in the new building. As it turned out, it was a wise decision; after the Gardens opened, the shares increased greatly in value, making many of them rich. Toronto's new sports palace was officially opened on November 12, a mere 196 days after construction began. Unfortunately, the Leaf team lost the first NHL game played in the new building. In fact, the first Leaf victory didn't occur until November 28, 1931. While the Gardens was best known for hockey games, there were lots of other visitors: the Dionne Quintuplets, Winston Churchill, the Ice Capades, Rameses Shrine Circus, Perry Como, the Beatles, and the Royal Ballet, to name just a few.

Since the opening of the Leafs' new arena, the Air Canada Centre, in February 1999, the city's historic Maple Leaf Gardens has fallen on hard times. Its future is anything but assured. This view looks southwest with Church Street in the foreground, Carlton to the extreme left. The Canada Life Building pokes skyward at the left of the view. Skimming the horizon (left to right) we see the O'Keefe brewing warehouse (Dundas and Simcoe), the Hospital for Sick Children (University Avenue), Mount Sinai Hospital (University Avenue, now the Toronto Rehab Hospital), Eaton's College Street store (with the paired windows), the rising steelwork of the new addition to the Toronto General Hospital, and the Ontario Hydro Building (the latter two structures on University just south of College).

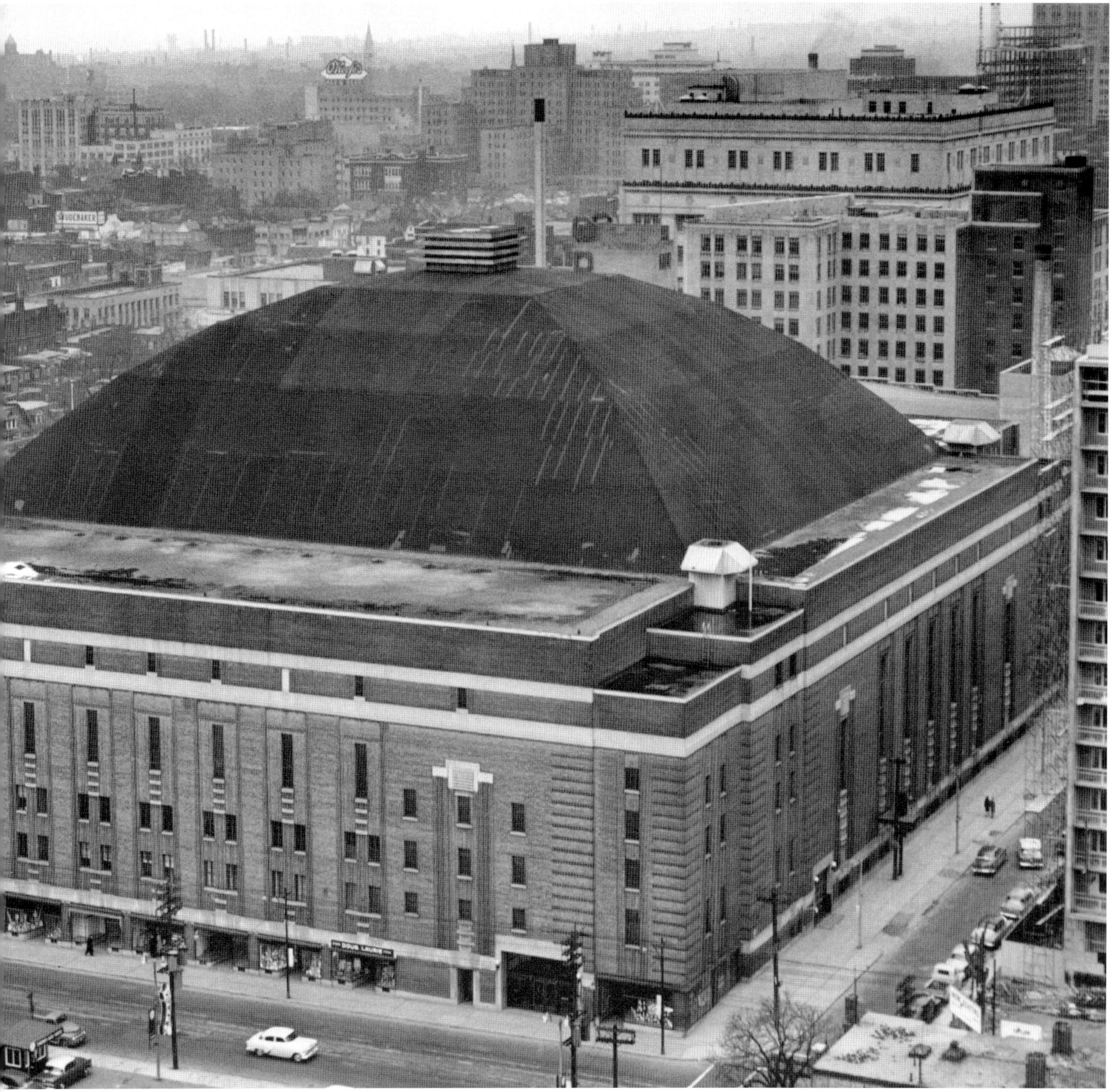

Toronto was an extremely busy place during the war years. A variety of aircraft were quite literally flying out of both the De Havilland factory in North York Township and the Victory (later AVRO Canada) plant at Malton Airport, guns emerged by the thousands from the old Massey-Harris tractor factory near the CNE grounds, and millions of shell fuses emanated from the sprawling GECO plant on Eglinton Avenue East in Scarborough. Truck and automotive products spewed forth from fabricating plants all over town, while the manufacture of highly classified optical parts and intricate components for the newly discovered radar made suburban Leaside busy day and night. Torontonians were doing their part.

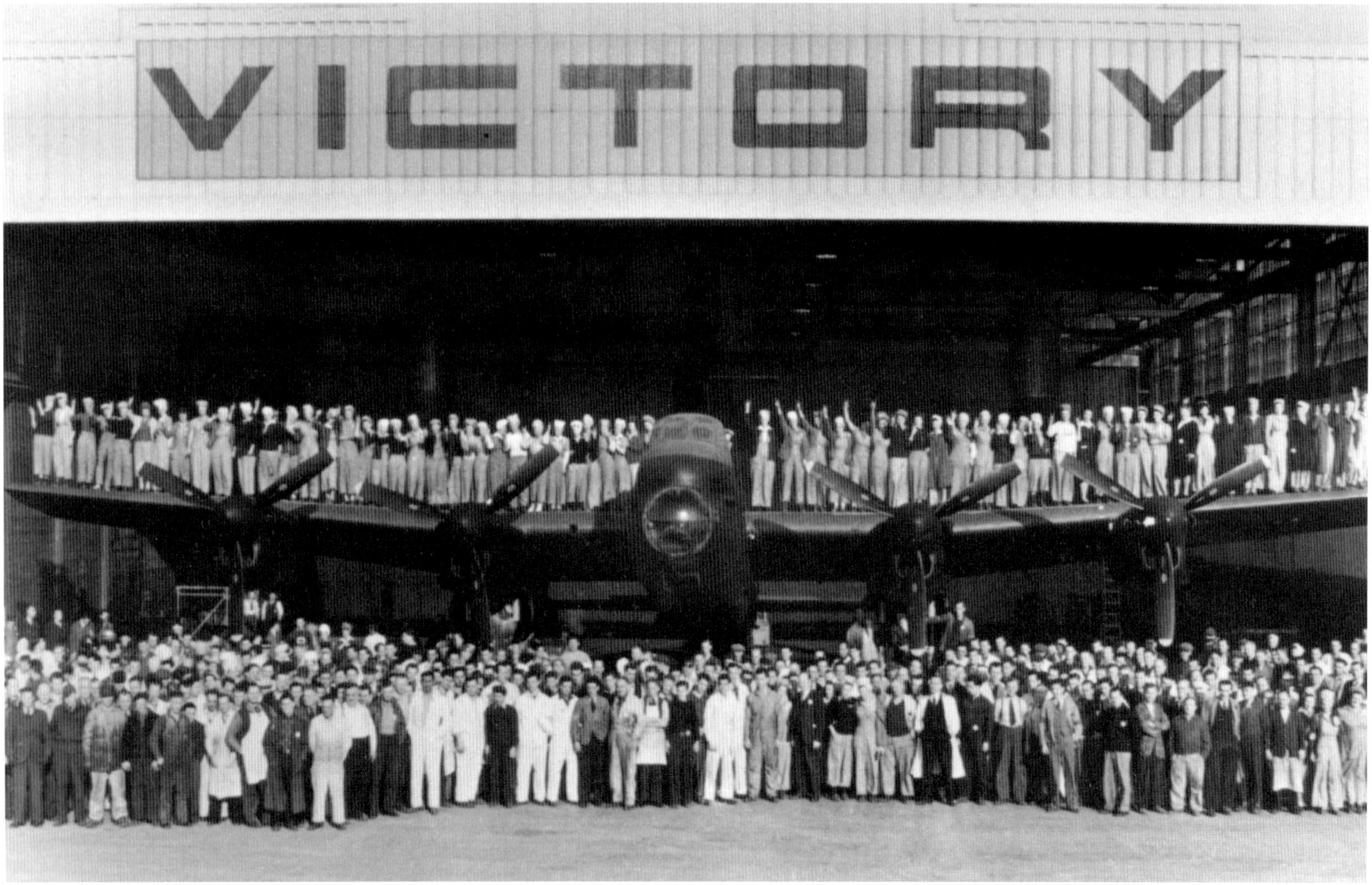

56 Workers pose for the photographer as the one-hundredth Lancaster bomber is rolled out of Victory Aircraft's Malton factory, 1944.

One of Canada's major contributions to the war effort was the manufacture of 430 Lancaster heavy bombers at Victory's Malton, Ontario factory, located at the north end of today's Pearson International Airport. The first of the Canadian Lancasters to take to the air was KB-700, dubbed the "Ruhr Express." It rolled off the assembly line on August 1, 1943. During peak production (one Lancaster per day) the Victory factory employed ten thousand workers. The aircraft shown in this unique photograph, KB-799, was taken on strength by the RCAF in October 1944. It joined 419 (Moose) Squadron based at Middelton St. George, England and was lost, with its crew of seven, during a raid on the oil refinery complex at Merseberg, Germany on January 14, 1945.

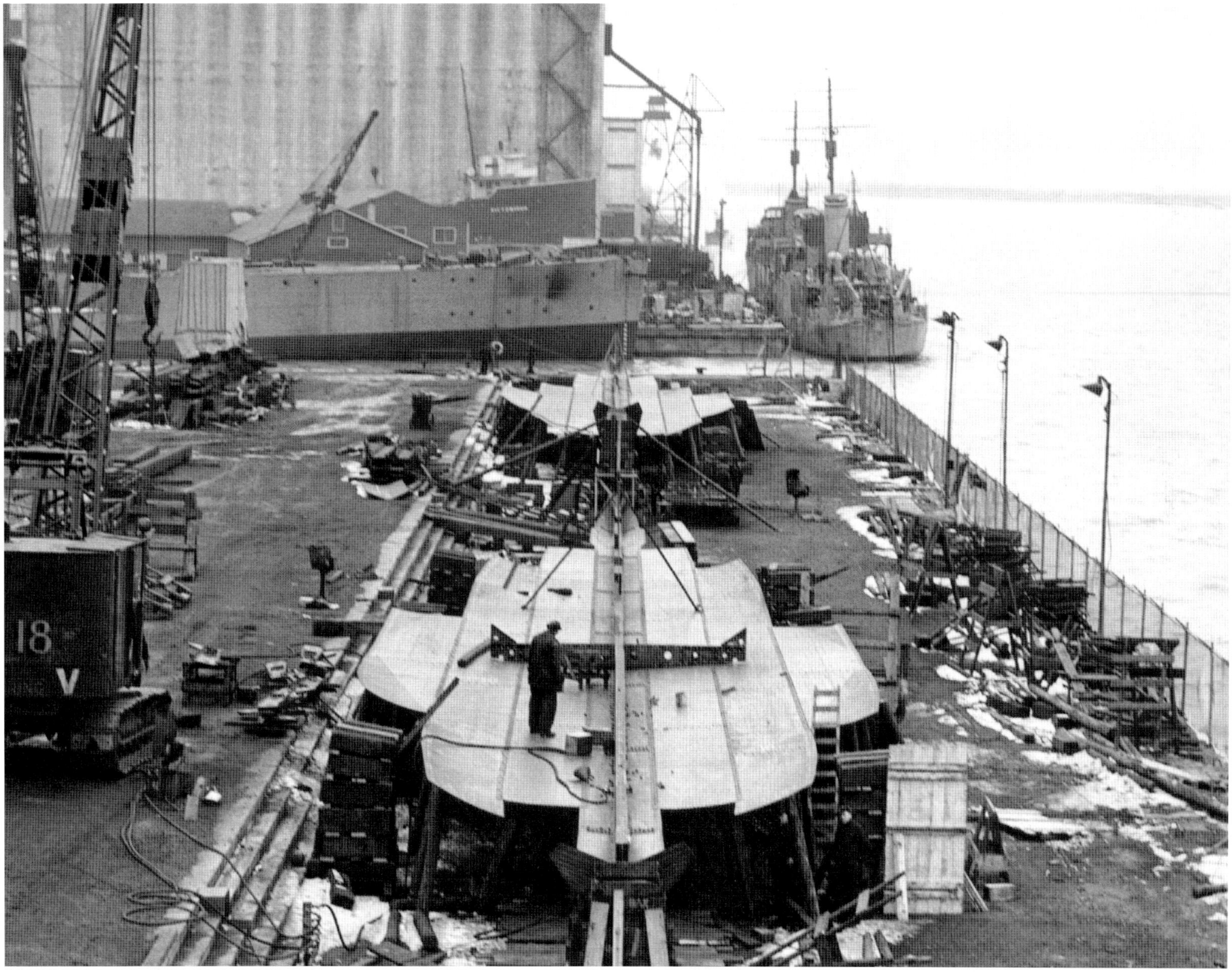

57 Laying the keel of a new warship at the foot of Spadina Avenue, sometime in 1942.

Located on the water's edge, about where the stately King's Landing condominium now stands (landfilling has drastically changed the shoreline), stood a busy wartime shipyard that under a trio of names (Dufferin Shipbuilding, Toronto Shipbuilding, and Redfern Construction) turned out fifty-six Bangor and Algerine class minesweepers for the Royal Canadian Navy and Royal Navy. The first vessel, HMCS *Burlington*, slid into the waters of Toronto Bay on November 23, 1940, and the last, HMS *Nerissa*, exactly four years and two days later. At peak production almost three thousand workers toiled night and day at this ambitious Toronto waterfront factory. In this view both the Spadina slip and the 1928 grain elevator complex owned by the Toronto Elevator Company are visible. Recent realignment of Queen's Quay West has resulted in the thoroughfare now passing south of the war plant. This photograph, perhaps taken without authority, is only dated with the year.

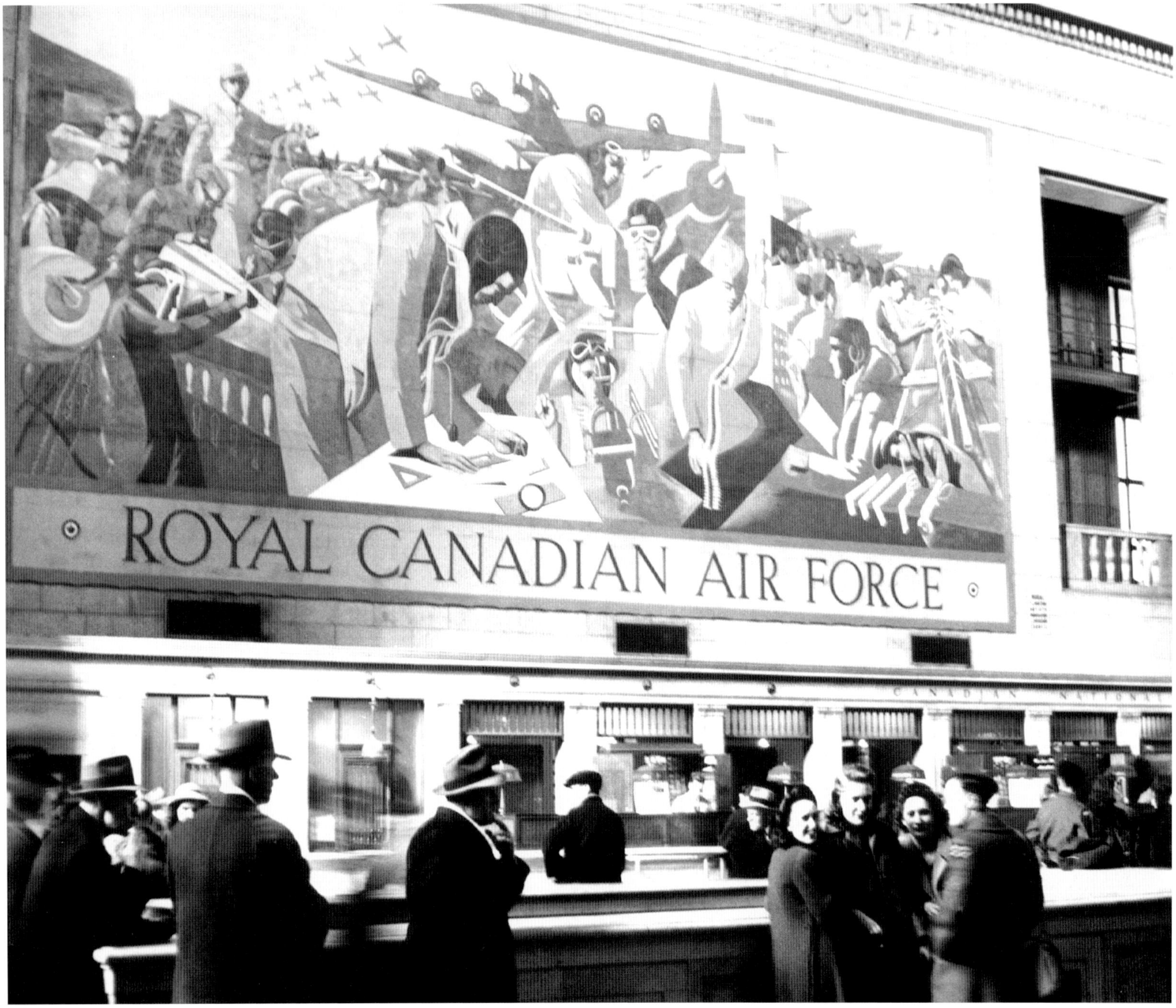

58 Royal Canadian Air Force mural in the Great Hall of Toronto's imposing Union Station, March 1943.

This 8.2-metre by 17.7-metre (27-foot by 58-foot) mural was the creation of Nancy Burden, a young Toronto commercial artist, and was commissioned by the Writers', Artists', Broadcasters' and Musicians' Council as a memorial and artistic contribution to the war effort. Burden's work, for which she was awarded $150, featured the various phases of training undertaken by RCAF recruits and was prominently displayed on the north wall of the station's Great Hall. Unfortunately, the ultimate disposition of this interesting example of Canadiana is unknown.

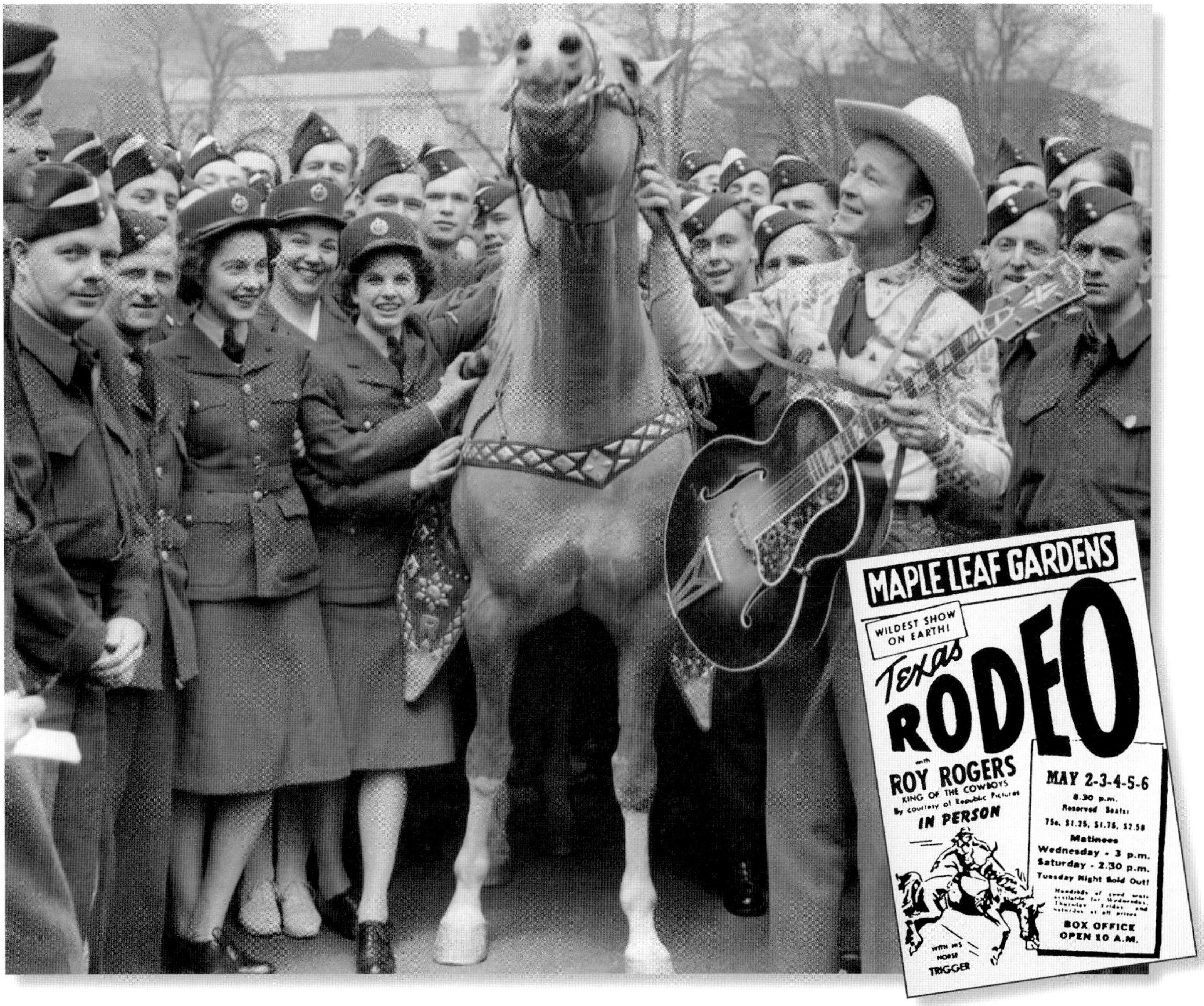

59–60 Roy Rogers and his golden palomino, Trigger, perform for armed forces personnel during his visit to Toronto in May 1944.

"The King of the Cowboys" was in Toronto to perform at a rodeo at Maple Leaf Gardens. Roy agreed that the proceeds of one of the afternoon performances would be donated to the British War Victims' Fund (BWVF), which was established early in the war by the city's *Evening Telegram*. Interestingly, most of the money from the Fund (almost $3 million) was used to build replacement housing for senior citizens throughout England who had lost their homes during bombing raids. All of these new housing complexes incorporated the name "Toronto" in their titles and are still to be found in such cities as Liverpool, Sheffield, Southampton, and Exeter.

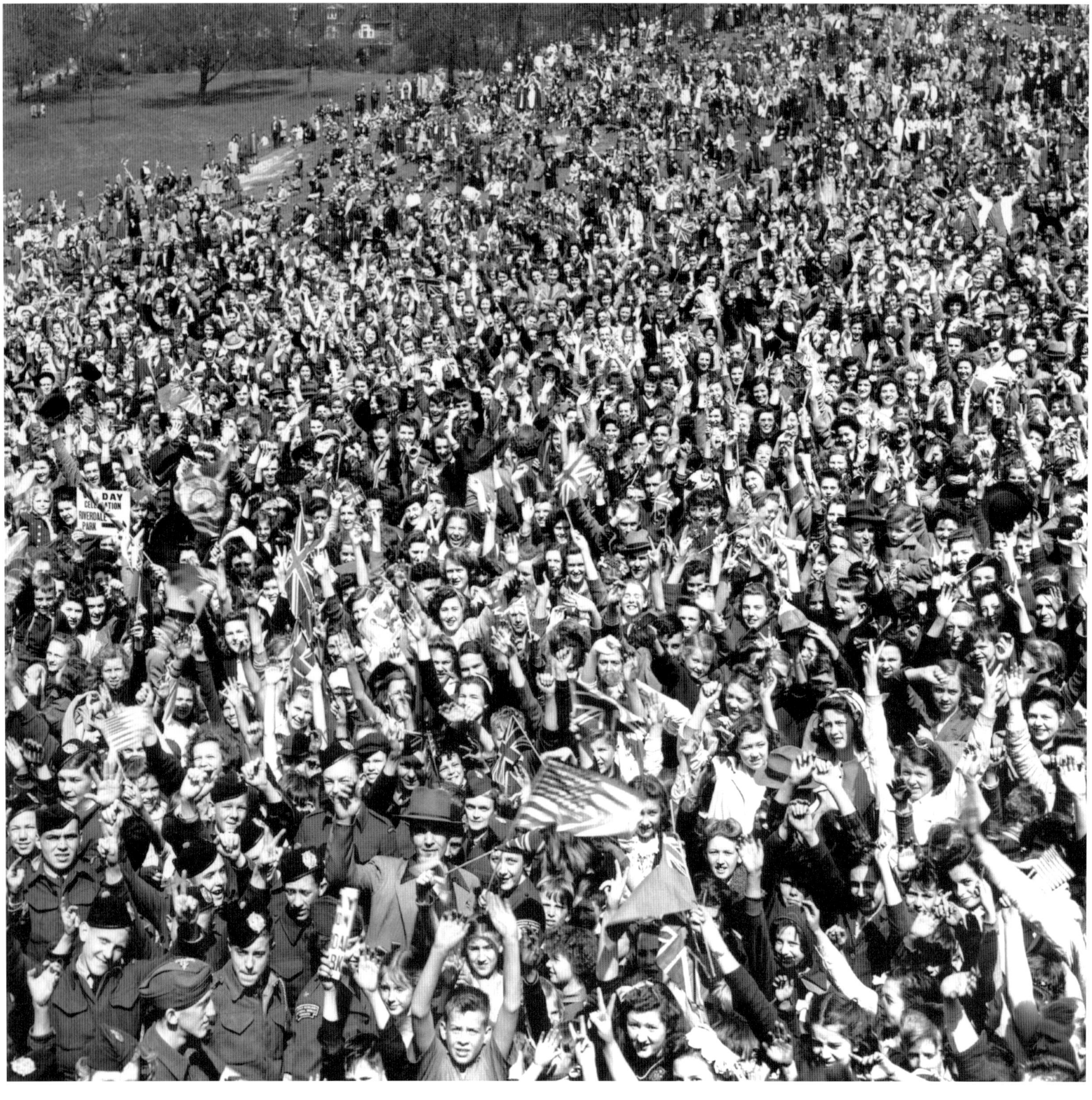

61 Victory in Europe celebrations in Riverdale Park, May 7, 1945.

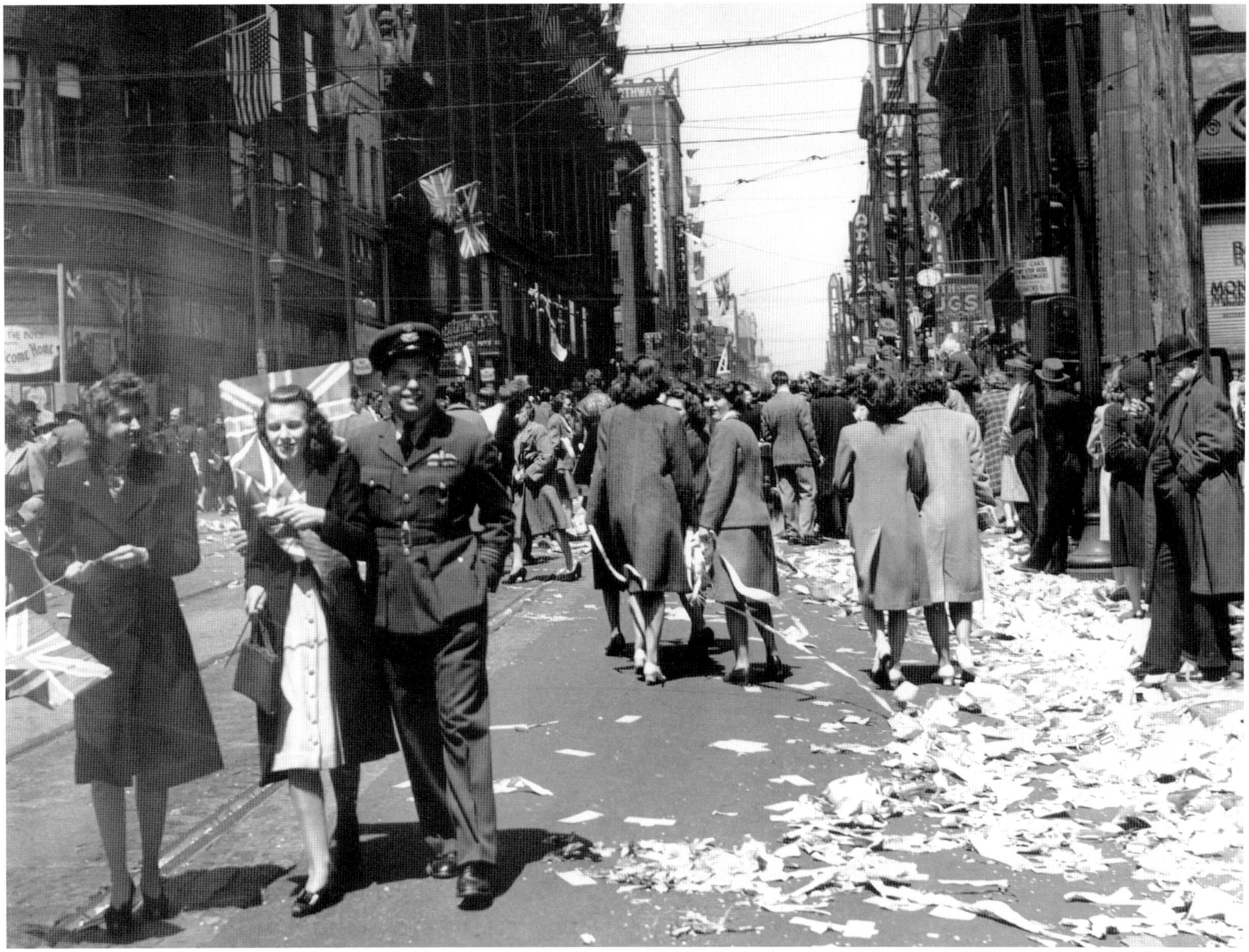

62 Victory in Europe celebrations on Yonge Street south of Queen, May 7, 1945.

As the spring of 1945 arrived, it appeared that the Allied forces in Europe would declare victory over the enemy at any moment. Anxious to get a "scoop," a few radio networks announced the war's successful conclusion prematurely. With obvious embarrassment in their voices, newscasters would then retract the bulletin. Cheers turned to sighs. Finally, at 9:30 in the morning on May 7, an official statement announced that the war in Europe was over. To say that the city went wild would be an understatement. Within half an hour downtown traffic was snarled while streams of ticker tape began to block out the sun shining down on a frantic Bay Street. Patients in the Christie Street Military Hospital burst into patriotic songs while overhead Canadian-built Mosquito bombers dropped leaflets with Mayor Robert Saunders's proclamation that the war was finally over and that the following day, May 8, would be observed as VE-Day. Once the euphoria had worn off thousands attended open-air church services held in several city parks where they honoured those who would never return.

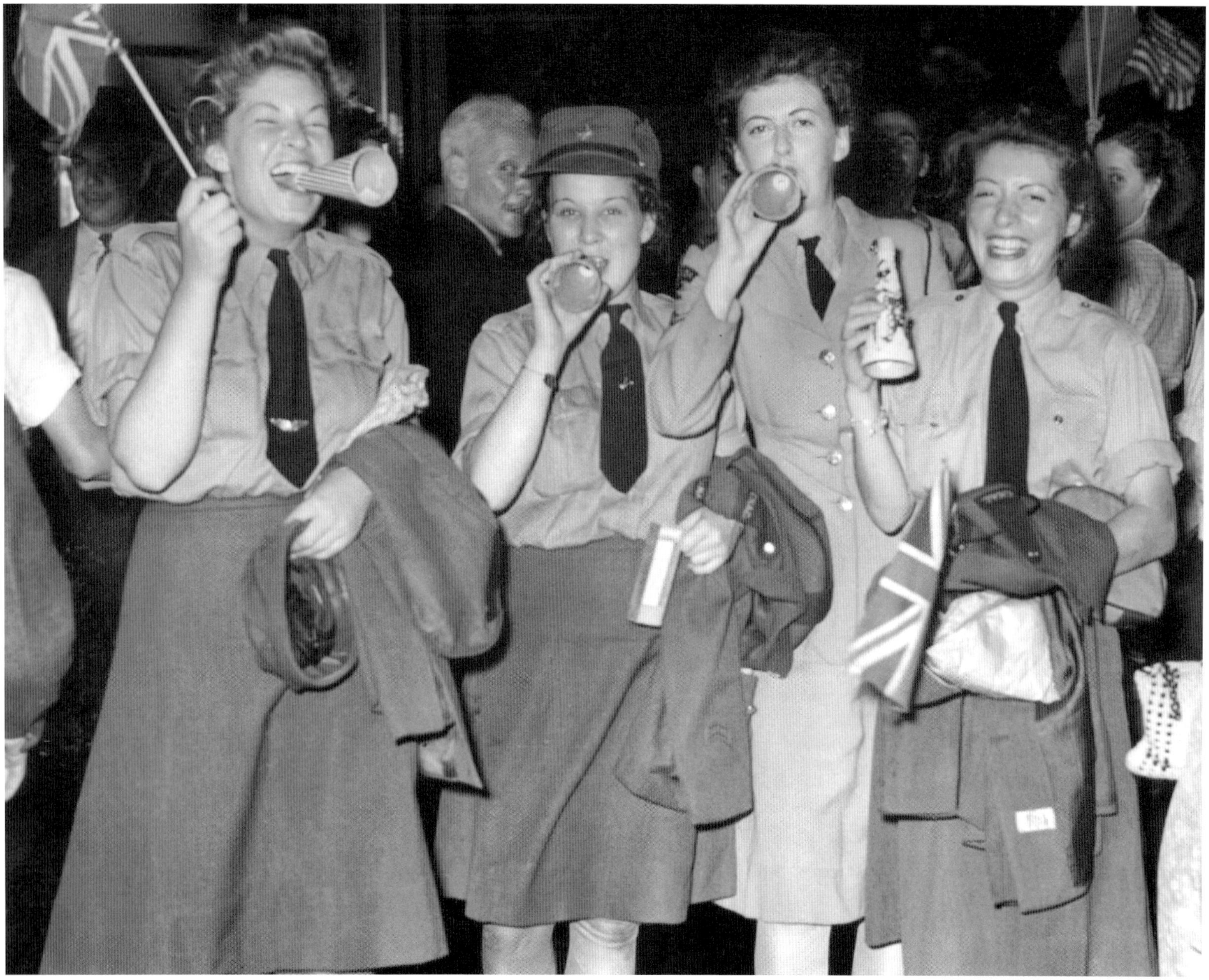

63 Four members of the Canadian Women's Army Corp celebrate VJ-Day in Toronto, August 15, 1945.

As they did after hearing that the war in Europe was over, Torontonians celebrated when victory over Japan was announced on August 15, 1945. There were spontaneous parades and street dancing, but all that changed with the terrible realization that thousands of Canadian men and women who had made the supreme sacrifice in battles all over the world would never return home. One of the largest events held that hot August day was at Kew Beach Park, where more than ten thousand people, led by the ministers of the nearby Kew Beach United Church and the Church of the Resurrection, prayed and sang. At Greenwood and Riverdale parks hushed crowds listened solemnly as patriotic and religious music was played by the quickly assembled bands of the Queen's Own Rifles and Governor-General's Horse Guards.

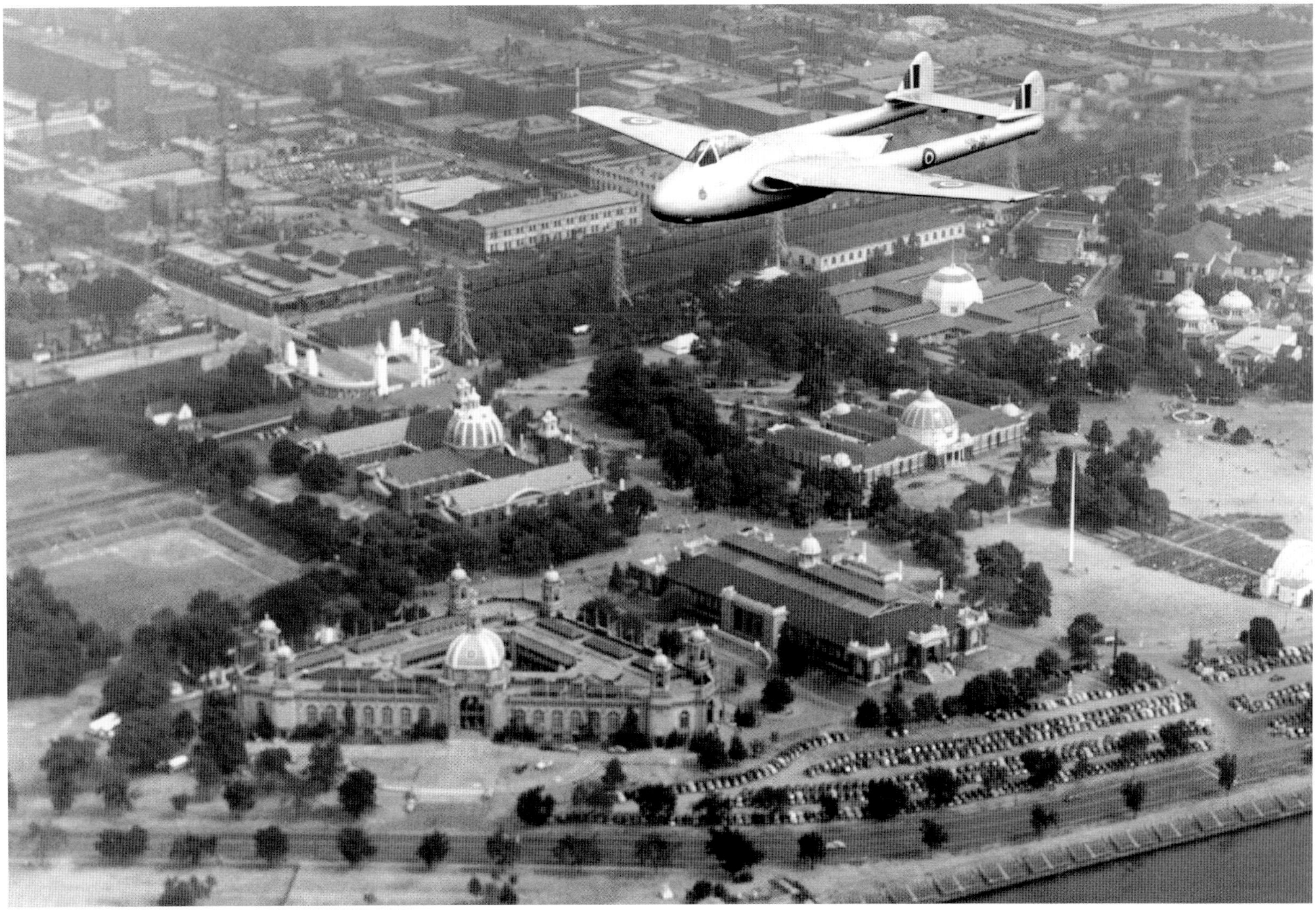

64 A Vampire jet soars over the CNE grounds, 1948.

The De Havilland Vampire was developed in England and first flew in the fall of 1943. After briefly considering another pioneer jet fighter, the Gloster Meteor, the Canadian government decided to enter the jet age by equipping the RCAF with eighty-six of the new De Havilland Vampires. This revolutionary aircraft had a top speed of 500 to 550 mph, and in 1948 two were assigned to 400 City of Toronto (Auxiliary) Squadron, replacing its six "ancient" Harvards. Vampire was replaced in the mid-1950s by the T-33 Silver Star, which was in turn was replaced by the F-86.

400 Squadron traces its history back to 1932; in 1940 it became the first RCAF squadron to go overseas. At that time it was redesignated 400 City of Toronto Squadron and throughout the war flew Lysanders, Tomahawks, Spitfires, and Mustangs. Now, as 400 Tactical Helicopter Squadron, this proud member of Canada's defence team operates a fleet of seven Bell CH146 Griffon helicopters. Visible in this aerial view of the west end of the CNE grounds are several now-demolished Exhibition buildings: (centre left) Dufferin Gate, (centre bottom) the International Building, and (under the Vampire's left wing) the General Exhibits Building and Art Gallery. The two buildings at centre left are the Government Building (later the Arts, Crafts and Hobbies Building) and, closer to the waterfront, the Ontario Government Building (later the Carlsberg Pavilion). Today they are Medieval Times and the wonderfully restored Liberty Grand, respectively.

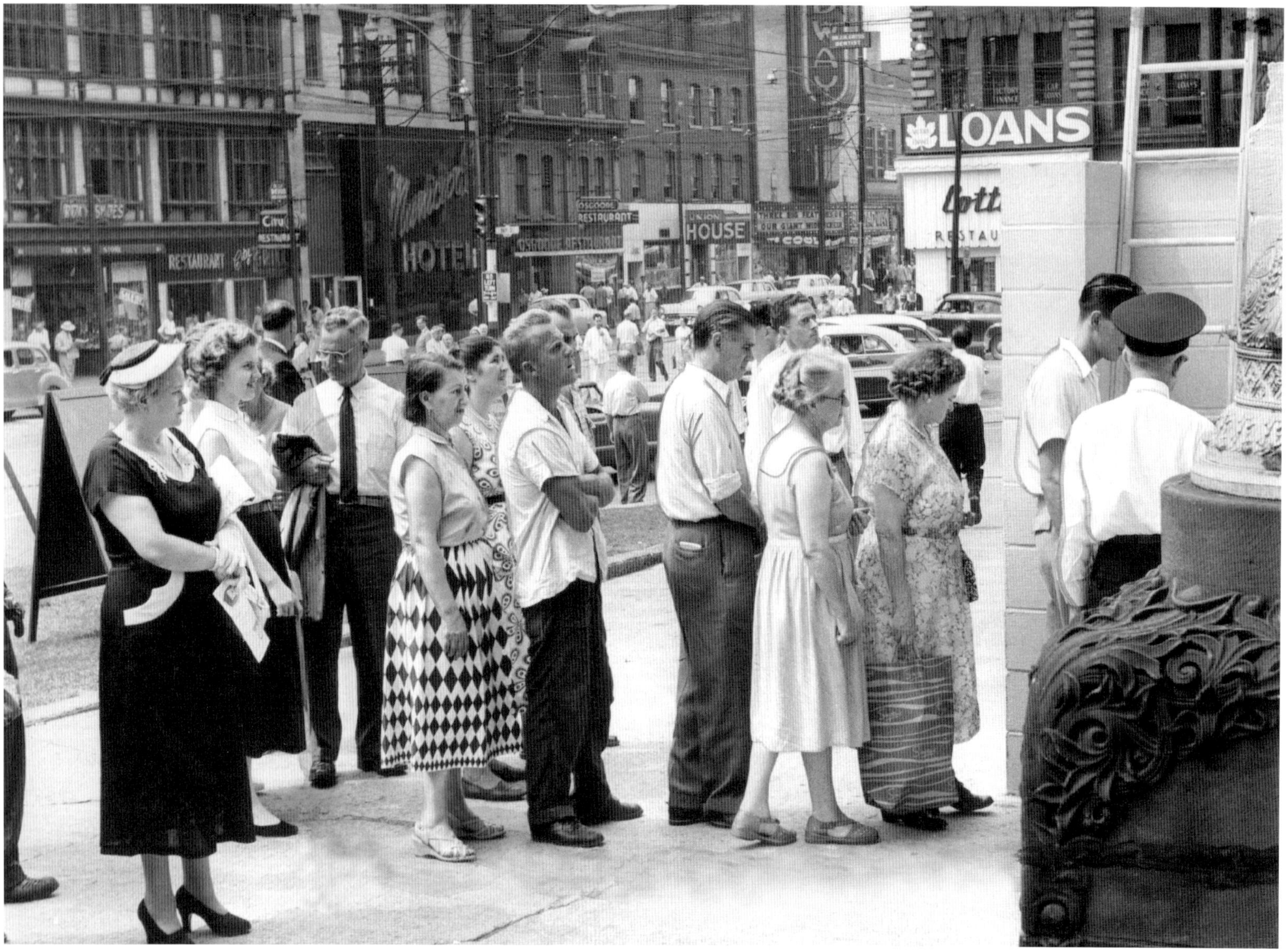

65 Curious Torontonians visit a model H-Bomb shelter set up in front of City Hall, August 1955.

The advent of the Cold War resulted in many Canadians taking a closer look at what they might do to protect themselves and their families should a nuclear attack be imminent. Across the country, numerous civil defence organizations were set up, while here in Toronto, the *Telegram*, one of the city's three daily newspapers at the time, sponsored a full-size, fully equipped H-bomb shelter. It was officially opened by General "Fighting Frank" Worthington, head of the nation's civil defence organization. Over a period of two weeks in the summer of 1955 the shelter was inspected by more than fifty thousand curious (and frightened) members of the general public. In the background of this photograph we see some of the myriad of old shops, stores, restaurants, and theatres that stood on the south side of Queen Street opposite the site of the new City Hall. Included in the mix were the Broadway and Casino theatres and Henry Stein's little pawnbroking shop, which over the years has evolved into Henry's chain of photographic and digital equipment stores. All the old buildings were demolished and the area turned into parkland. The Sheraton Centre Hotel, which opened in October 1972, now occupies the site.

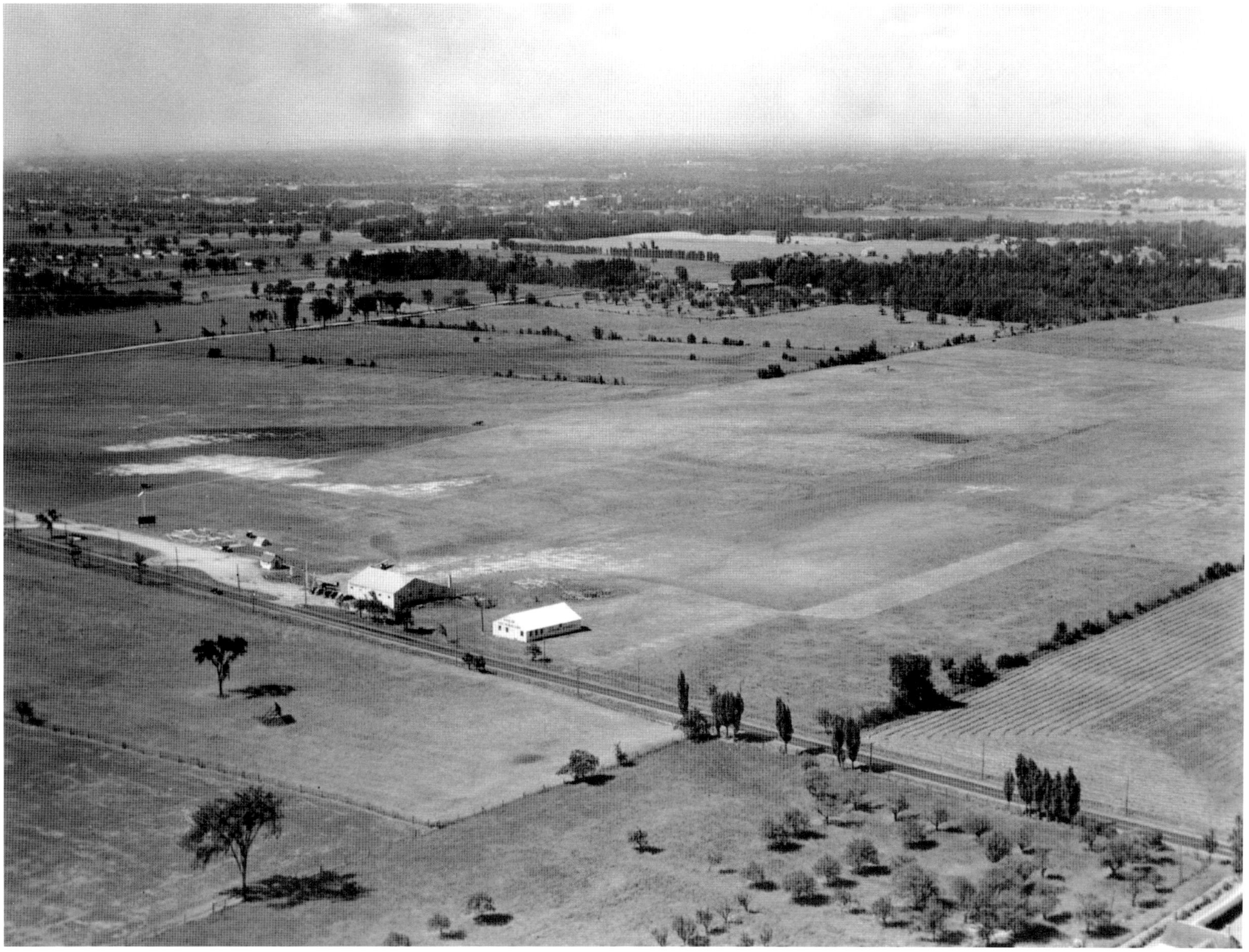

66 Barker Air Field, North York Township, 1941.

One of the federal government's ideas for Toronto's modern new airport was simply to enlarge Barker Field, which was located on the west side of Dufferin Street just north of today's Lawrence Avenue. Barker Field was first used as a flying field in 1927 and remained nameless until June 6, 1931, when Toronto Mayor William Stewart dedicated the field to the memory of First World War flying ace Col. W.G. "Billy" Barker VC, who had died in a flying accident at the Ottawa Airport the previous year. In its early years the field was used by Bishop-Barker Aeroplanes Limited, a pioneer aerial photography business that was co-owned by two Canadian First World War aces and Victoria Cross winners, Billy Bishop and Billy Barker. Later tenants included Century Airways (owned by future Toronto mayor and aviation enthusiast Allan Lamport), National Air Transport, and Leavens Brothers. Barker Field remained in operation until 1953, when it was squeezed out by the commercialization of what had been the tranquil farmland that had once surrounded the airfield.

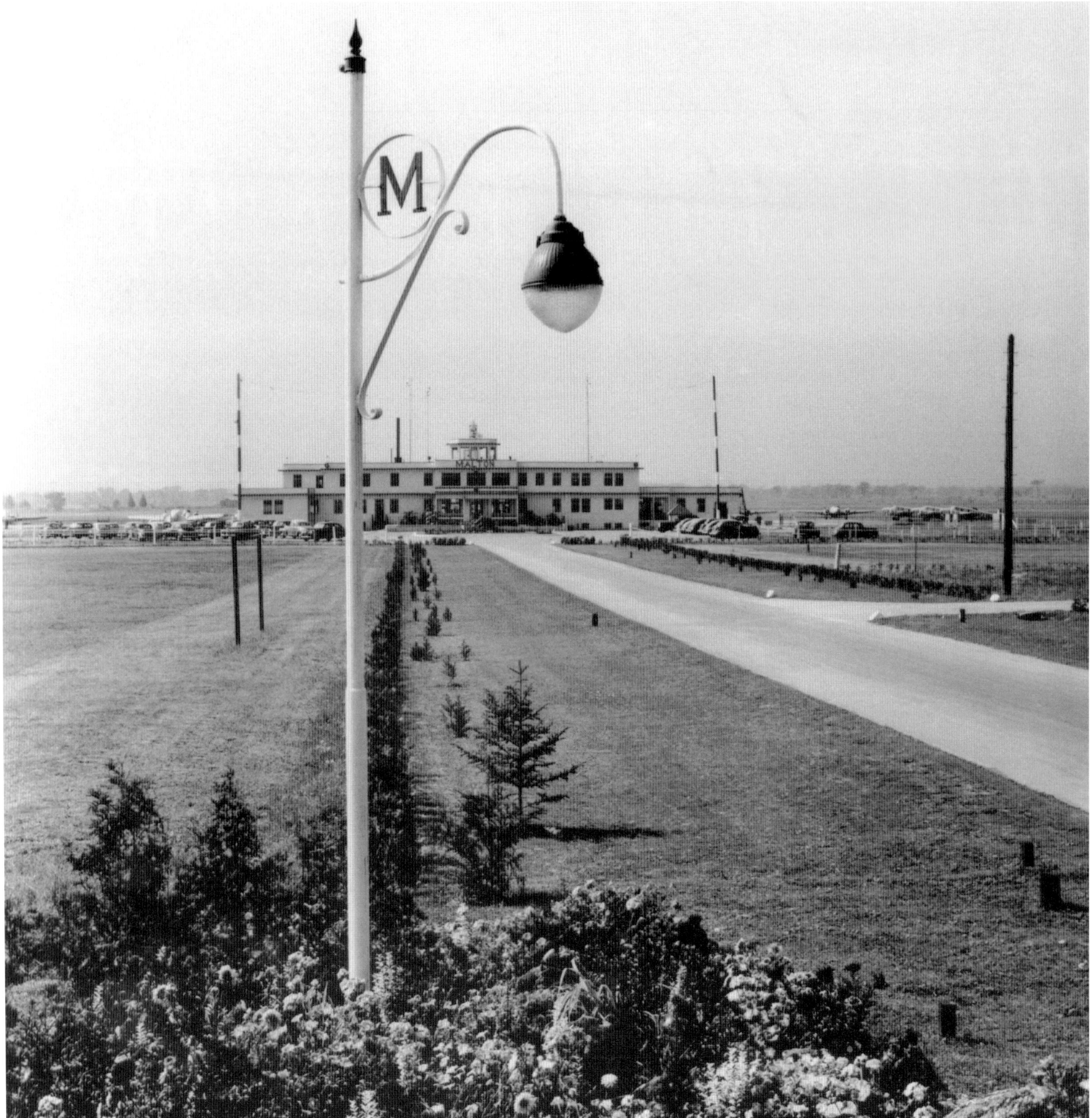
M

67 The new Malton Airport and its even newer Administration Building, circa 1939.

In the summer of 1910 a flying meet was held on the Trethewey farm northwest of the city. Aviation was in its infancy, and when aviator Count Jacques de Lesseps piloted his crude biplane over the City of Toronto on July 13 citizens were totally flabbergasted. Over the years, numerous small, grass-covered airfields sprang up all around the city. None, however, was suitable to accommodate the larger planes that were now able to provide inter-city passenger and freight handling services. Even more time went by, and Toronto continued to be ridiculed for its lack of interest in the future of aviation. In fact, it wasn't until 1935 that the federal government finally got its act together and announced it would build a $1-million airport to serve the aviation needs of Toronto. Government press releases trumpeted that it would be "the finest in all Canada." But where would it be built? That was still the question. Eventually, the government announced that it was considering two possible sites, both of which were in the still rural Township of North York. The first would involve the expansion of an existing airfield on the west side of Dufferin Street, a mile or so north of today's Lawrence Avenue West. (At that time, both thoroughfares were still nothing more than dirt trails.) The second possibility was the creation of an airport on a large piece of farmland at the northeast corner of Dufferin Street and Wilson Avenue that was owned by the Toronto Flying Club. In the meantime, Toronto city council had developed its own agenda and was eagerly promoting a new "Air Harbour" that would be laid out at the west end of Toronto Island. To advance its desire city council was able to convince Prime Minister R.B. Bennett to approve the construction of a $1-million tunnel to serve this proposed airport. However, just two weeks after a large steam shovel began preliminary digging for the new tunnel at the foot of Bathurst Street, the federal government in Ottawa changed hands and the new prime minister, W.L. Mackenzie King, ordered all work on the tunnel stopped. Within hours the gaping hole was no more. Talks on where to build the city's new airport continued. Finally, in June 1937, officials representing both the city and the federal government announced the location of not one, but two new airports to serve the city. The main field would be located at Hanlan's Point on Toronto Island, the same site originally promoted by the city. A second, or what was termed at the time an "auxiliary airport," would be located at a site not even in the running when plans and possible sites were announced several years before. This airfield would cover more than fifteen hundred acres of farmland in Toronto Township not far from the small farming community of Malton, Ontario. Officials insisted, however, that it was only to be used in the event that fog closed down the main airport on the Island. Work proceeded, and the first flight landed at the new Toronto Island Airport on February 4, 1939. Soon after, the airport's name was changed to Port George VI to honour of the reigning monarch's first Canadian visit. That name has long since vanished, and the facility is now known as Toronto City Centre. Today, this airport's future is very much in doubt. The first landing at Malton Airport had occurred several months earlier, on August 29, 1938, when a "giant" American Airlines twin-engined, twenty-one-passenger DC-3 landed at the still unfinished airport. It brought special invited guests to Toronto to see that year's CNE. The new Administration Building (identical in design to the one under construction to serve the Island Airport) wouldn't open for another year. When it was suggested that the airfield at Malton be named in honour of Canadian air ace Billy Bishop VC, the federal government nixed the idea, saying airports should not be named for people but for the city they served. Nevertheless, what was Malton Airport from its opening to 1960, then Toronto International until 1984, is now known as Pearson International in tribute to Lester B. Pearson, Canadian prime minister from 1963 to 1968. The airport is now undergoing a 10-year, $4.4-billion redevelopment program that by 2020 will have 50 million passengers using its numerous moving sidewalks, 258 check-in counters, and 12,600 parking spaces annually.

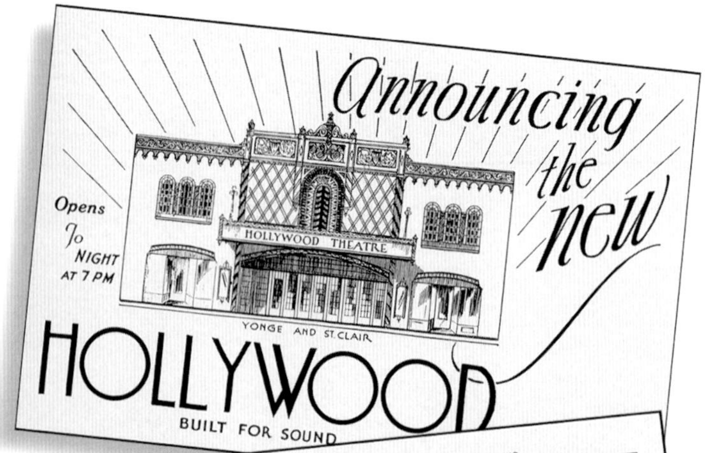

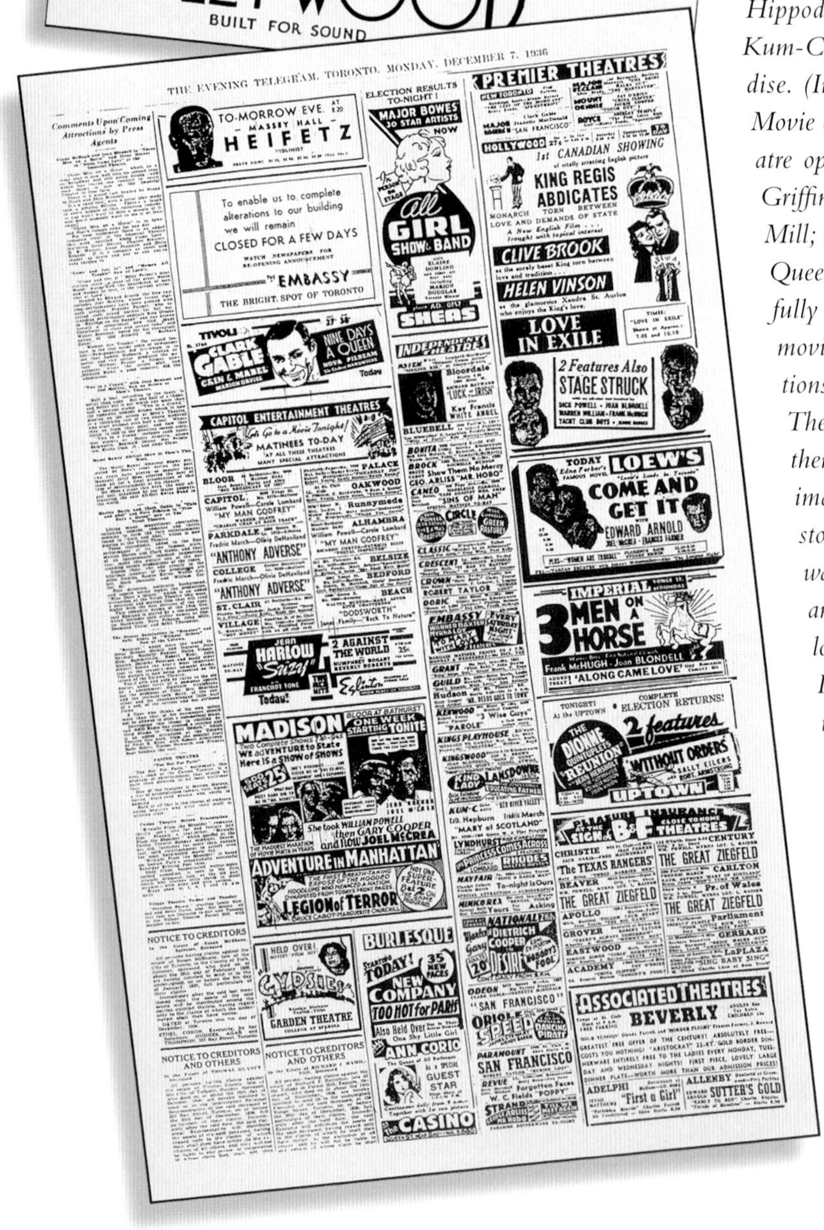

A quartet of popular Toronto motion picture theatres.

In the past, Toronto was often referred to as the "city of churches and chestnuts," a reference to the numerous houses of worship and lofty chestnut trees that could be found in abundance throughout the young city. Something that could have been added to that descriptive phrase might have been the words "movie houses," since in years gone by Torontonians had dozens from which to choose. From majestic downtown picture palaces, such as the Loew's, Uptown, Shea's Hippodrome, and Tivoli, to small neighbourhood theatres like the Kum-C, Mavety, Beaver, and Circle, Toronto was a movie-goer's paradise. (Incidentally, the Paradise was at 1006 Bloor Street West.) Movie experts agree that the nation's first regular motion picture theatre opened in Toronto in 1896. It was originally known as John Griffin's Nickelodeon, then the Theatorium, and later still the Red Mill; it stood on the east side of Yonge Street a few steps north of Queen and not far from the Ontario Heritage Foundation's beautifully restored Elgin and Winter Garden Theatre Centre. The first movies presented in Toronto were short, American-made productions for which patrons would pay an admission fee of five cents. They would enter what had been a small store a few days before then sit on uncomfortable kitchen chairs and watch out-of-focus images flicker across a large white sheet hanging on one of the store walls. So popular were the "movies" that before long there was a proliferation of these theatres, places where working men and women, and their children, could spend a little and enjoy a lot. As late as 1951, the Year Book of the Canadian Motion Picture Industry listed more than 125 theatres in Toronto ranging in size from the tiny 325-seat Avon at 1092 Queen Street West to the mammoth 3,373-seat Imperial on Yonge, south of Dundas. Today, neighbourhood movie houses are few and far between, although an intrepid few, like the Mt. Pleasant, Metro, and Belsize, continue to soldier on.

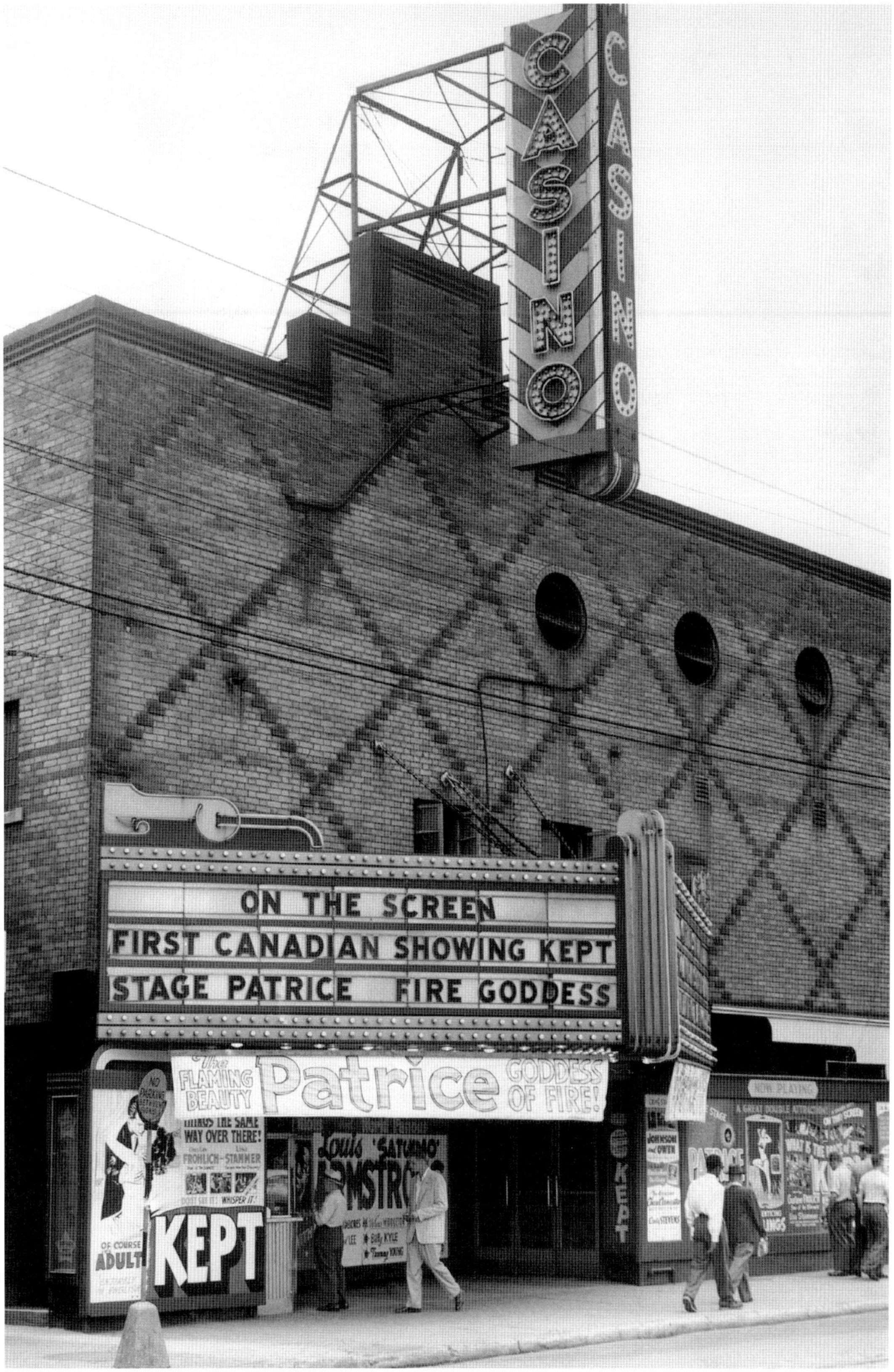

68 The popular Casino theatre on the south side of Queen Street West, directly opposite today's New City Hall.

The Casino opened in 1936 as a vaudeville and burlesque house. After nearly two decades in that business, theatre management changed its policy and began offering customers a place to see and enjoy young up-and-coming recording stars and not-so-young, on-their-way-down movie actors and actresses. A so-so movie was usually thrown in to help clear the place so a new batch of paying patrons could see the next show. A few of the performers who played the Casino were Kay Starr (August 1950), Rudy Vallee (June 1951), Tony Bennett (July 1951), Nat King Cole (January 1952), Basil Rathbone (October 1952), Toronto's own Four Lads (December 1952), Mickey Rooney (June 1953), Christine Jorgensen (the original cross-dresser, December 1953), Johnnie Ray (the other Prince of Wails, June 1953), Louis Armstrong (February 1953), and Eddie Fisher (July 1955). Before its closure and subsequent demolition the Casino tried showing strippers and then, as the Civic Square and later the Festival theatres, tried plays and international films. This time there were few takers. Finally, in 1965, as the movie *My Name is Ivan* flickered out, so too did the Casino.

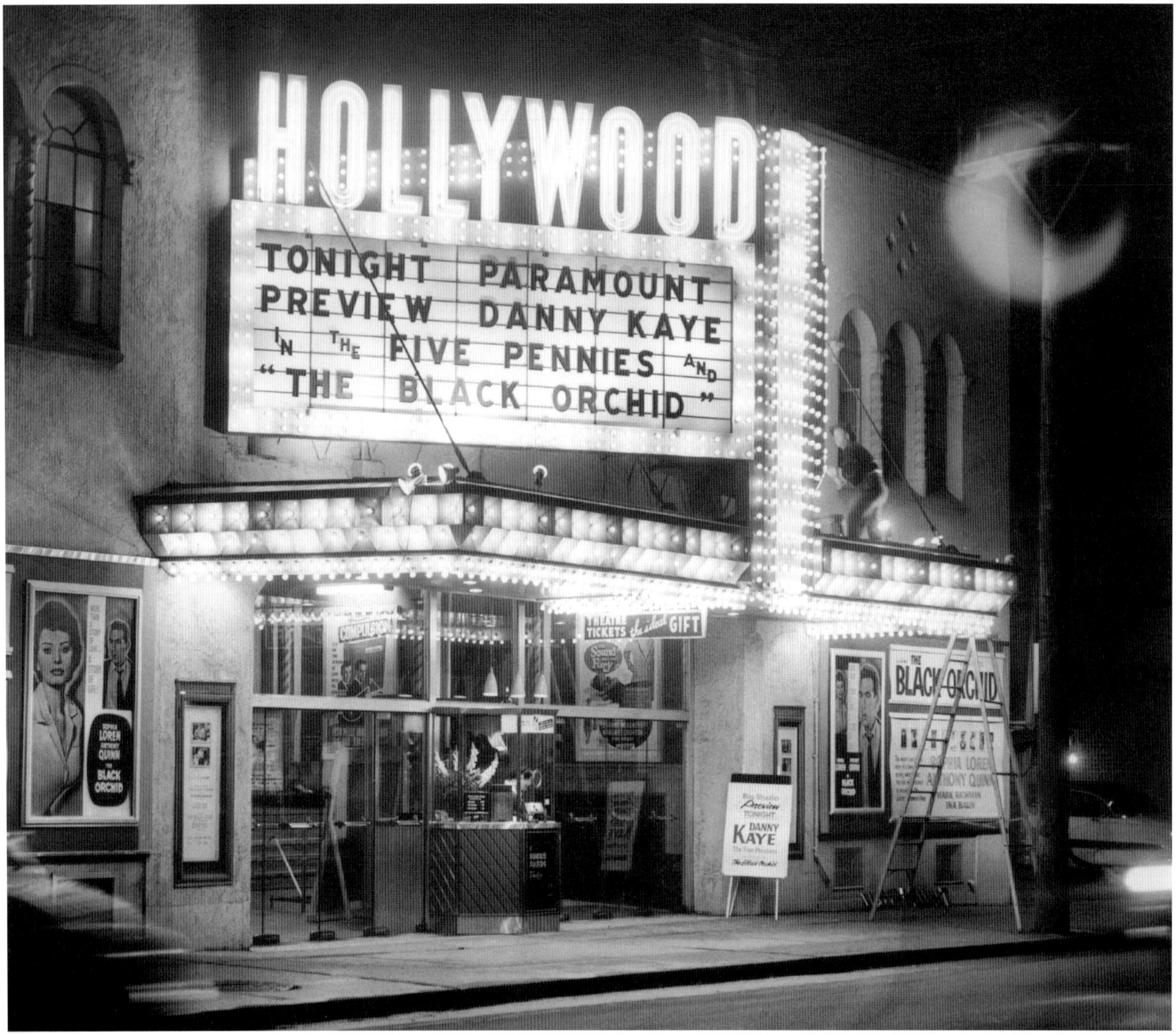

69 Famous Players' Hollywood Theatre, Yonge Street north of St. Clair Avenue, 1959.

When the Hollywood opened on the evening of October 27, 1930, it had the distinction of being the first theatre in Canada to be built specifically for the showing of the recently introduced "all talking" movies. Until then, all Toronto theatres had been constructed as silent film houses. The Hollywood's brightly illuminated marquee was specially designed to make this part of Yonge Street look like a little patch of New York City's "Great White Way." The theatre was demolished in early 1999.

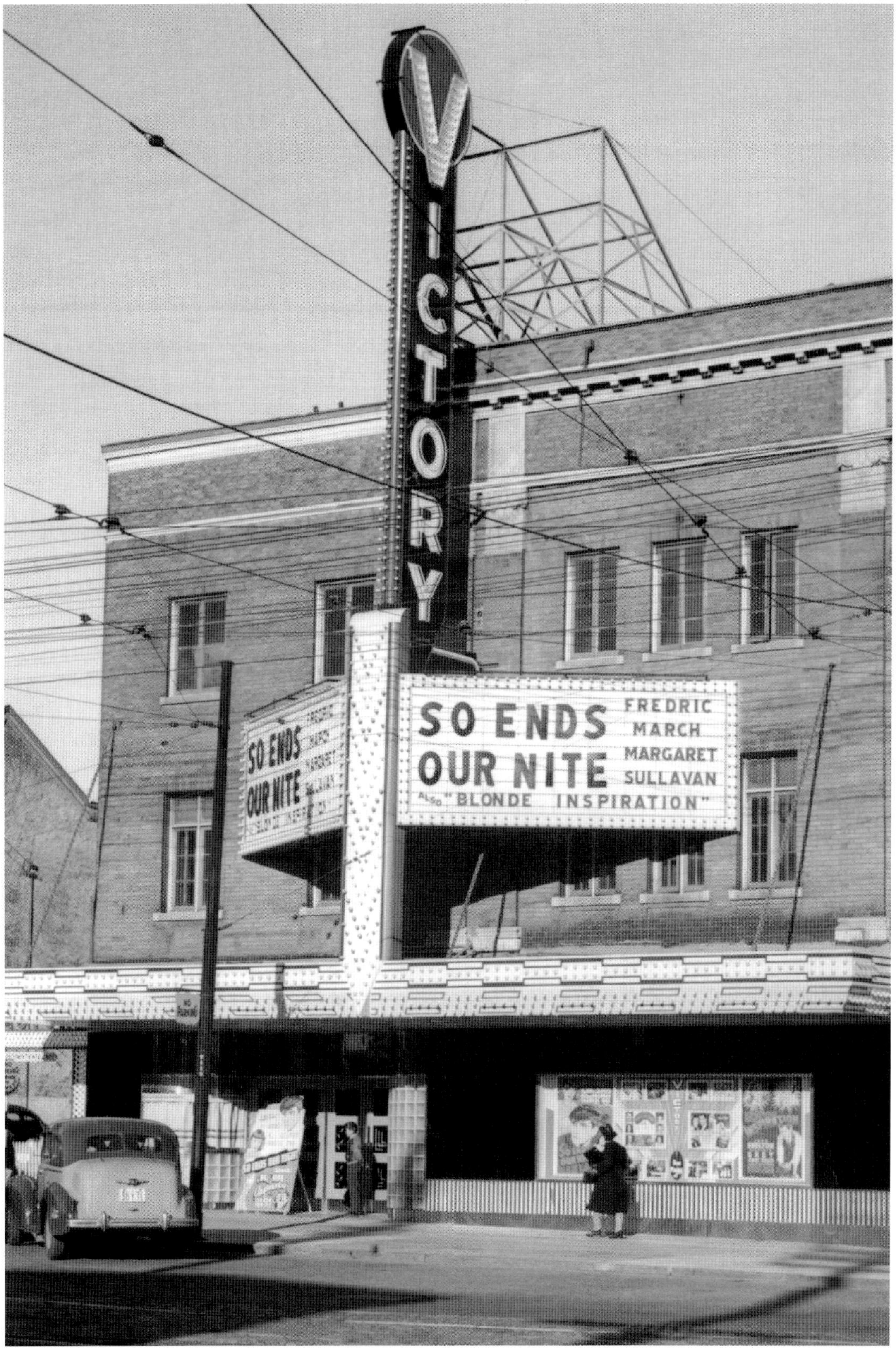

70 Victory Theatre, northeast corner of Spadina Avenue and Dundas Street West, 1941.

The Victory was originally opened as the Standard on August 30, 1922. Its debut was described in the newspapers of the day under the headline "Hebrew's Open Theatre" as "a legitimate theatre for the presentation of Jewish plays" and a place where "no refreshments or children would be allowed." The theatre's name was subsequently changed to the Strand and then, in mid-1941, to the Victory in anticipation of an eventual victory over Nazi Germany (Japan was not yet at war with the rest of the world). The Victory presented the "best in burlesque" but became better known for its "Amateur Strip" nights. In later years the theatre was known as the Golden Harvest, where legitimate plays were presented for the enjoyment of the nearby Chinese community. The old structure still stands, but has been converted to a variety of business uses.

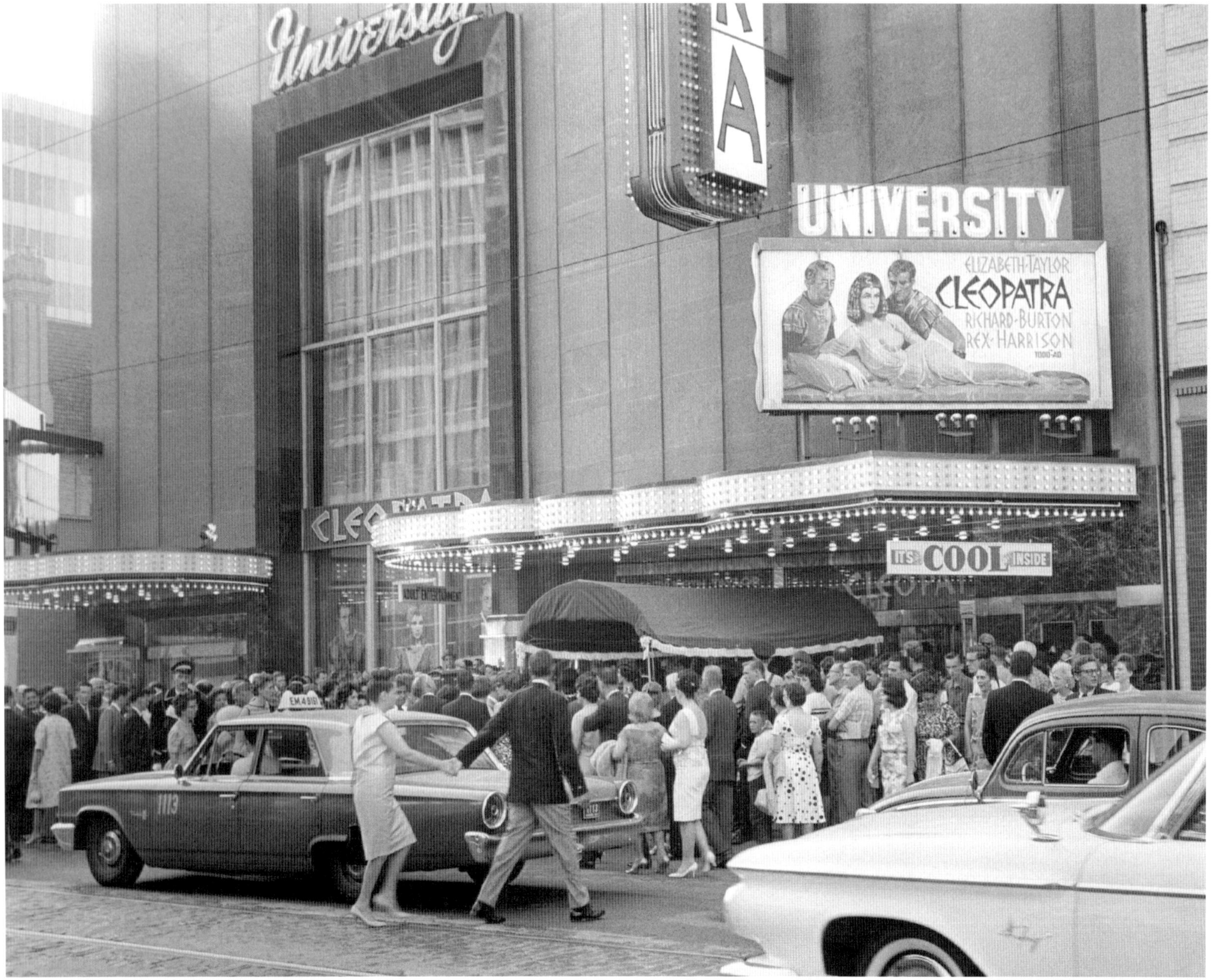

71 University Theatre, Bloor Street West, 1963.

The University Theatre, which opened on March 25, 1949, was described in the Toronto newspapers of the day as Famous Players' new "Theatre of Distinction," boasting many "unique post-war developments" that included a "spacious promenade and lounge areas" and "deeply upholstered push-back seats." Smoking was permitted in the Upper Circle and Loge Section. The University opened with the film *Joan of Arc*, starring Ingrid Bergman. Admission prices were 75 cents for matinees and $1.20 for evenings. Students' and children's tickets were 60 cents at all times. There was no mention of special prices for seniors. Following the theatre's closure, numerous plans were put forward to retain elements of this once-fashionable theatre in any future development. It was all talk. Today nothing remains of what was once one of the city's most prestigious theatres — nothing, that is, but memories.

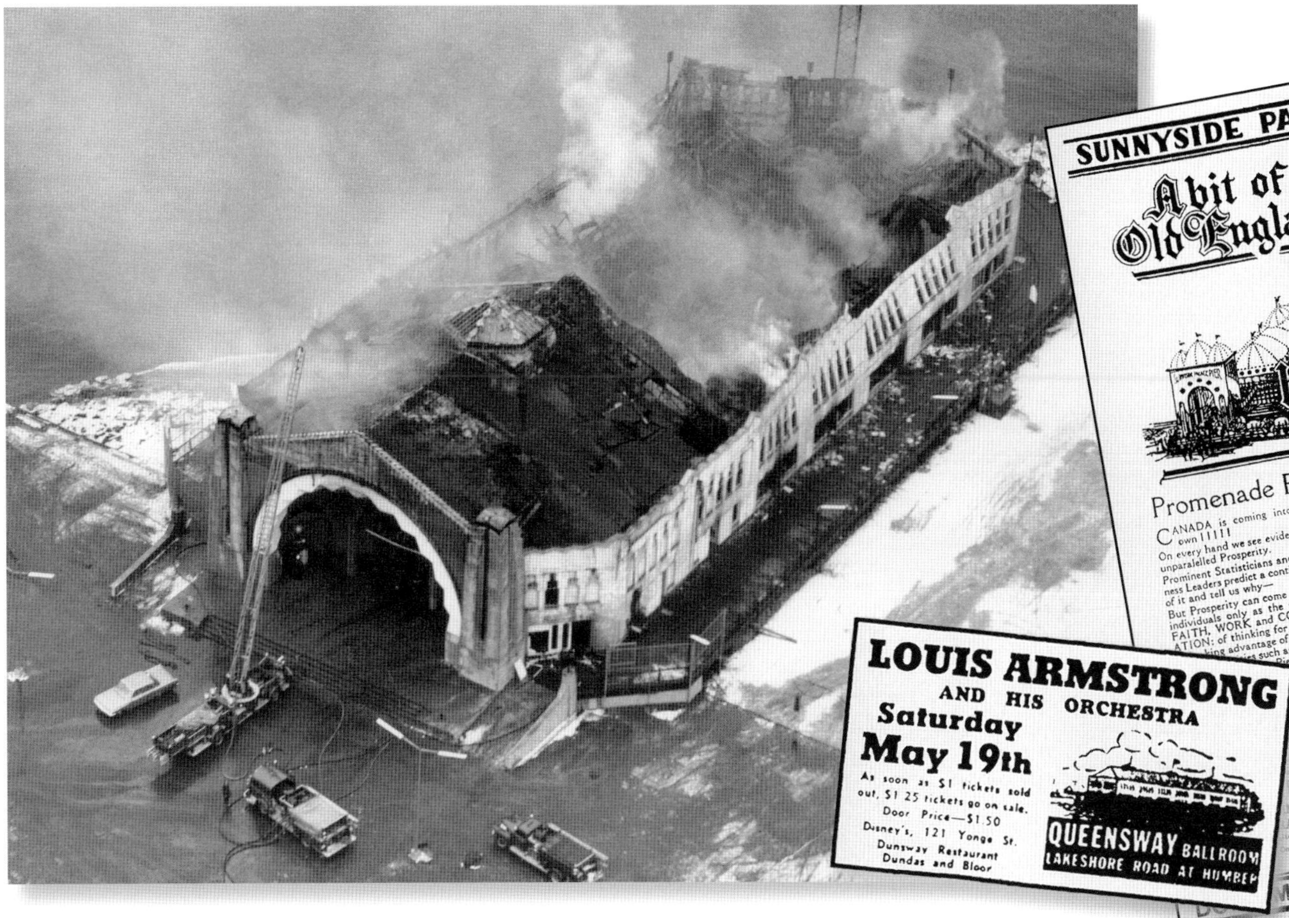

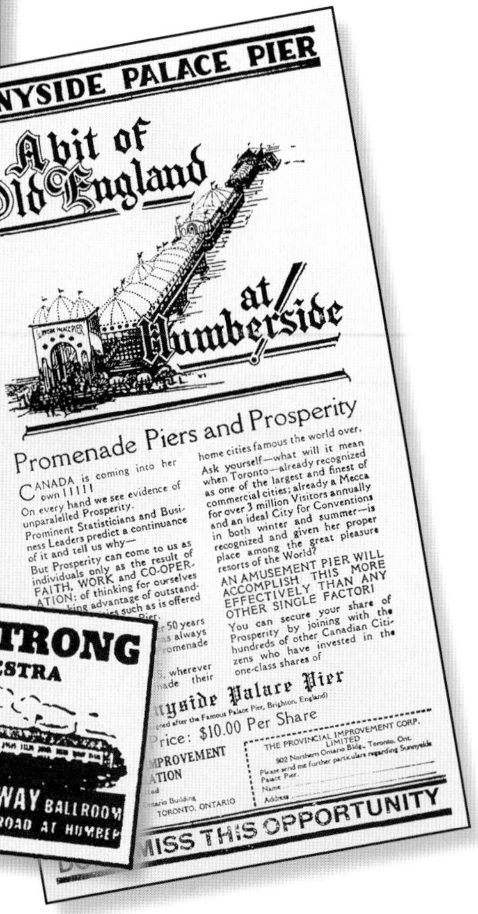

72–74 Smoke still rises from the ill-starred Palace Pier, January 7, 1963.

Located on the shore of Lake Ontario just west of the mouth of the Humber River in Etobicoke Township, the Sunnyside Palace Pier was a project originally put forward in 1927 by the Provincial Improvement Corporation. The company described it as a "promenade and entertainment pier" that would be similar to, but an improvement on, those found in various coastal cities in England. Toronto's pier would stretch 548 metres (1,800 feet) out into Lake Ontario and would feature a large dance and assembly hall, motion picture cinemas, a bandstand, and a large amusement arcade. Having promoted the new structure locally as "similar to the immensely popular Palace Pier in Brighton, England" and "a major new addition to Toronto's attractiveness as a tourist destination for free-spending Americans," the company began offering shares in the project to the general public. Some money was raised, just enough to allow construction to began in early 1931. Unfortunately, financial difficulties soon resulted in only a much abbreviated version being completed before the promoters (and most of the money) vanished. The pier then sat empty for years while the courts considered its future. It finally opened on June 18, 1941, with a roller skating carnival. Comedian Bob Hope, who happened to be in town promoting his new movie, was encouraged to visit the new pier, where he became the first person of note to skate the length of the shiny new floor. The building continued to operate for many years under a variety of names: Palace Pier, Strathcona Palace Pier, Club Queensway, Lakeshore Ballroom, and then back to Palace Pier. It was a dance hall (where big bands led by such luminaries as Tommy Dorsey, Les Brown, Duke Ellington, Louis Armstrong, and Canada's own Trump Davidson performed their magic) and, in its later years, a creaky old venue for such eclectic events as boxing and wrestling matches, high school proms, and religious revival meetings. The end came on January 7, 1963, when a crazed arsonist set fire to the structure. The gutted building was razed and the present condominium complex was eventually built on the site.

Two of Toronto's pioneer shopping centres

Something we take for granted in this day and age of rush, rush, rush is the number of strip malls, shopping plazas, and large regional malls located in and around Toronto. Virtually anything a consumer wants or needs can be acquired through this one-stop method of shopping. But it wasn't always that way. Not that long ago, a shopping trip usually meant a short drive down the block for a loaf of bread, a longer trip uptown for some meat, and another journey all the way across town for a new suit or dress. For many, all that changed on May 15, 1952, when the new Sunnybrook Shopping Centre, located at the northeast corner of Eglinton and Bayview avenues in the Toronto suburb of Leaside, opened. It was the first planned shopping centre to open anywhere in the province. Visitors to Sunnybrook could simply park their cars in the centre's spacious paved lot and do virtually all their shopping in one place and all at one time. This idea doesn't sound like much today, but it was a revolutionary step into the future for Torontonians of 1952. In fact, it wouldn't be a stretch to say that Sunnybrook Shopping Centre was the forerunner of the two to three hundred megamalls of today.

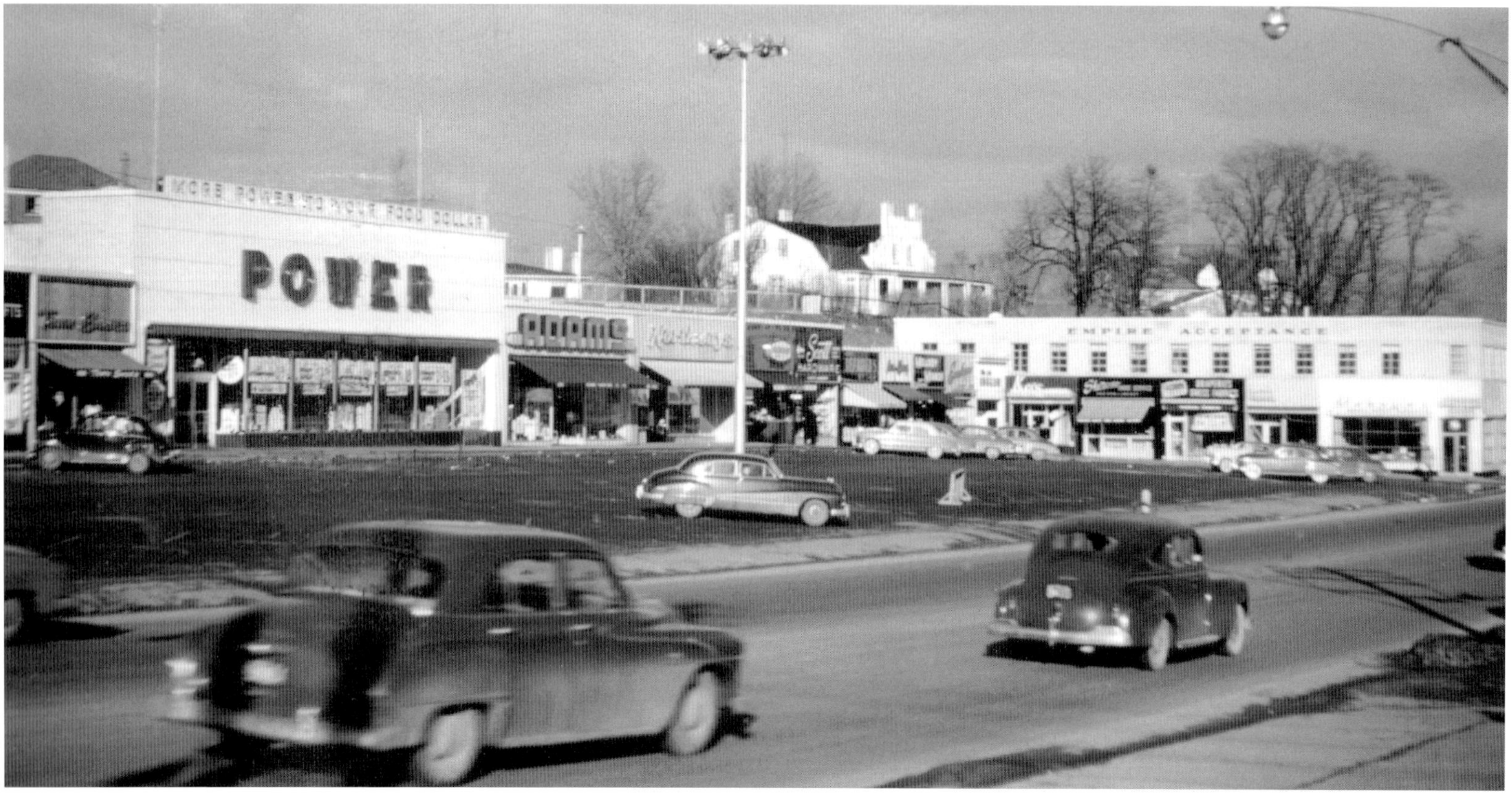

75 Sunnybrook Shopping Centre at the northeast corner of Eglinton and Bayview avenues, 1953.

The most prominent feature of this new shopping centre, aside from the large free parking lot and youthful attendants who cleaned the windshields on visitors' cars, was the mammoth Power Super Food Market, the largest by far in the chain of Power stores started by Leon Weinstein in 1933. Soon after this photograph was taken, Power was acquired by the huge Loblaws organization. Other tenants in the original Sunnybrook Shopping Centre were Ira Berg (ladies' clothing), Kerns (jewelry), John Northway (department store), Tamblyn's (drug store), Scott Hardware, and the Canadian Bank of Commerce. The latter two, now with slightly different names, continue as tenants of this historic plaza. As part of the centre's opening ceremonies on May 15, 1952, an ultramodern black-and-white television set was donated to the Sunnybrook Military Hospital (now Sunnybrook and Women's College Health Sciences Centre) located just north of the shopping centre.

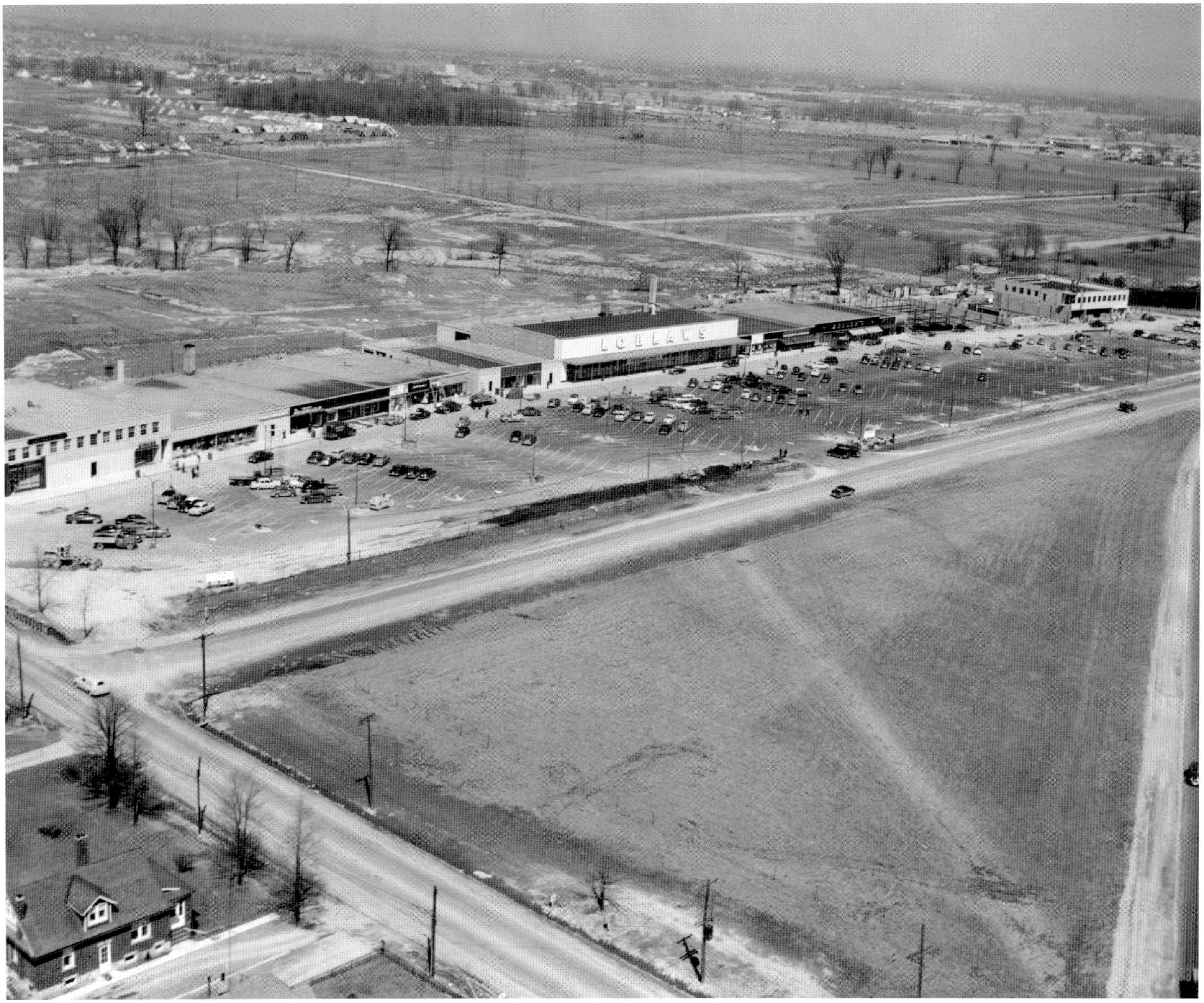

76 Golden Mile Plaza, Eglinton Avenue east at Victoria Park Avenue, Township of Scarborough, 1954.

One year after opening Sunnybrook Shopping Centre, its owner, Principal Investments Limited, opened Toronto's second, the much larger Lawrence Plaza, which was located at the northwest corner of Lawrence Avenue West and Bathurst Street. The company opened a third in 1954. This one, the Golden Mile Plaza at the northeast corner of Victoria Park and Eglinton avenues in Scarborough Township, was, at the time, the largest in Canada. It covered twenty acres of former farmland, had a total of thirty-five stores, and had parking for more than two thousand cars. As part of the plaza's opening celebrations, a brand new Ford Skyliner hardtop convertible was awarded to a lucky visitor to Metropolitan Toronto's newest plaza. Metro Toronto was new that year as well.

77 Queen Elizabeth II pays a visit to the Golden Mile Plaza, 1959.

A special visitor to Scarborough's Golden Mile Plaza was Queen Elizabeth II, who, during her visit to Toronto in 1959, asked to see the plaza's new Loblaws store. Store officials offered the Queen a selection of store items, which she politely declined. To the Queen's left in the photograph is Frederick Gardiner, the first chairman of Metropolitan Toronto (and the person for whom the Gardiner Expressway is named), and to his left is Ontario Lieutenant Governor Keiler McKay.

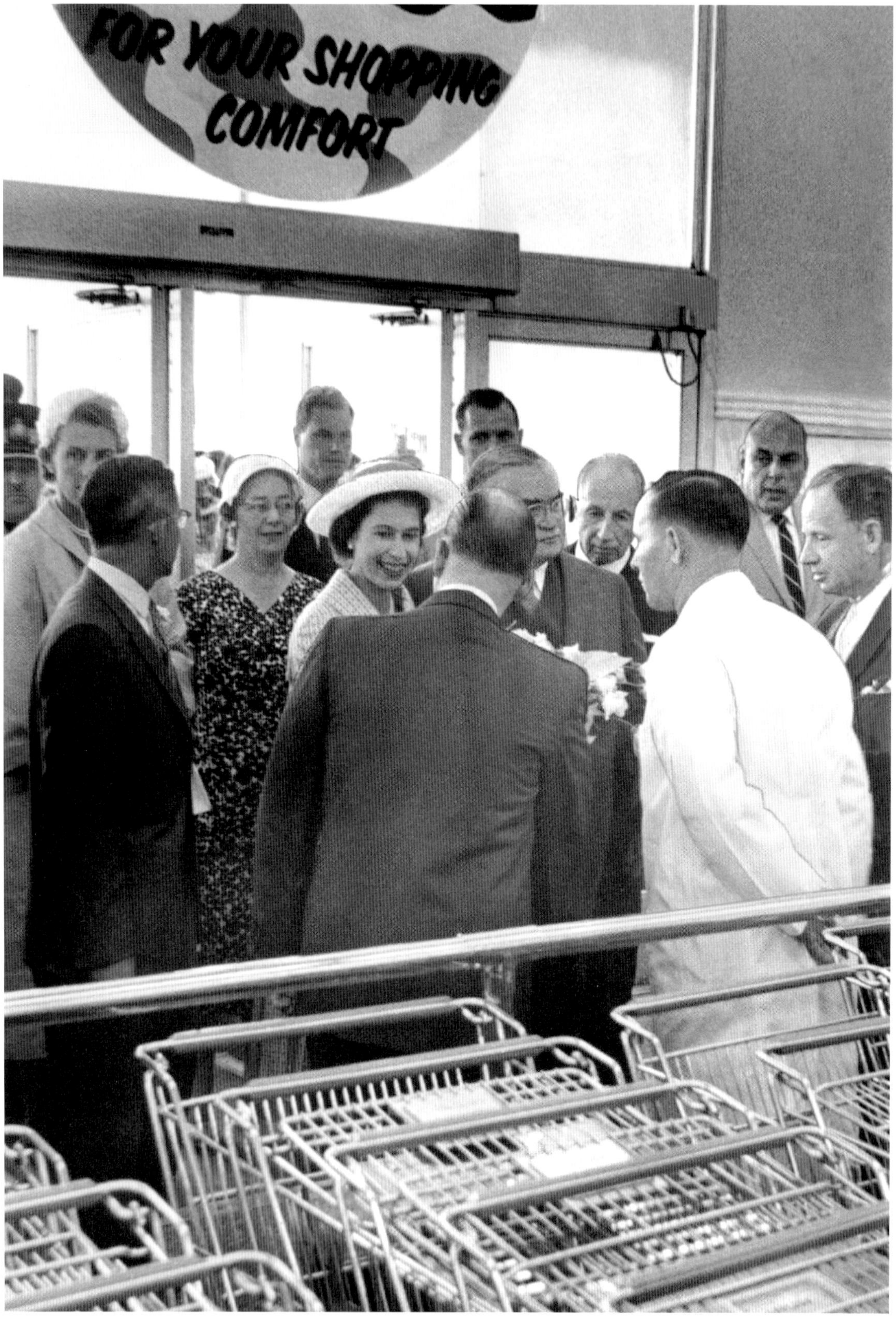

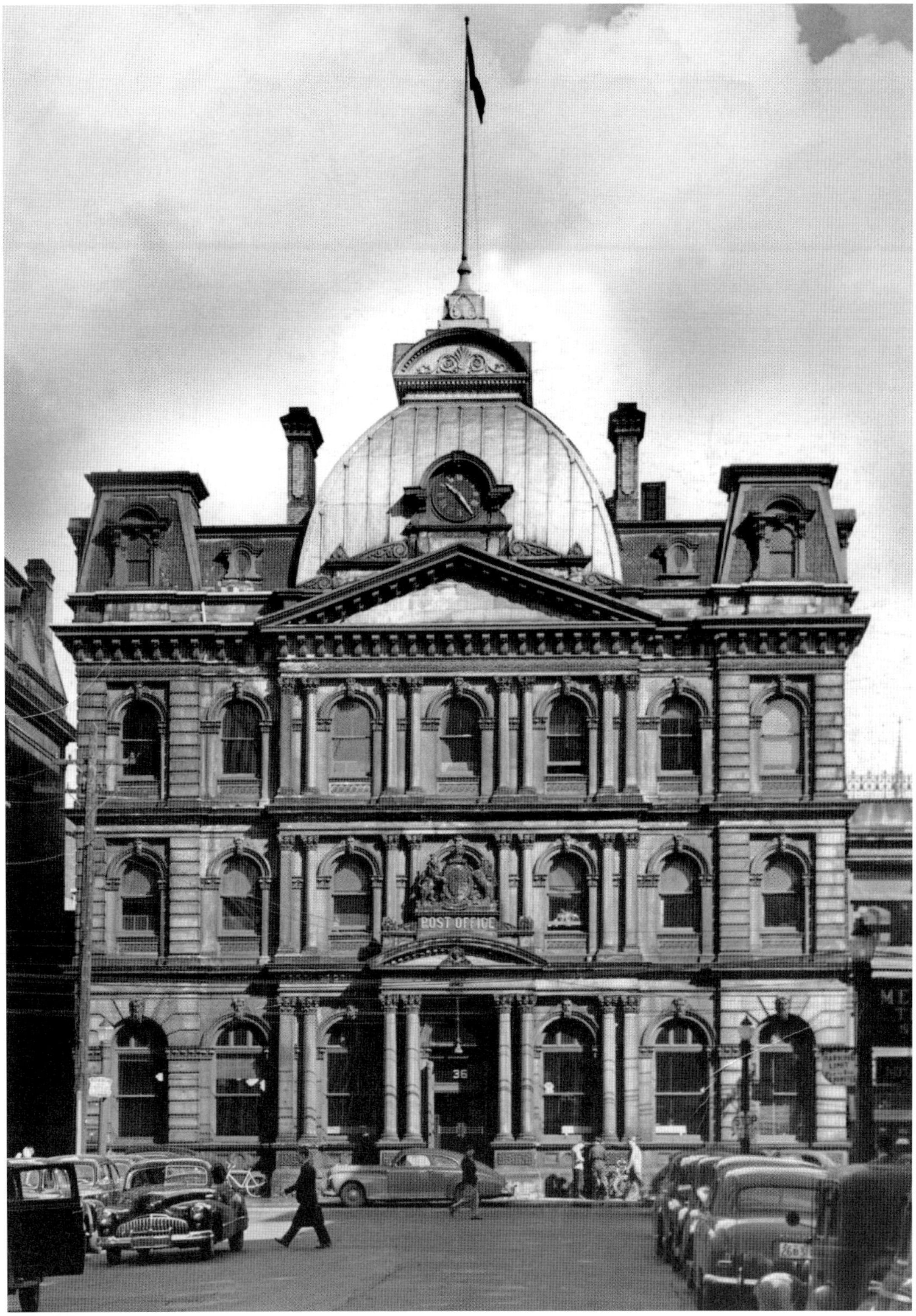

The 1960s were not kind to many of Toronto's historic old buildings. In its wild rush to be new and exciting, the city frequently paid little heed to what few architectural treasures it still had. Here are some that vanished in the name of progress. Dare I say that if they had survived, these buildings would be regarded as untouchable today.

78 Eighth Toronto Post Office, Adelaide Street East between Victoria and Church streets, 1947.

The Eighth Toronto Post Office, which was completed in 1873, stood on the north side of Adelaide Street East directly opposite little Toronto Street, a one-block long thoroughfare that, for many years, was one of the most architecturally rich streets in the city. The building shown here served as the city's main postal facility until 1930. It was demolished in 1957, and another, though less imposing, government building was erected on the site. This latter building has recently been converted into an office building bearing the less-than-Canadian title of State Street Financial Centre. In the photograph we can see a beautiful carving of the nation's coat of arms proudly displayed over the old building's main entrance. This beautiful work of art still exists, though it is now squirrelled away at the back of the new building.

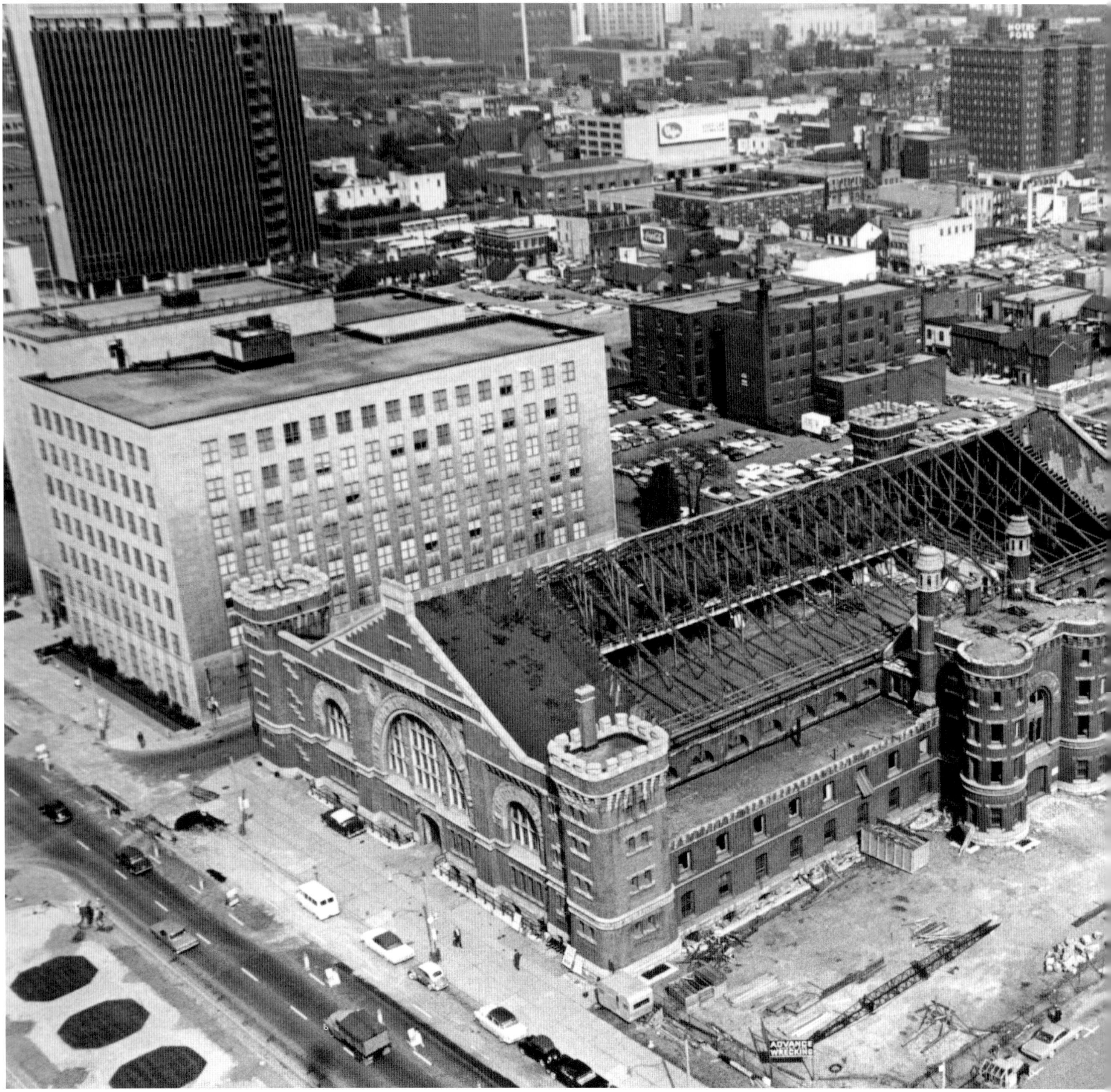
HOTEL FORD
ADVANCE WRECKING

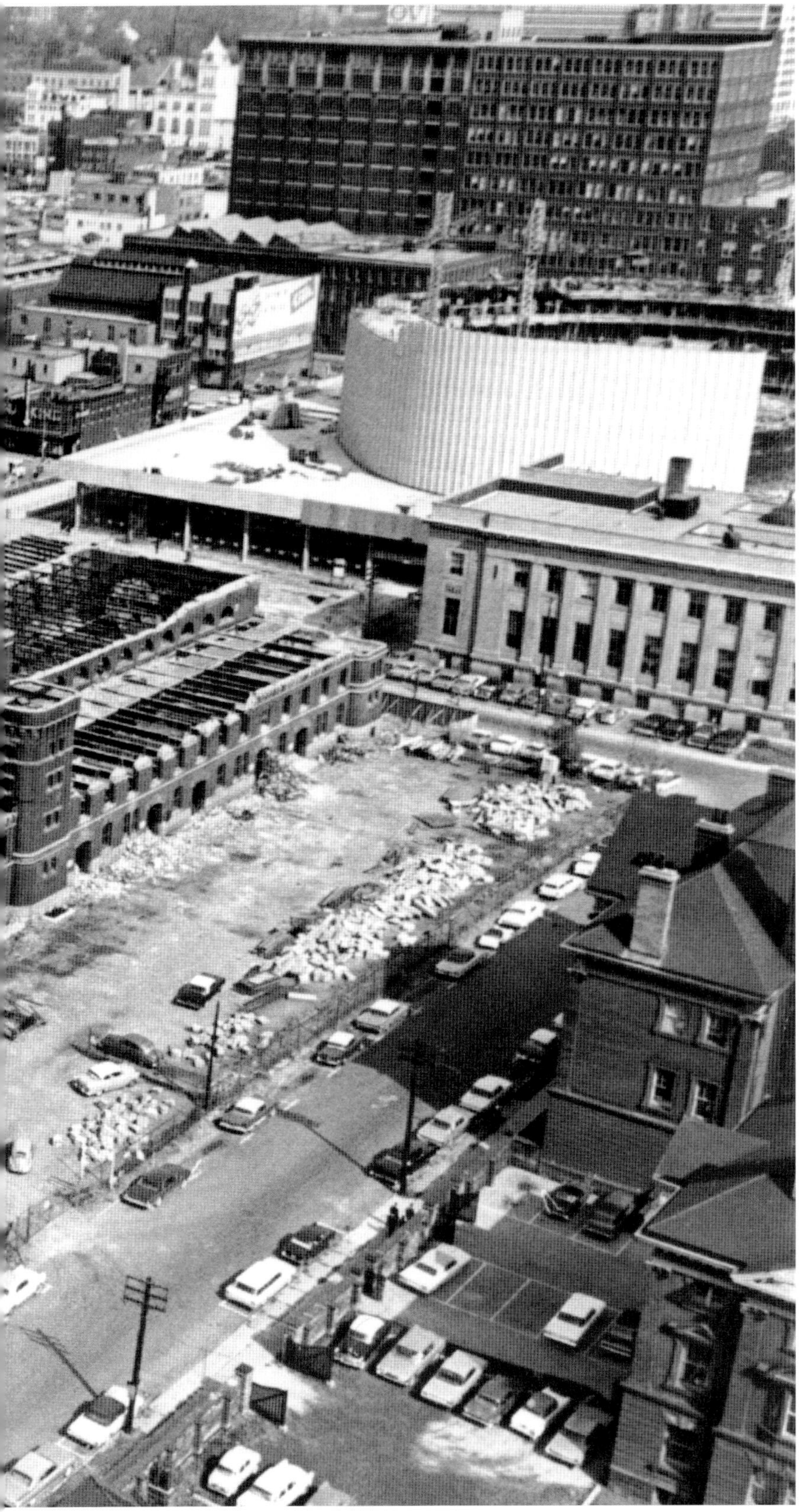

79 Demolition of the University Avenue Armouries, 1963.

The University Avenue Armouries stood on the east side of the city's widest thoroughfare and just up the street from the historic Osgoode Hall. While similar, though less imposing, military buildings were to be found in various towns and cities across the country, Toronto's was the nation's largest. It was here at the University Avenue Armouries that the local militia units would rally in time of need eager to help defend the "Mother Country" and, in later years, the Dominion of Canada itself. Built over a two-year period, the Armouries opened on May 17, 1894, with a spectacular Military Tournament featuring several proud Toronto regiments: the Queen's Own, 48th Highlanders, Royal Regiment, Royal Dragoons, Toronto Field Battery, and the Governor-General's Body Guard. Just five years later several of these same regiments would assemble in the Armouries to rush to Britain's aid as she battled the Boers in South Africa, the first time Canadians fought on foreign soil. In 1914, troops once again rallied at the Armouries as Britain and Canada went to war with Germany and her Kaiser. In 1939, another war, another call-up, and troops gathered once more at the Armouries. But it wasn't just war that brought people to the University Avenue Armouries. Numerous horse shows were held within its massive walls, as was Toronto's first automobile show. By the 1960s, the land on which the Armouries stood had become far too valuable for a building as old-fashioned as a military armoury. When it was announced that the old building would be demolished, rallies of another kind took place — this time focused on preserving the historic structure. But they were to no avail, and in 1963 the University Avenue Armouries was demolished. Today, a nearby street and historical plaque are the only things left to recall the important role this building played in the maturation of Toronto. In the centre background of this photograph is the Ford Hotel at the northeast corner of Bay and Dundas streets. To the extreme right are the hulking warehouses and factories of the T. Eaton Company. Like the Armouries, these buildings also no longer exist. Just in front of these structures Toronto's new City Hall can be seen taking shape.

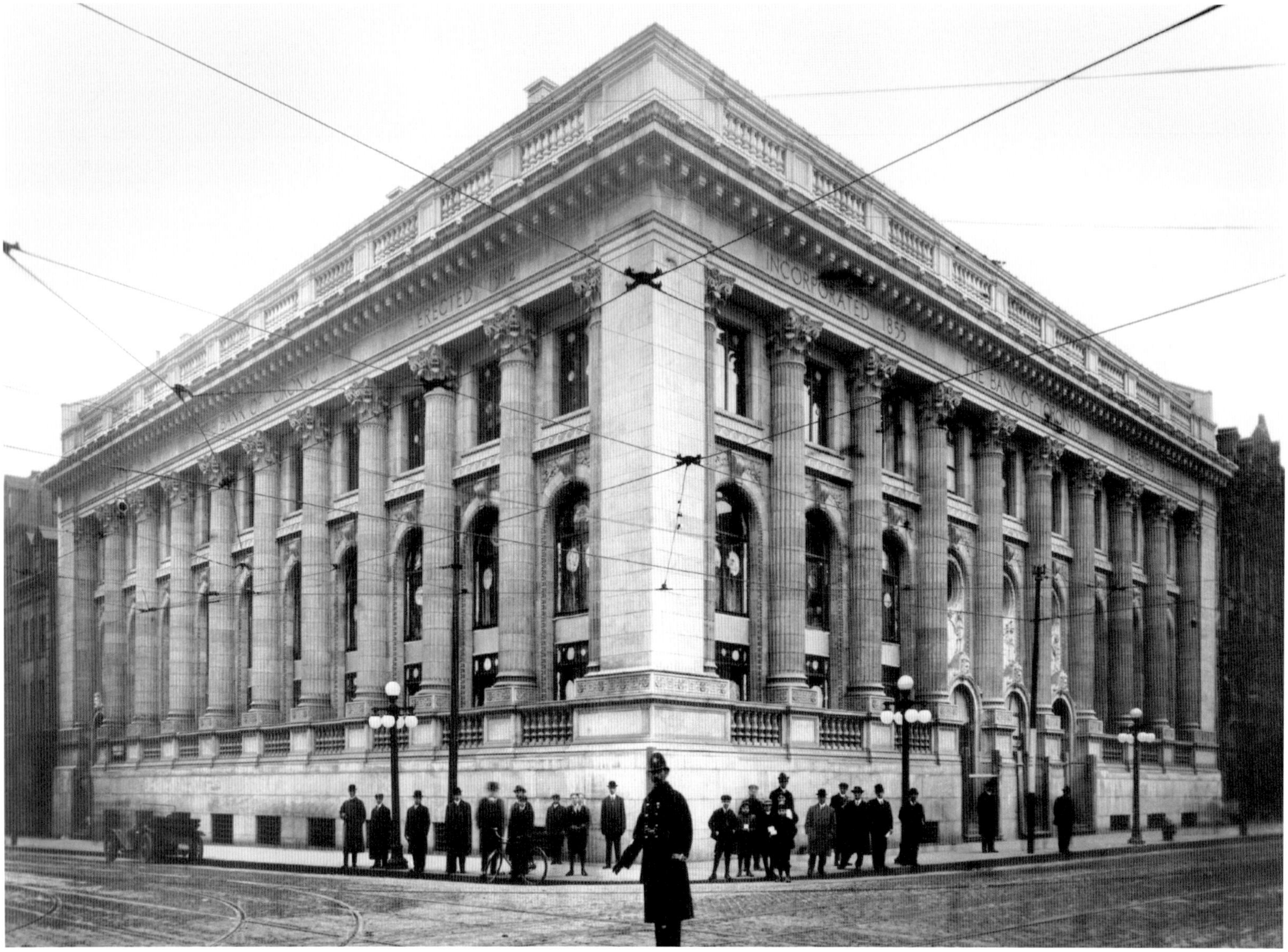

80 Bank of Toronto, southwest corner King and Bay streets, circa 1913.

In the 1960s, as Toronto tried very hard to become a "world class city," civic officials continued to turn a blind eye to the ongoing destruction of the community's few remaining architectural treasures. One of the saddest losses was the unceremonious flattening of the Bank of Toronto's magnificent building at the corner of Bay and King streets in the heart of the city. This grand structure was designed by the American architectural firm of Carrere and Hasting (whose other Toronto work, the Traders Bank at the northeast corner of Yonge and Colborne streets, one-time champion of tall buildings in Canada, still stands). Completed in 1913, the building served as the Bank of Toronto's head office for the next forty-two years. It continued to do so under a new corporate identity following the amalgamation of the Bank of Toronto with the Dominion Bank to form the Toronto-Dominion Bank. Unfortunately, when plans for Toronto's first modern skyscraper were being finalized the developers could find no place in the mammoth project for the old building. Private enterprise as well as all levels of government had yet to see any value in heritage preservation. Pity. The T-D Centre would have been much more impressive had the old been allowed to share the site with the new.

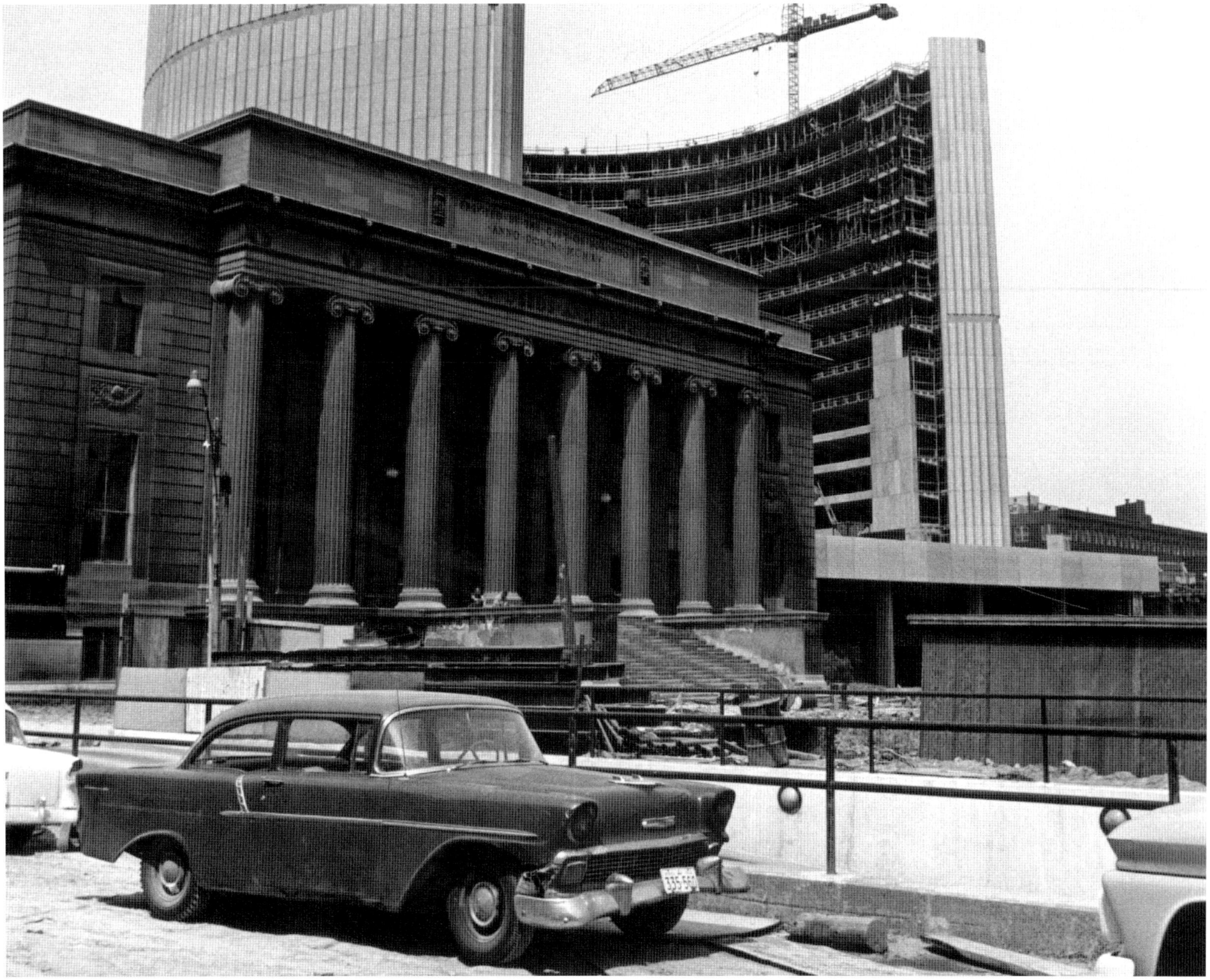

81 Old Registry Office and New City Hall, July 1964.

Another victim of progress was the Registry Office, a temple-like structure that opened in 1917 as the first and, as it would turn out, only structure in a civic government square proposed for a two-block area west and north of the City Hall of the day (today's Old City Hall). For a variety of reasons the civic square plan never made it past the design stage. This resulted in the impressive Registry Office standing on a side street surrounded by deteriorating shops and houses. Years later, when the city approved another civic square plan, this one complete with a new city hall, the old Registry Office was found to be in the way. While there were some half-hearted attempts to move the structure, this idea was found to be far too costly. Even as Viljo Revell's New City Hall was going up, the Registry Office was coming down.

82 Royal York Hotel soon after its official opening on June 11, 1929.

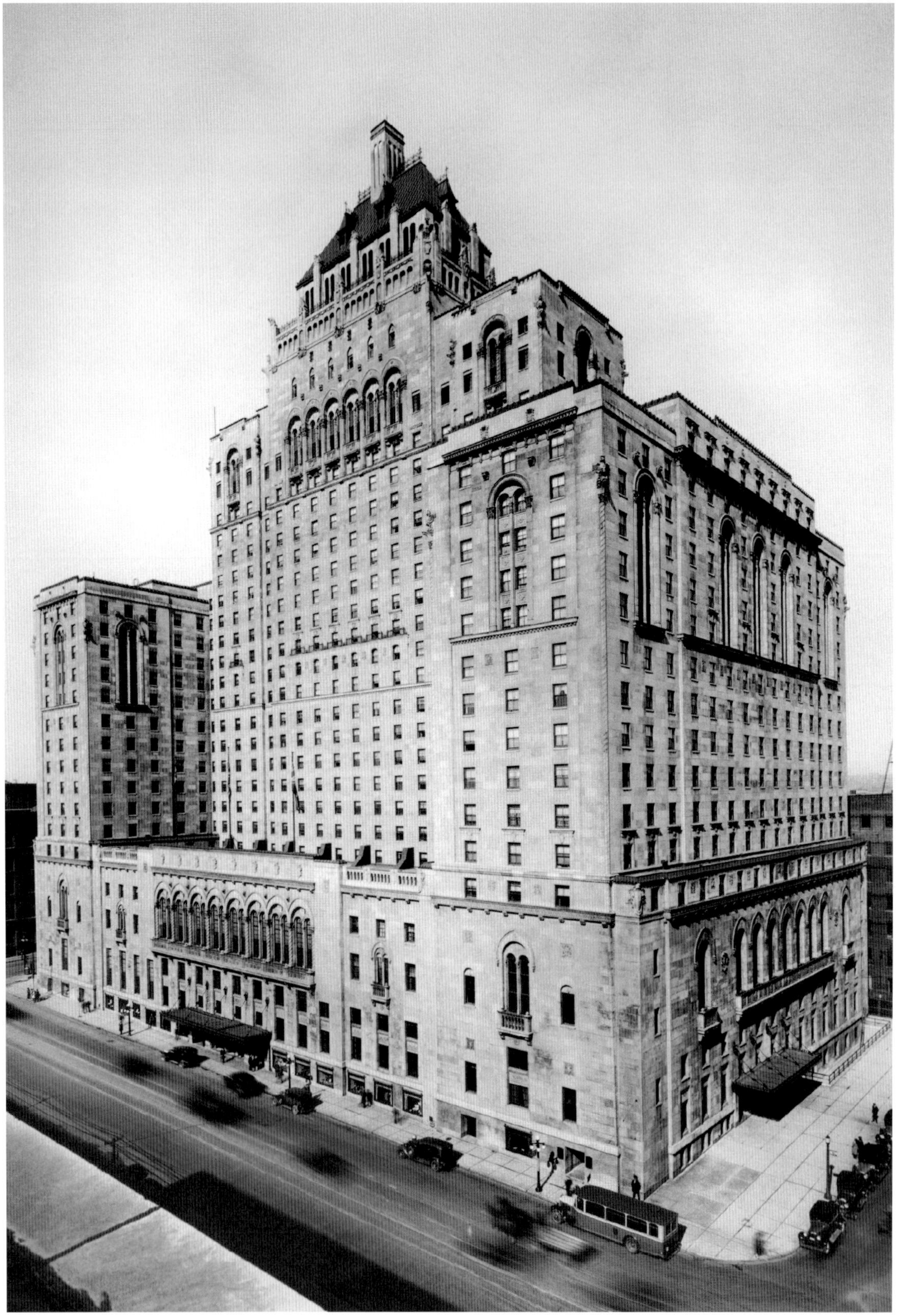

In the 1950s and '60s, while buildings of architectural and historic merit were being flattened all over town, the twelve-hundred-room Royal York Hotel managed to evade the wrecker's ball. It even grew in size, with two additions, the first soon after the hotel's opening in 1929 and a second, the 17-storey, 400-room East Wing, in 1957. And while there was never any official pronouncement that the "ancient" structure was to be replaced (after all, it was getting on in years) things were happening so fast that such a possibility was not out of the question. The hotel was named, albeit indirectly, in honour of Frederick, the Duke of York, second eldest son of King George III, who was the reigning monarch when Toronto was first settled by the British in 1793. Lieutenant-Governor Simcoe did not appreciate many of the place names used by the First Nations people. As a result, on August 26, 1793, he changed the name Toronto to York, ostensibly to honour the Duke, who had been victorious over the French in a battle at Flanders, but in reality to schmooze the Duke's father, King George III. Other "Yorks" would follow: a county, a township, a city, and a street, not to mention a suburb (Yorkville), a shopping centre (Yorkdale), and, of course, a distinguished downtown hotel.

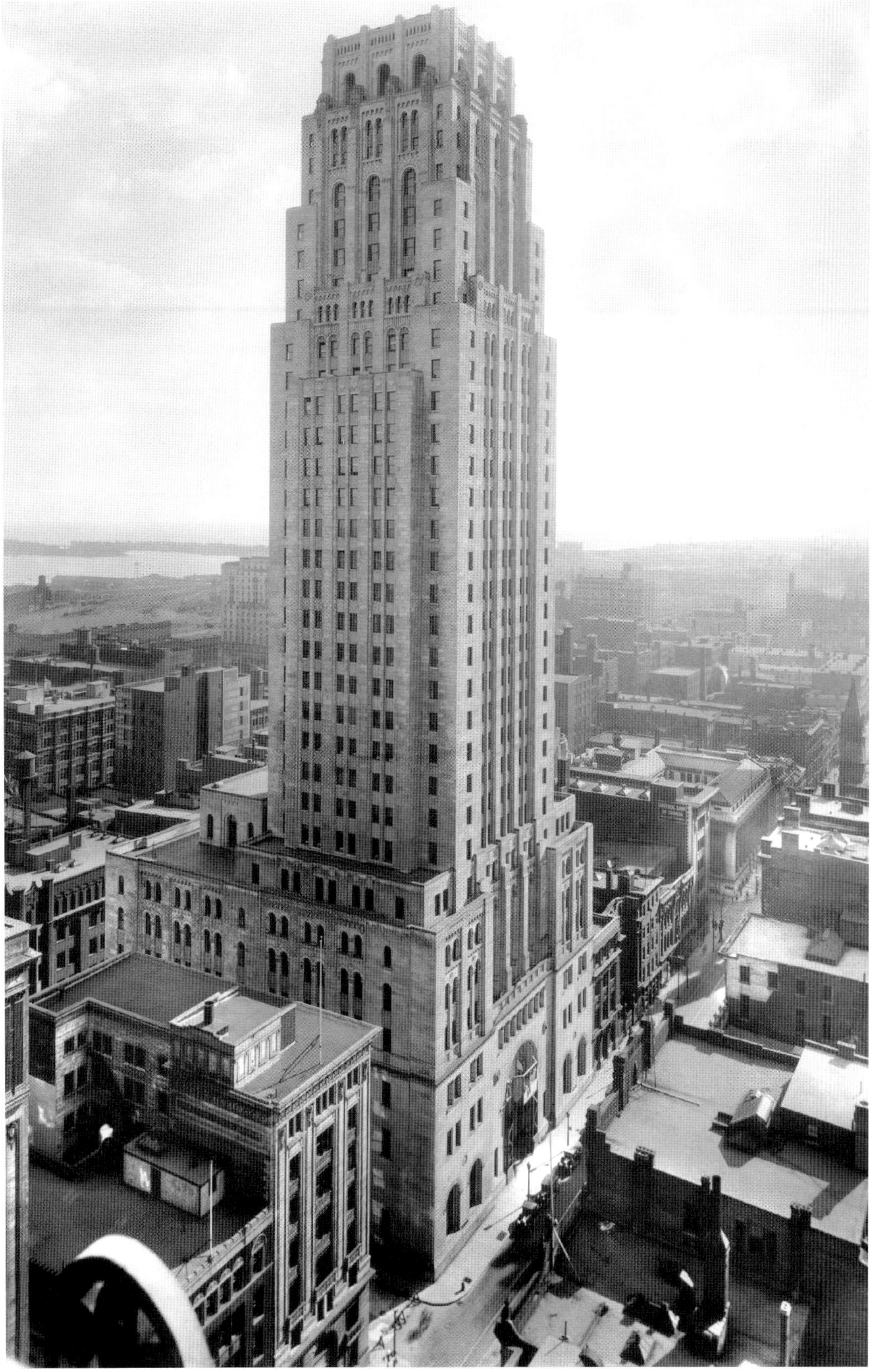

83 The Bank of Commerce Building, 25 King Street West, circa 1930.

Established in Toronto in 1867, the Bank of Commerce merged with another Toronto-born bank, the Imperial Bank of Commerce, in 1961 to form today's Canadian Imperial Bank of Commerce, one of the largest of the nation's thirteen domestic banks. Since 1890, the head office of the old Bank of Commerce was located at the southwest corner of King and Melinda streets in the heart of the city. In the late 1920s, bank officials decided to demolish the old head office building and erect a new building in its place. But the replacement would be no ordinary office building; it would be the most modern possible. Not only that, it would stand taller than any other structure in the city. In fact, it would rise 132.3 metres (434 feet) above sidewalk level, making it the tallest building in the entire British Commonwealth. Interestingly, this true Toronto landmark never had an official opening. The closest it came was when the bank's directors and shareholders met for the first time in the new building on January 13, 1931, the date of the 1930 annual General Meeting. Other buildings of note in the photograph include (bottom left) Dominion Bank Building, recently converted into a condominium, (centre right) tower of The Mail Building, home of the *Mail* newspaper, which later amalgamated with *The Globe* to form the *Globe and Mail*, (to the left of The Mail Building) the Bank of Toronto Building, and (extreme right) the Toronto Star Building.

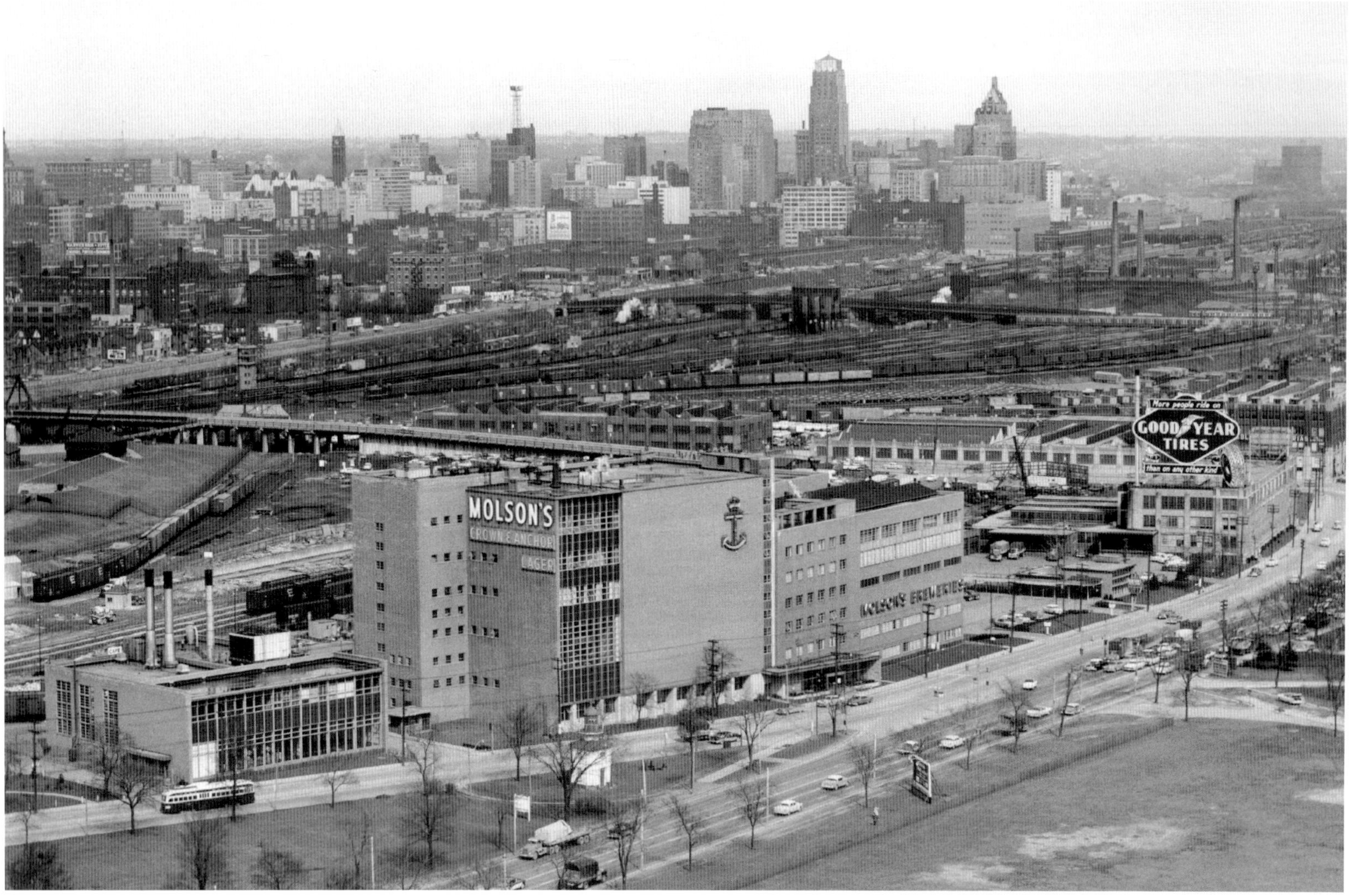

84 The new Molson Brewery and the Toronto skyline, March 21, 1958.

The land on which Molson erected its new Toronto brewery in the mid-1950s was land that didn't even exist some forty or so years earlier. In fact, until the newly created Toronto Harbour Commission began reclaiming this part of the city's waterfront in 1912, the site was actually in Lake Ontario. That fact was a major problem for the brewery designers, since the water table was less than four feet below ground level. Construction of the $11-million project began in early 1954 with the driving of dozens of six-metre-long (twenty-foot-long) steel piles to bedrock. That was followed by the erection of the service building, brewery, and retail store, all of which were completed in a record fifteen months. The first product out of the new plant was Crown and Anchor lager beer, which first began flowing on April 11, 1958. Molson closed the brewery several years ago, and while it appeared for a time that the plant would be converted for "dot-com" purposes, it now seems likely that the previously state-of-the-art complex will be demolished and condominiums built on the site. Other buildings and structures of interest in this photograph are (left to right on the skyline) the Canada Life Building with its new weather beacon, clock tower of Old City Hall, new Lord Simcoe Hotel (under construction), Bank of Commerce Building, and Royal York Hotel. In the foreground is the historic Queen's Wharf lighthouse, which was erected near the foot of Bathurst Street in 1861 and moved to its present site in 1929, where it still stands. One of the Toronto Transit Commission's PCC Streamliner streetcars approaches what is still known as Lighthouse Loop.

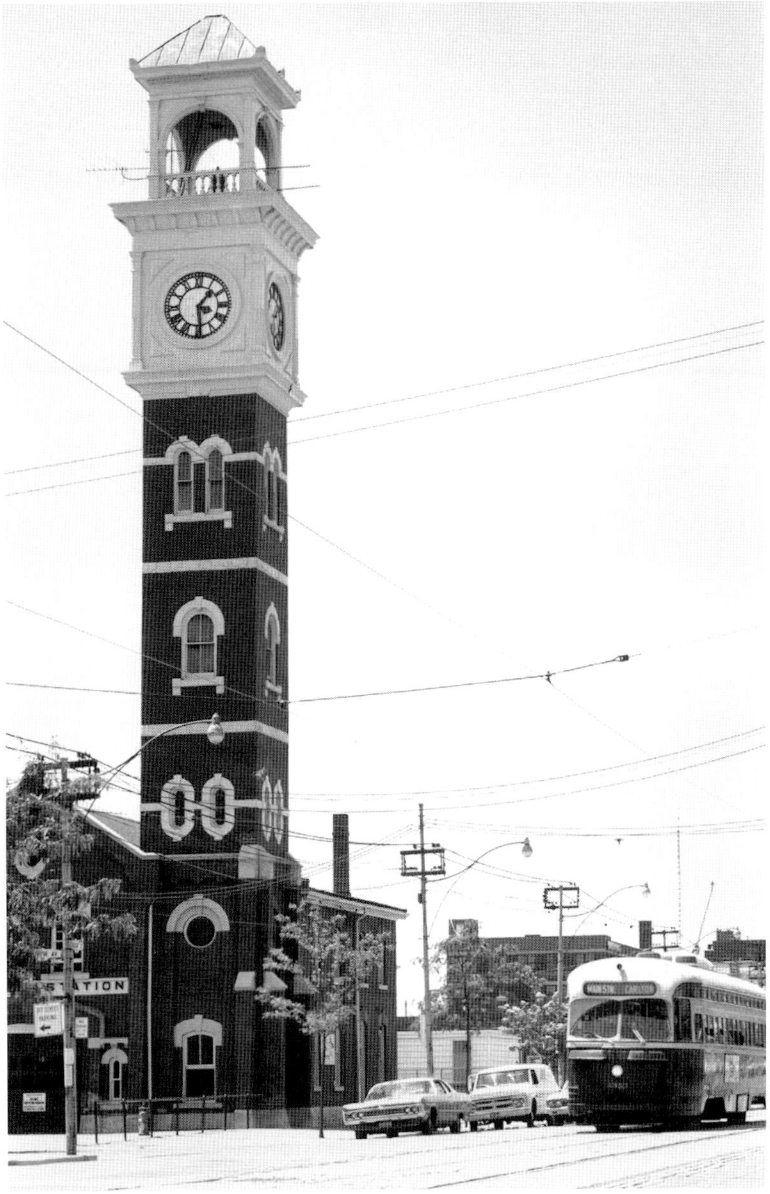

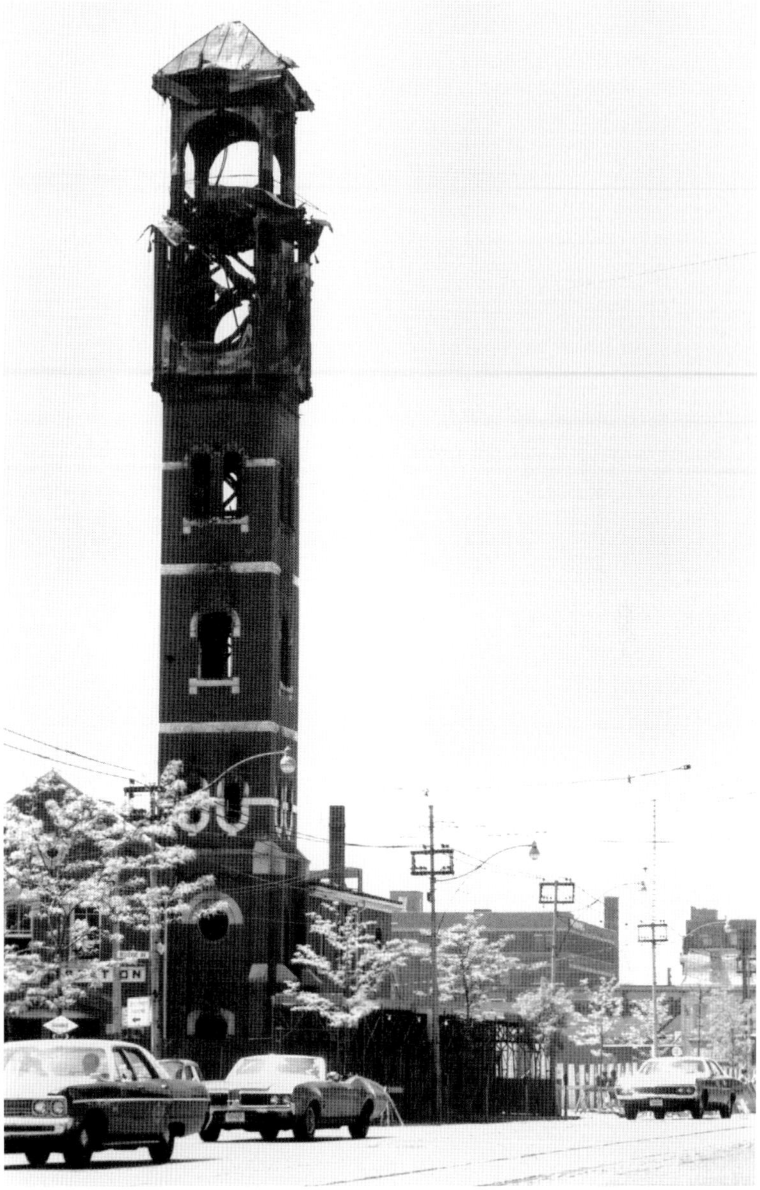

85–86 Number 8 fire hall at College Street and Bellevue Avenue before and after the May 1972 fire.

When this glorious fire hall was built in 1878, its tower served three distinct but equally important functions. First, in those pre-telephone days, spotters would be stationed atop the tower to watch for signs of trouble. Second, after "running a fire," the water-soaked hoses would be hoisted into the tower and allowed to drain dry. The third, and perhaps most obvious, function was to contain the large four-sided clock, which was, and continues to be, the neighbourhood timepiece. After the modern hall next door was constructed, officials decided to convert the old hall into a fire museum. Early in the morning of May 28, 1972, a blaze broke out in the tower, destroying the clock and much of the support structure. It was then that Fire Chief Ben Bonser, the Toronto Historical Board, and other interested citizens persuaded city council to continue with the restoration project, and today the historic fire hall (renumbered Station #315 following amalgamation of Toronto and area fire departments in 1998) is with us still as one of the city's true architectural gems.

A vision for Toronto's future

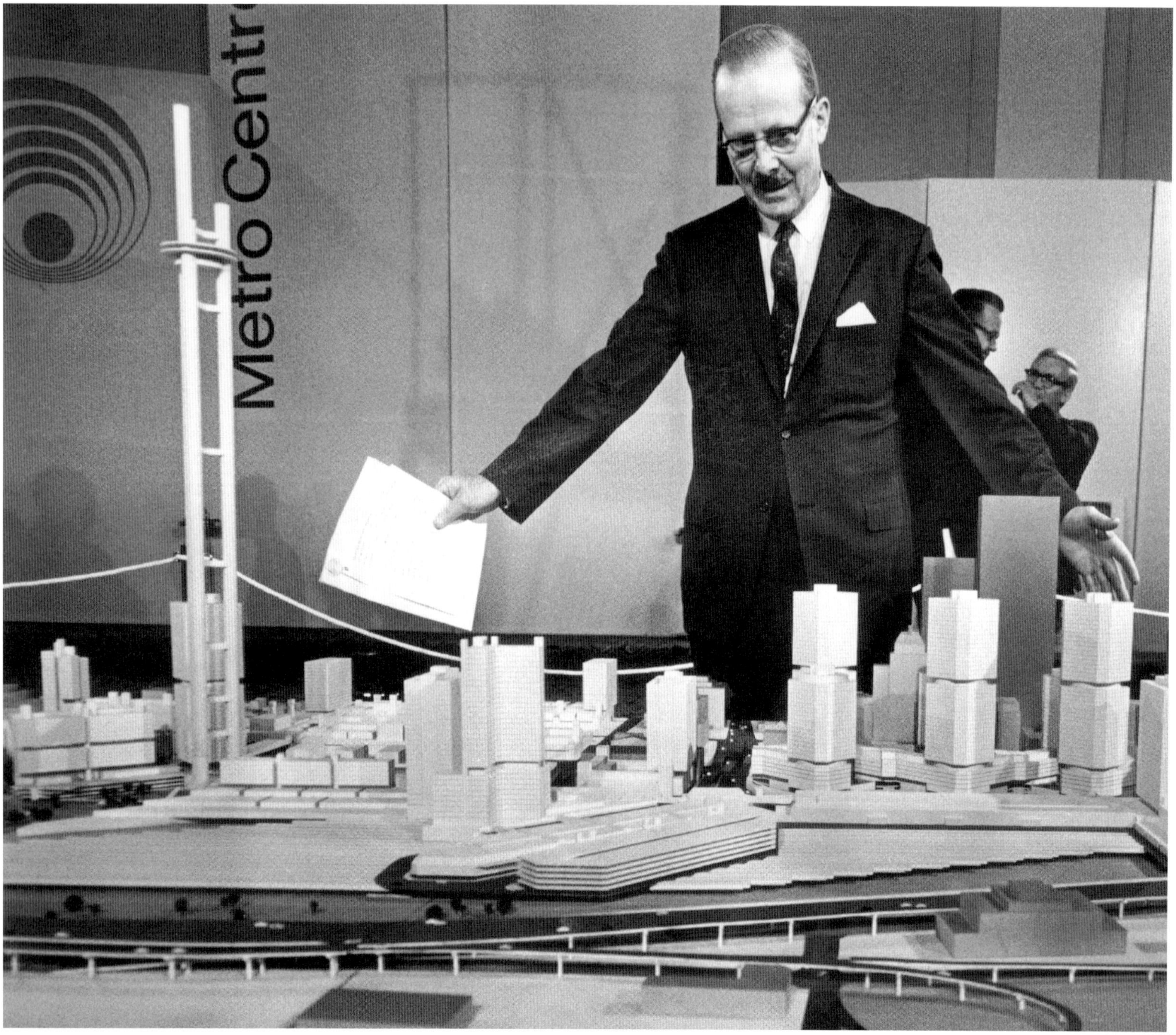

87 Mayor William Dennison beams as he unveils a model of the proposed Metropolitan Centre, December 20, 1968.

Note that a major component of the project was a lofty communications tower, the precursor of today's CN Tower.

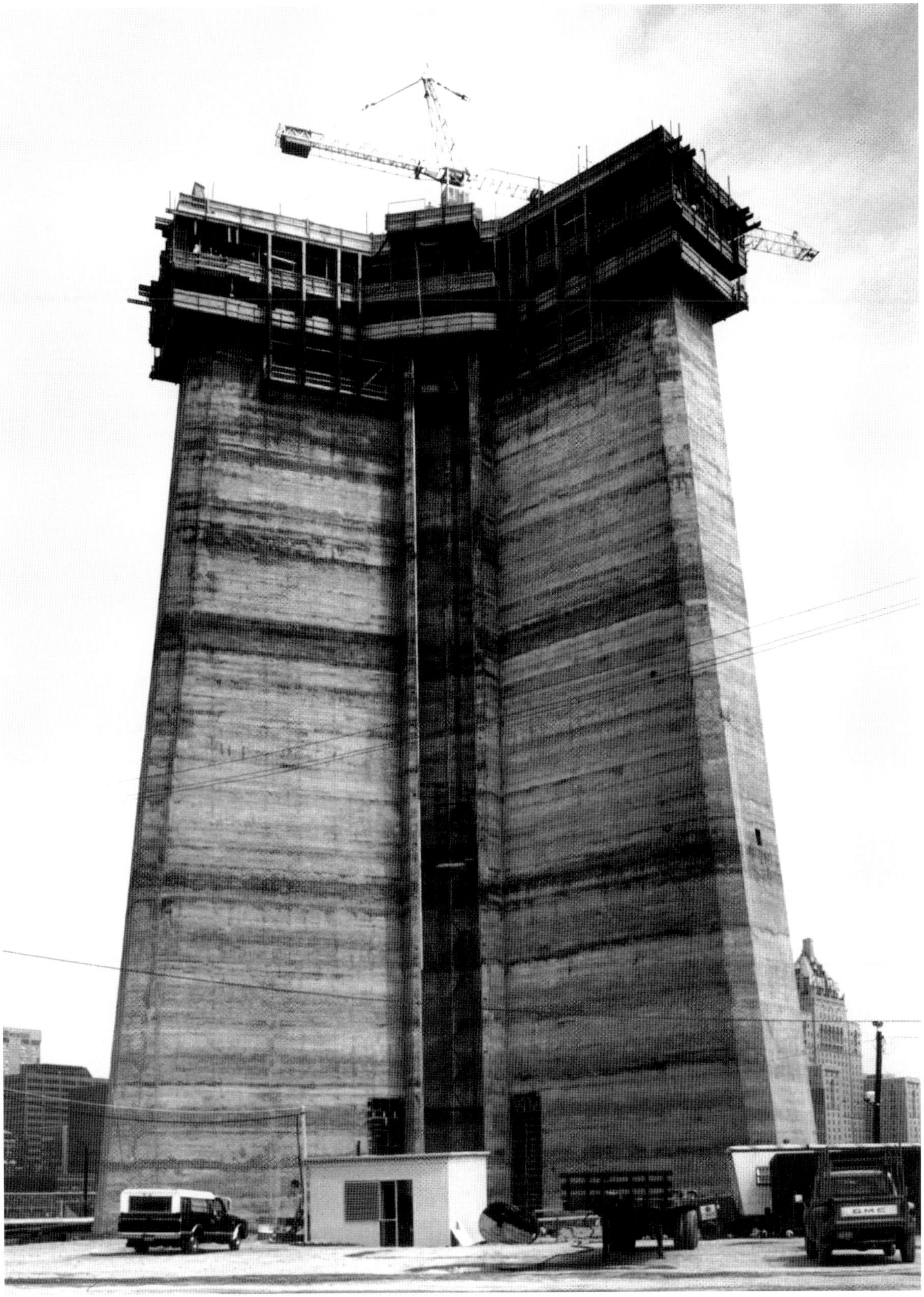

88 Work on a future city landmark, the CN Tower, is well underway in this photograph taken in the summer of 1973.

During the early stages of tower construction, several dark bands encircling the structure began to appear. These were caused by the thick grease that was used to help in the repositioning of the heavy slipform into which the concrete was poured. As this repositioning was scheduled for weekends, at which time no concrete was poured, the bands came to represent weekly intervals in the tower's climb skyward.

89 In the spring of 1975 a gigantic Sikorsky Skycrane helicopter, known affectionately to Torontonians as Olga, began the intricate job of topping off the CN Tower with a massive communications antenna. — *Courtesy Toronto Sun*

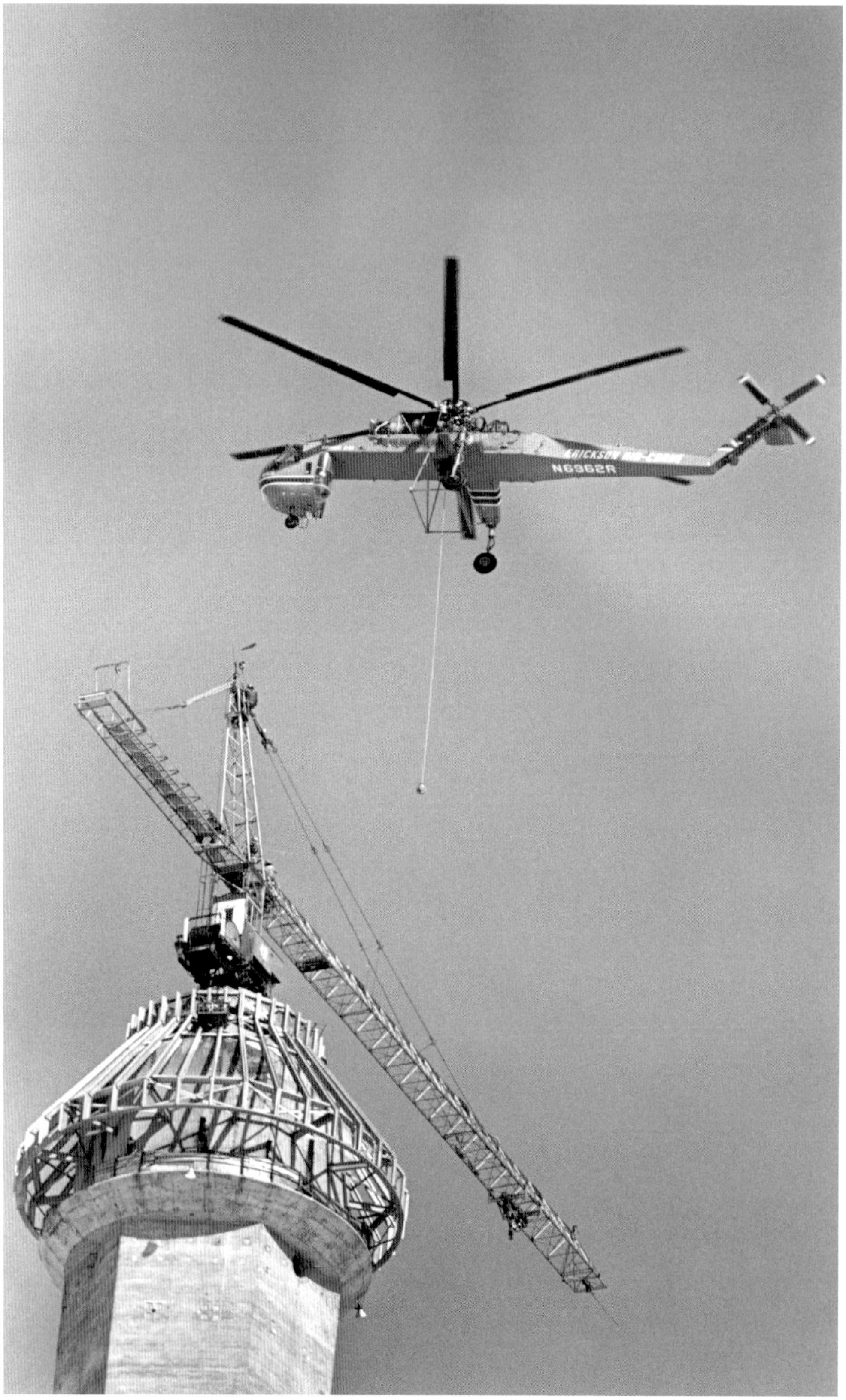

The idea of a communications tower soaring more than 450 metres (1500 feet) into the heavens was first proposed in 1968 as part of a billion-dollar redevelopment of 190 acres in the city's central waterfront area and the so-called railway lands. The main component of this project, known as Metropolitan Centre (later simply as Metro Centre), would be an ultra-modern communications facility. However, over the years a proliferation of high-rise buildings in and around the city core had created major problems with both the transmission and reception of television, FM radio, cellular telephone, microwave, and other commercial telecommunication signals. Therefore, crucial to the success of this proposed multi-million-dollar facility would be a giant new transmission tower that would overcome these problems. Work on the new CN Tower (named for Canadian National Railways, a partner in the Metro Centre project, who financed this component) began in 1973. But even as the new tower climbed skyward, plans for the Metro Centre project itself began to unravel. Ultimately, the project was cancelled, except for the communications tower, which was already well underway. It kept climbing, and on April 2, 1975, Toronto's spectacular CN Tower was topped-off at 553.4 metres (1,815 feet, 6 inches). *The Guinness Book of World Records* confirmed its status as the tallest "free-standing" structure in the world. On June 26 of the following year the city's newest landmark opened to the public. The tower was subsequently leased to the highly successful Canadian real estate developer TrizecHahn with the "CN" portion of CN Tower now standing for Canada's National Tower.

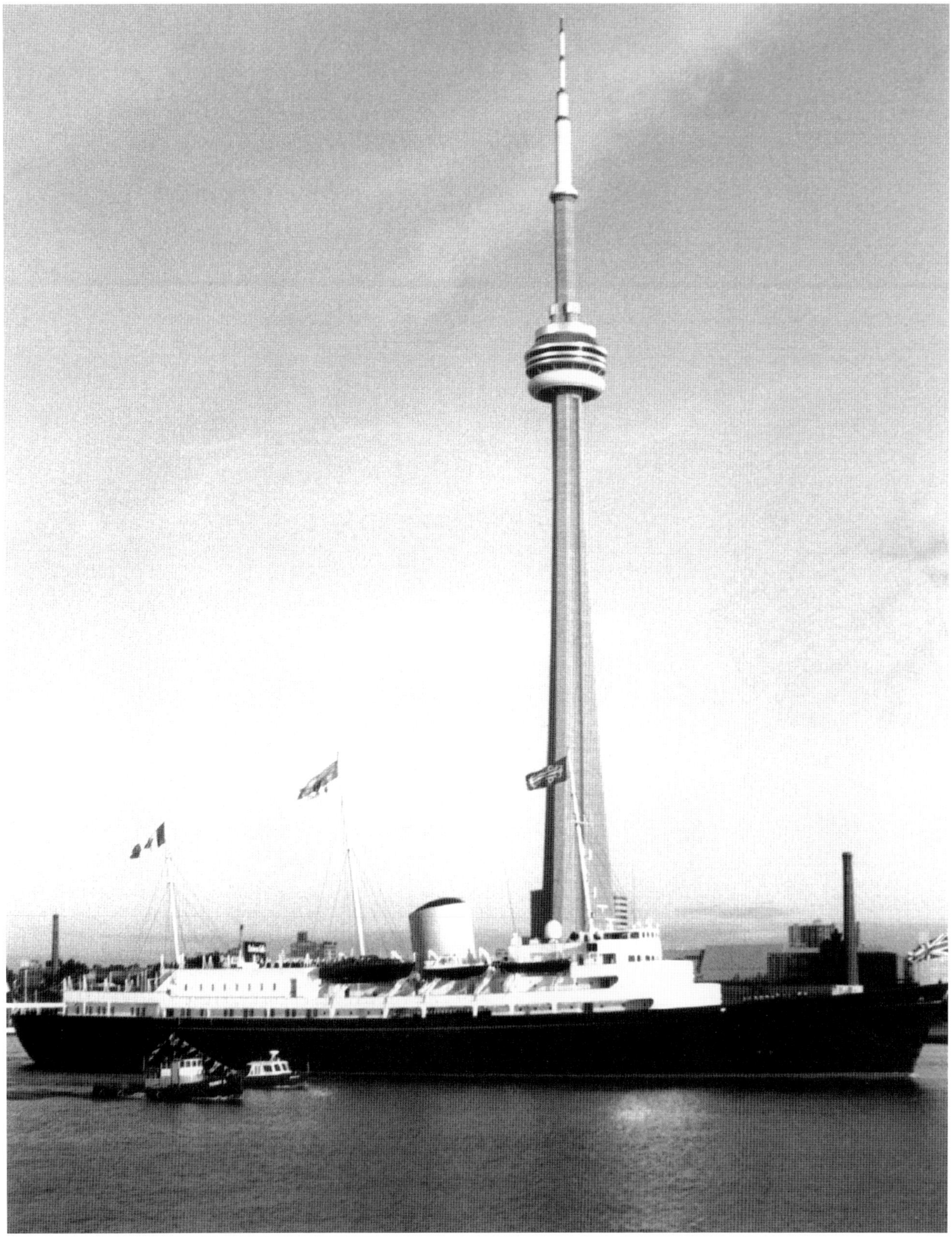

90 The CN Tower looms over the Royal Yacht Britannia *as the sleek vessel transports Queen Elizabeth II and Prince Philip to the city to participate in Ontario's bi-centennial celebrations, September 29, 1984.*

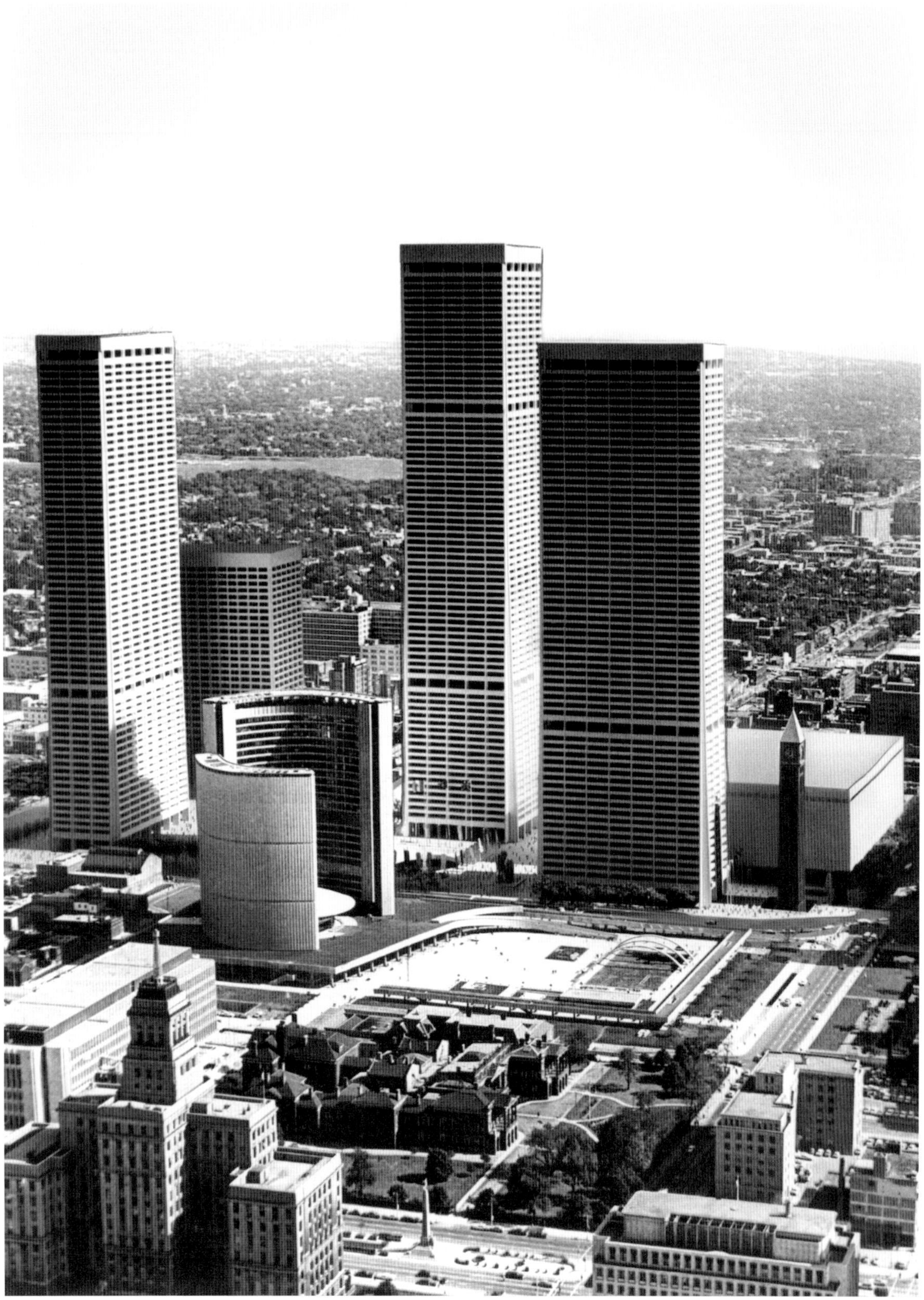

91 Composite photograph showing the original design for Toronto's new Eaton Centre, March 1966.

Just as the Metropolitan Centre project failed a few years later because of the planners' refusal to retain all of Union Station in the proposal, so too was the original Eaton Centre concept doomed when it was announced that Old City Hall would be replaced by an office tower and large retail store. In an attempt to appease an irate public, it was proposed by the developer that the Hall's clock tower and memorial Cenotaph, the only components of any merit, be saved. Thousands of citizens, and a few municipal politicians, reacted angrily to the proposed desecration, and eventually the developers abandoned the entire scheme. A few years later a condensed Eaton Centre plan was put forward; this time, all of Old City Hall was retained, along with the 1847 Church of the Holy Trinity and Dr. Henry Scadding's house (although the latter, which was built around 1861, was moved slightly to accommodate the new Eaton Centre). Toronto city council, with the enthusiastic backing of the public, approved the project. Not only did Toronto get its Eaton Centre (the first phase of which opened in 1977), it was able to hang on to a couple of its most cherished landmarks as well.

Royal visits to Toronto

The first visit to Toronto by a member of the royal family took place in 1860 with the arrival of Queen Victoria's son, eighteen-year-old Albert Edward, Prince of Wales (later King Edward VII), who stopped by the young city while on a three-month tour of North America. Though it has a minor spelling anomaly, tiny Berti Street, in the Queen and Church part of the city, reminds us of his visit, (Bertie, short for Albert, was the young prince's nickname), as does Queen's Park, which the young prince dedicated in honour of his mother. Since then various members of the British royal family have dropped by for a visit. Even though royal visits have almost always generated great public interest, many historians believe that the six-week-long, coast-to-coast tour of Canada in 1939 by King George VI and Queen Elizabeth remains the most popular in our nation's history. In a visit to our city that lasted a mere eight hours, the King and Queen were greeted on their arrival by thousands of loyal Torontonians at the CPR North Toronto Station, then at Old City Hall, Queen's Park, Woodbine Race Track, Riverdale Park, and the Christie Street Military Hospital; hundreds more cheered as the royal couple said goodbye to the city at Union Station.

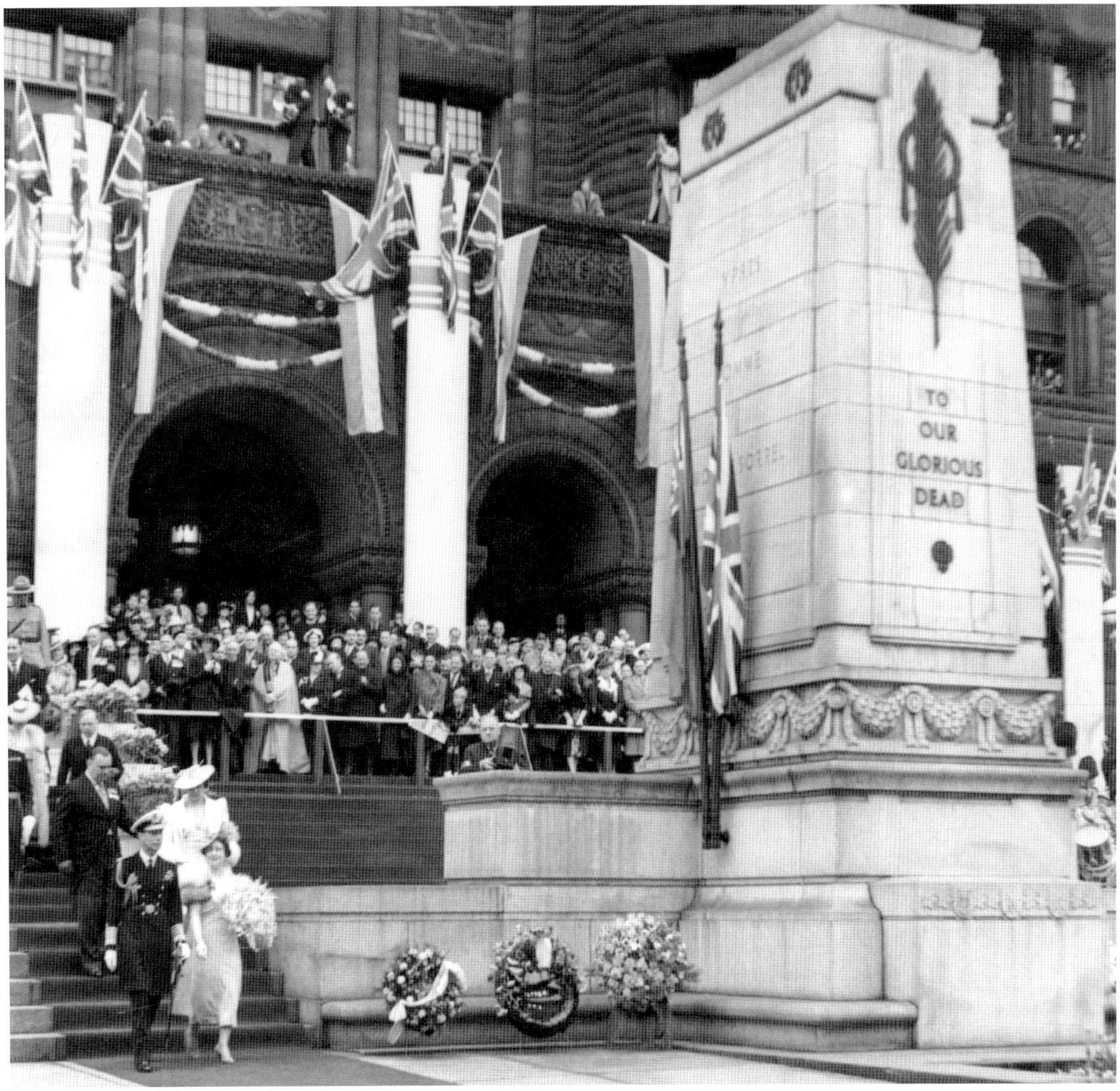

92 King George VI and Queen Elizabeth at Toronto City Hall, May 22, 1939.

They are followed down the steps by Mayor Ralph Day and Prime Minister Mackenzie King.

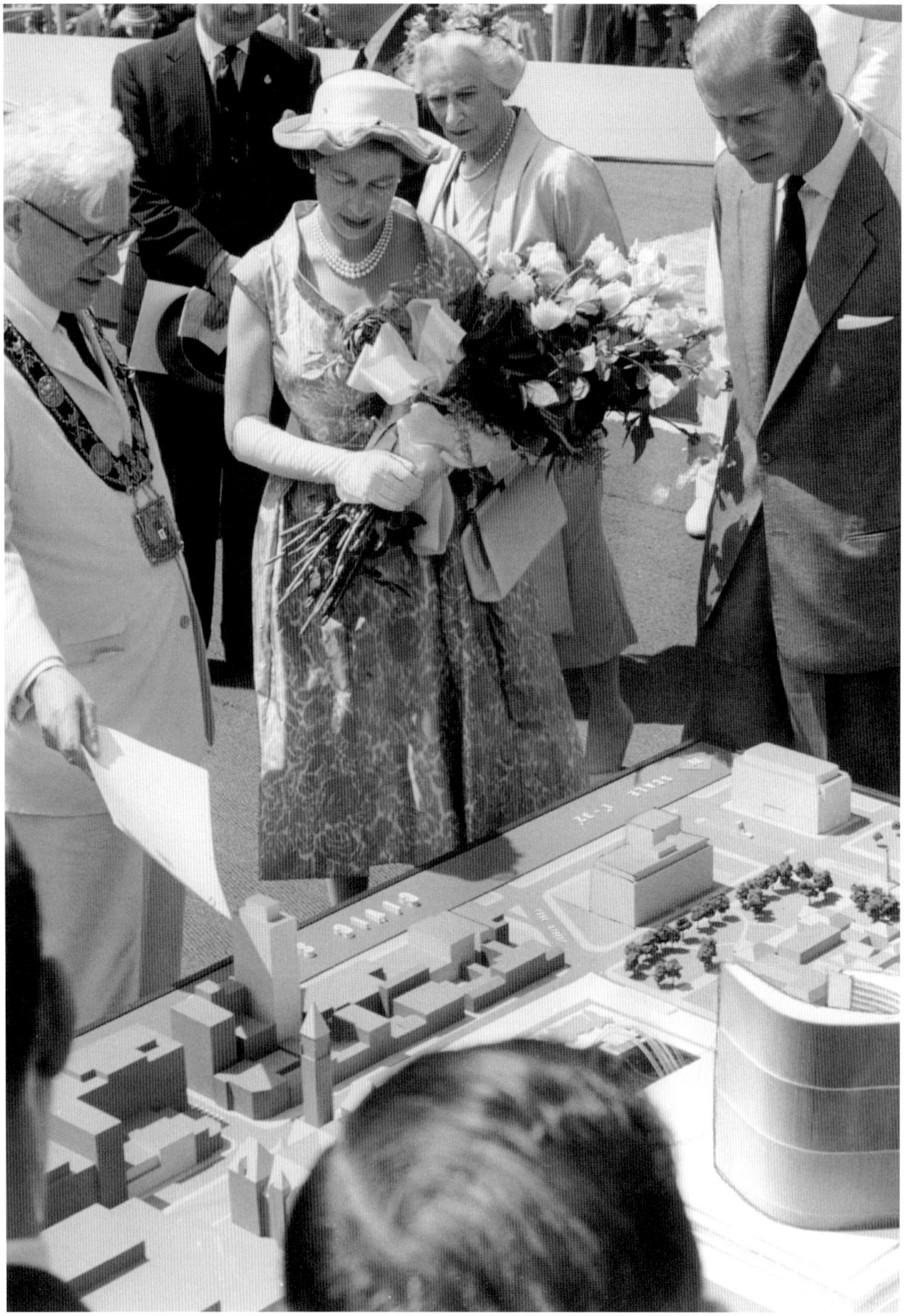

93 Queen Elizabeth II and Prince Philip examine a scale model of Toronto's New City Hall while commentary is provided by Mayor Nathan Phillips, June 29, 1959.

This was the Queen's second visit to Toronto; the first occurred in 1951 while she was still Princess Elizabeth. One of the main features of the 1959 visit was her participation, with American President Eisenhower, in the official opening of the new St. Lawrence Seaway. During their two-day stay in Toronto, the Queen and the Prince visited Kew Beach Park, where they met thousands of children, and beautiful High Park, where they were met by Toronto and area Boy Scouts and Girl Guides. Then it was on to the CNE Grandstand, where the royal couple reviewed the 48th Highlanders of Canada. That was followed by a tree planting ceremony in Coronation Park (just across Lake Shore Boulevard). The park was originally dedicated in honour of her father's coronation in 1937. The following morning the Queen visited the veterans at Sunnybrook Hospital.

The availability of affordable housing is not a new problem for Toronto, as this trio of photographs will prove.

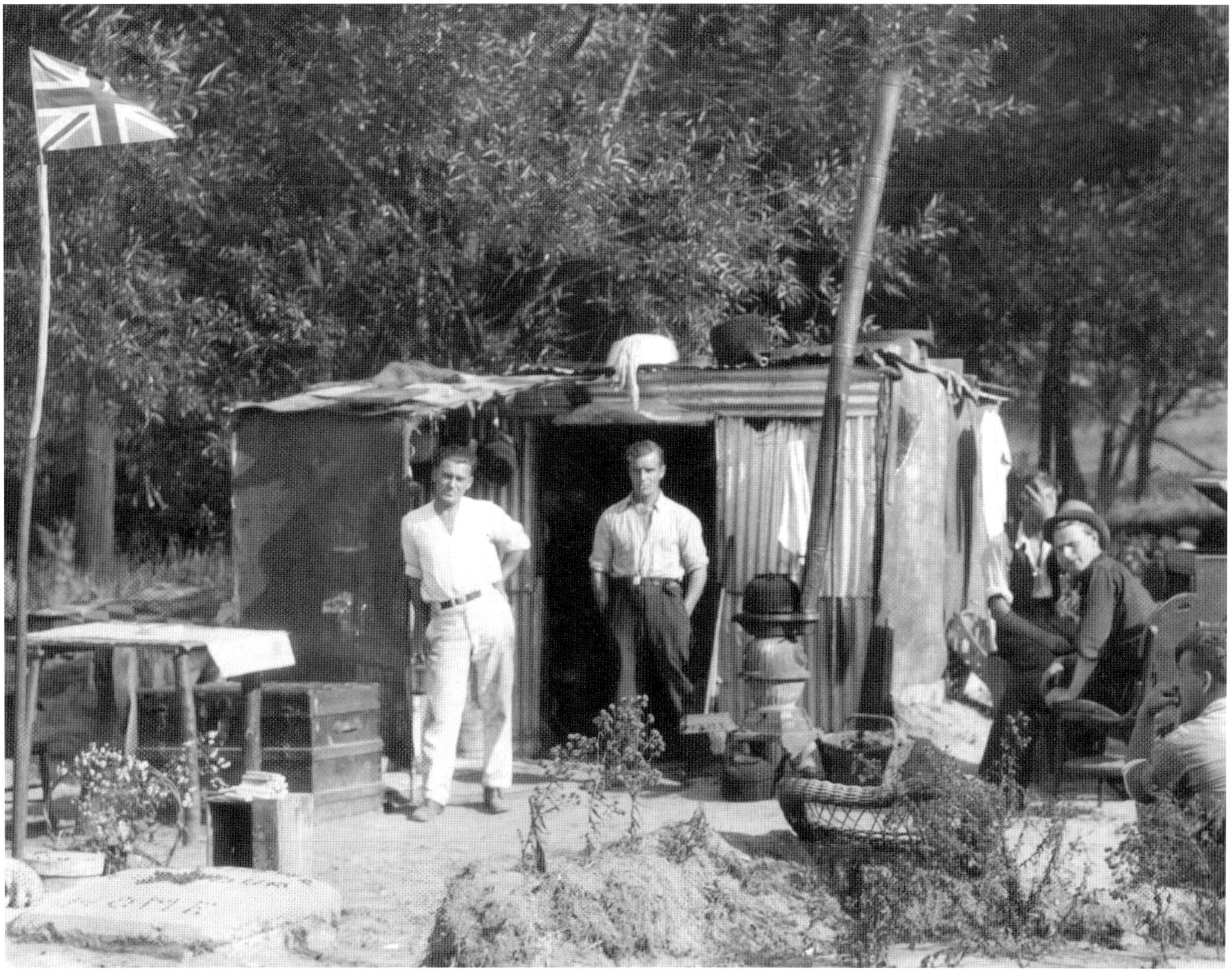

94 The Great Depression brought thousands of unemployed to Canada's cities in search of work.

Many were forced to live in shacks such as these in the Don Valley, 1931.

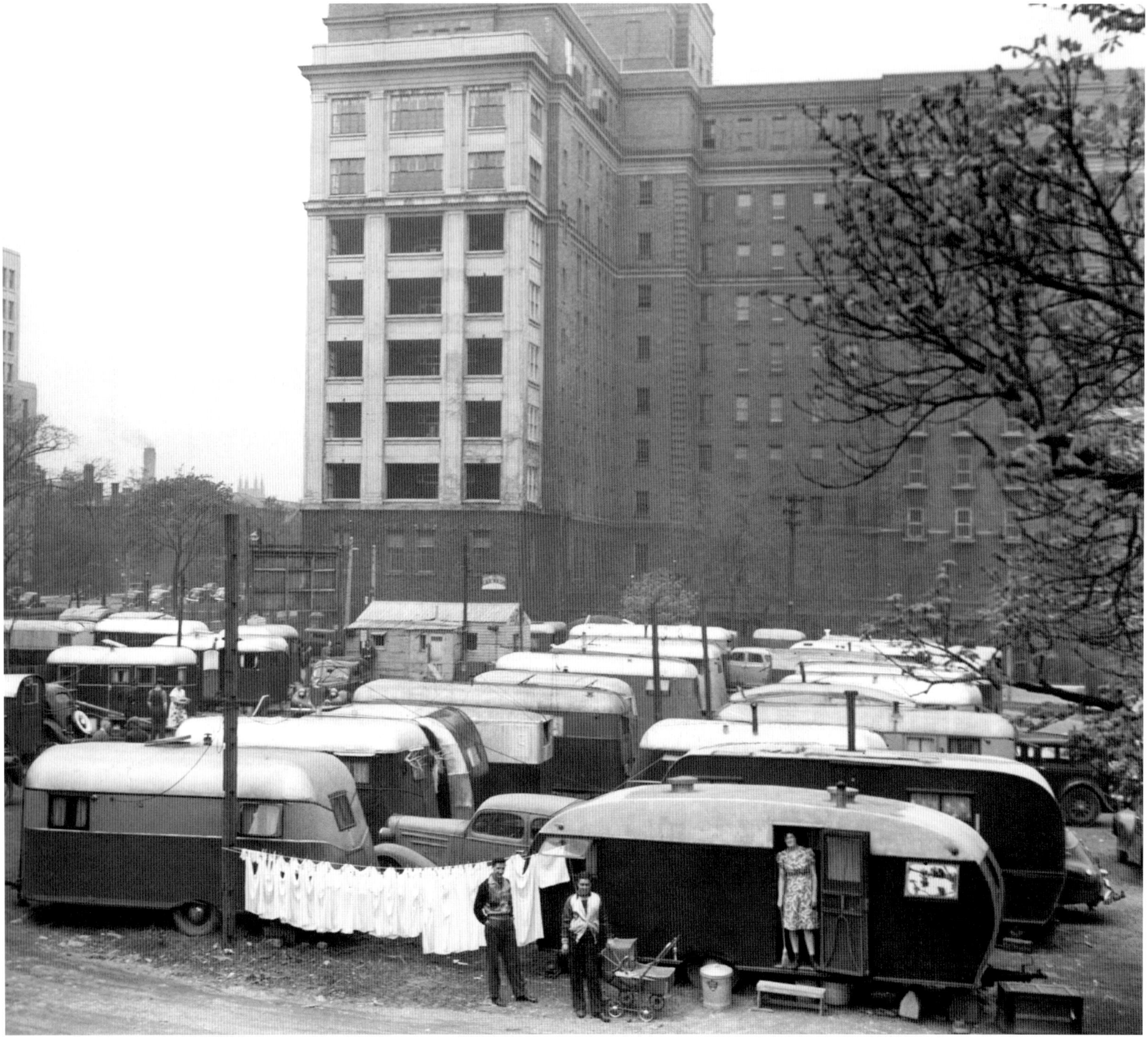

95 Housing was a major problem once again during the Second World War.

A total of thirty families found themselves living in this trailer park on the east side of University Avenue, steps from the Toronto General Hospital, 1943.

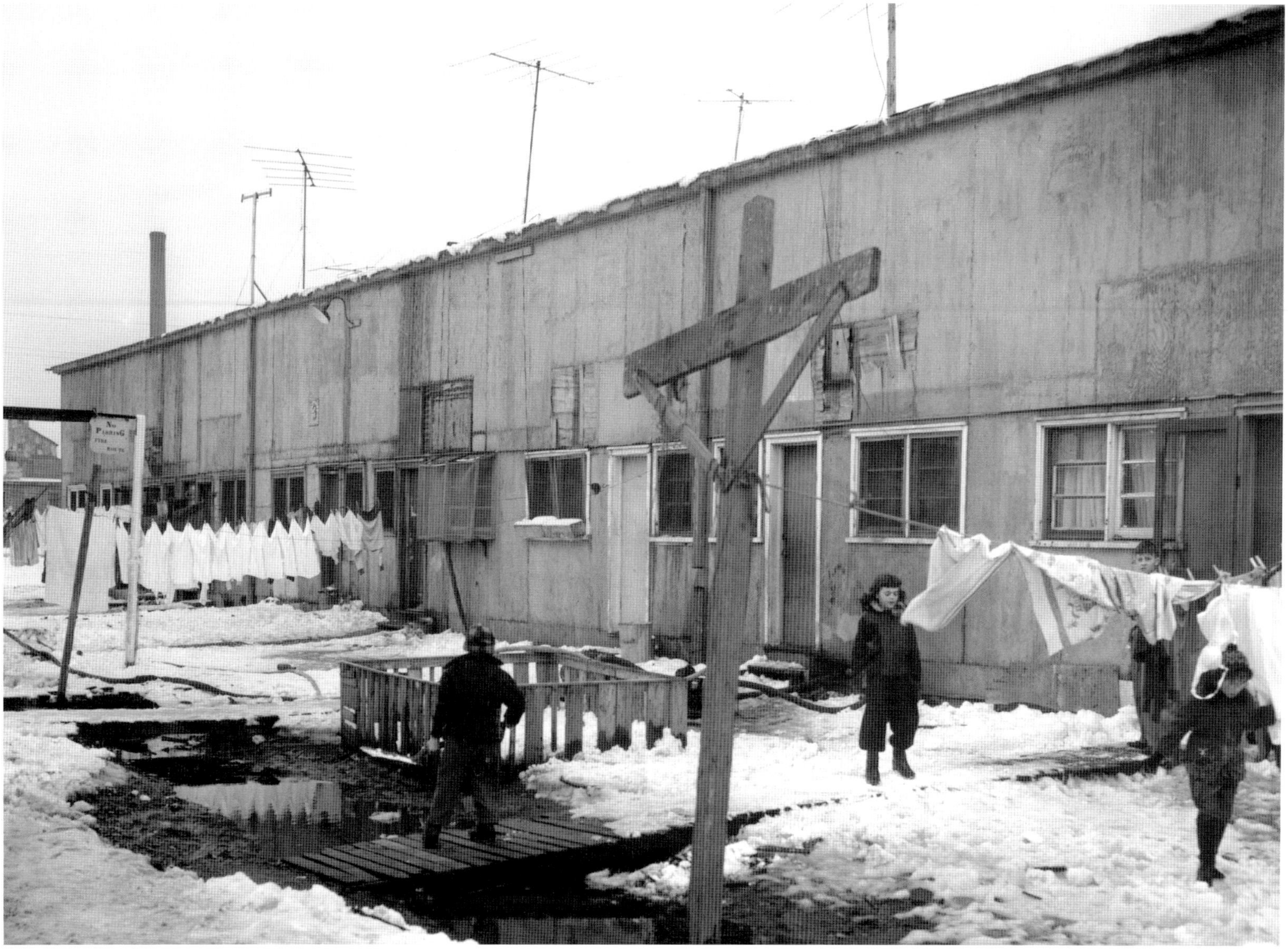

96 Even after the war ended housing remained scarce.

This forced officials to establish emergency housing sites at the foot of Bathurst Street (Little Norway), in the various buildings that made up Stanley Barracks in the CNE grounds, and at the former GECO (General Engineering Company) ammunition factory on the south side of Eglinton Avenue East, east of Warden Avenue. It was here that many Torontonians turned out millions of tracer shells for the war effort. While housing shortages prevailed during the war, the armistice did little to ease the problem. Through an arrangement with the federal government, the various buildings in the GECO complex in Scarborough Township were converted for "temporary" residential use. In early 1946, families began moving, and within a few years more than two thousand people were living in structures that had been used for the production of ammunition. Other structures on the property were used as a grocery store, a fire hall, and schoolhouses. As the housing picture improved, the need for the GECO property decreased, and by late 1954 only 148 people remained on site. Soon everyone had moved on, leaving only a few of the old buildings as reminders of a once busy community.

One of the city's most enjoyable attractions is Toronto Island. And while most people consider the Island to have just three components (Ward's Island, Centre Island, and Hanlan's Point) it actually consists of more than twenty islands, some large, some very small. For centuries, Toronto Island (or the Peninsula, as it was known prior to the 1858 storm that breached its narrow connection with the mainland, turning the isthmus into an island) had been a welcome retreat for the First Nations people as well as some of the early European explorers. With the arrival in the early 1800s of more permanent inhabitants, a variety of residences began appearing on the Island, especially on Ward's. Initially these tents and cabins were used mainly on weekends, but soon the Island was boasting a year-round population, with many of Toronto's elite removing to their new mansions for the hot summer months. During the Second World War years and a few years following, the ongoing housing shortage in the city had civic officials promoting Toronto Island as a year-round place to live. That all changed following the creation of Metropolitan Toronto in 1953, when the decision was made to convert all of Toronto Island into parkland for the use of all of the people. Demolition of the large houses at Centre Island began, with the small homes at Ward's soon to follow. However, the second part of that transformation process was halted for a variety of reasons, and today a community of more than seven hundred people still enjoys life on Ward's Island.

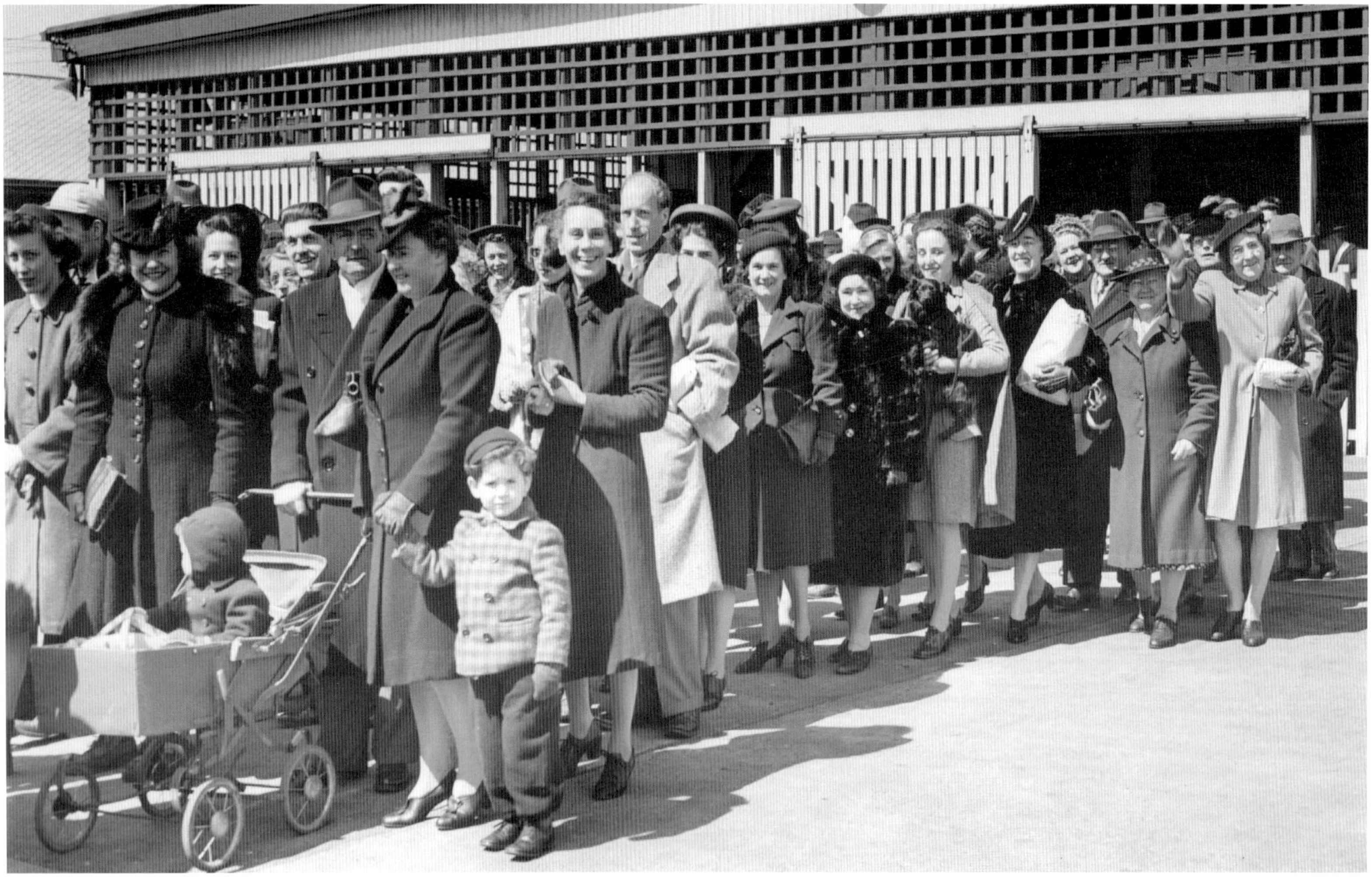

97 Even though war is still raging, spring is in the air as visitors and residents of Toronto Island wait to board the ferry at the old Island Ferry Docks, April 4, 1944.

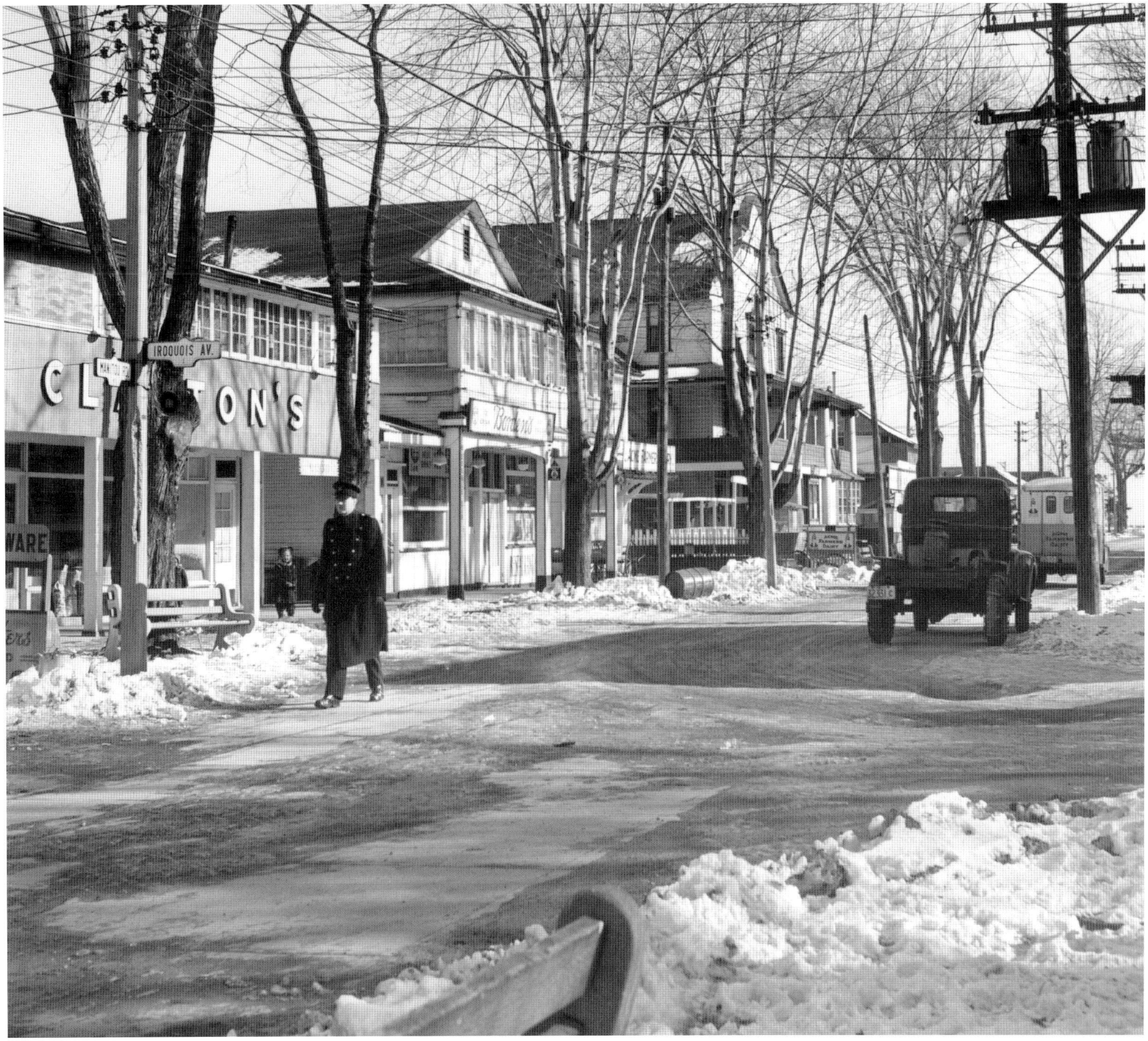

98 A city constable walks the beat on Toronto Island's main street, Manitou Road, 1952.

Note the can of milk on the back of the truck parked by the curb as well as the snow chains to help the driver get around when heavy snowfalls blanketed the unploughed streets. All the buildings in this view were demolished as Centre Island was turned into parkland. Today, the Avenue of the Islands has replaced Manitou Road.

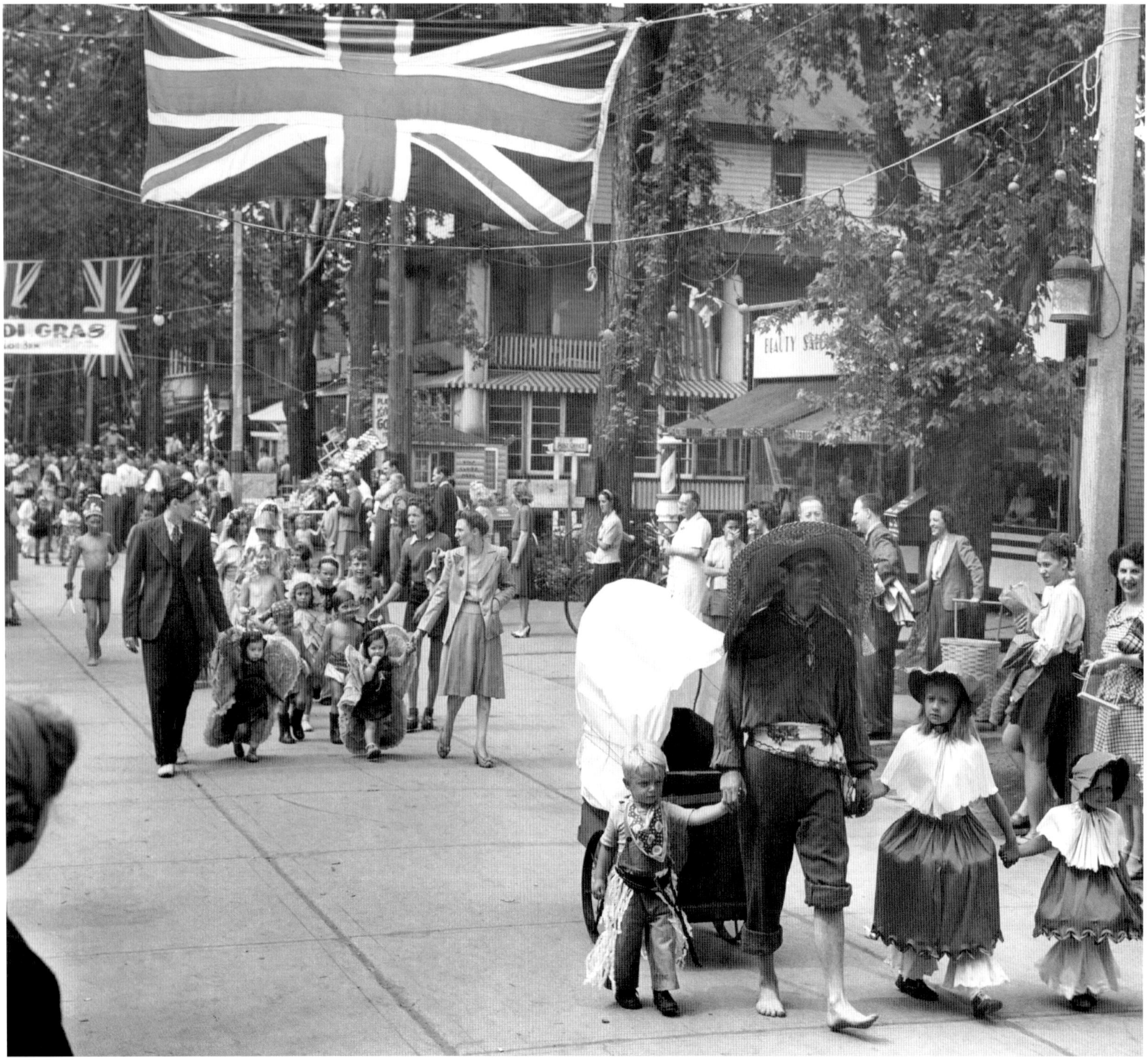

99 It's the summer of 1953 and the Centre Island community "soldiers on" even though the new Metropolitan Toronto corporation will soon be asked to turn Toronto Island into parkland, demolishing most of the houses, shops, and other buildings in the process.

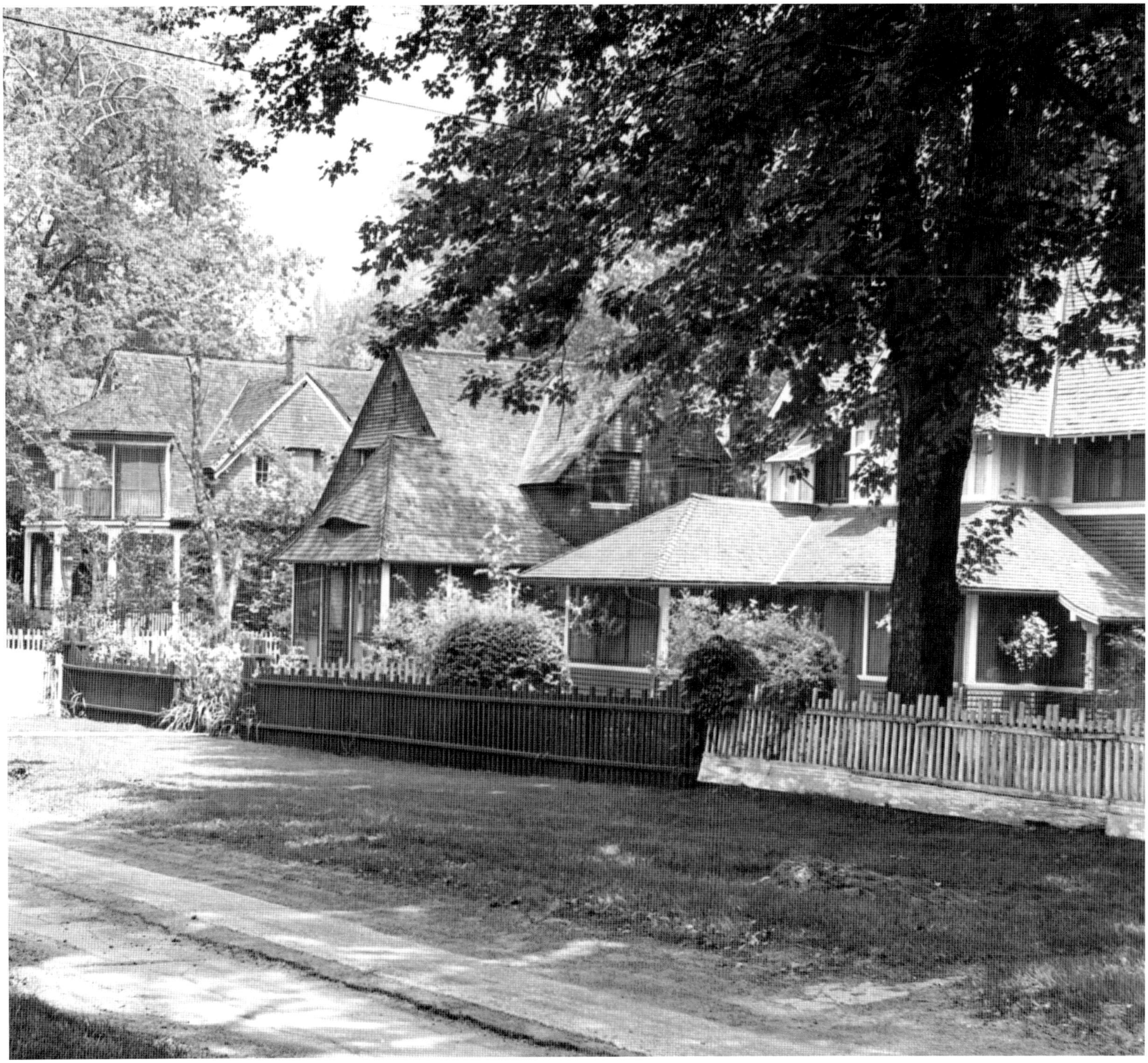

100 This summer 1963 photograph shows a row of Centre Island houses that was soon to be flattened as Metropolitan Toronto got on with the process of converting the Island into parkland.

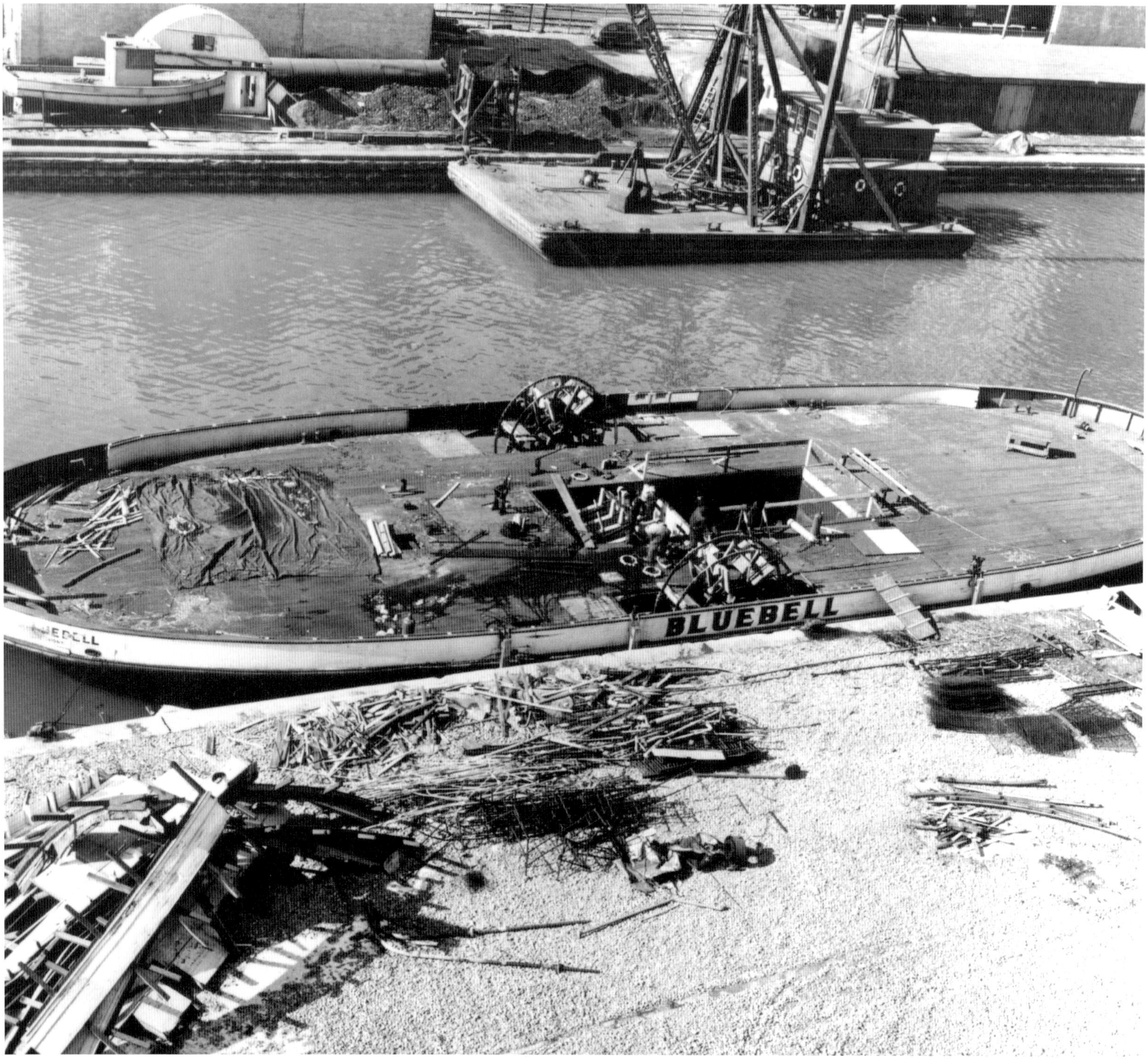

101 In the mid-1950s, with fewer and fewer people heading for Toronto Island and with a surplus of modern diesel ferry boats, officials decided to convert the "ancient" ferry Blue Bell *into a garbage scow.*

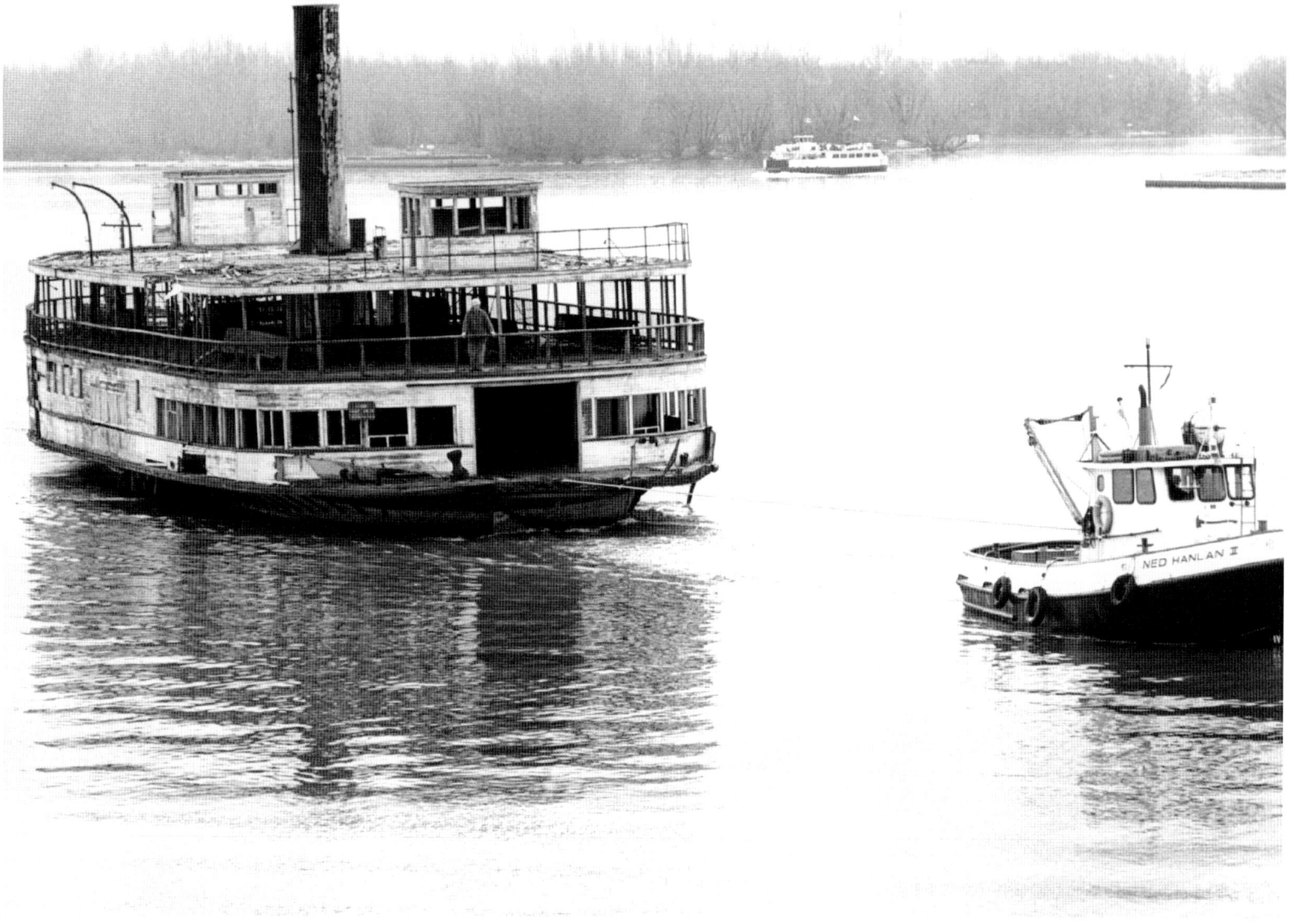

102 A similar fate awaited Trillium, *but nostalgia and good sense won out when Metro Council decided instead to restore the 1910 paddle-wheeler and return it to special service.*

In this December 1973 photograph, *Trillium* returns to the mainland after spending years languishing in an Island lagoon. *Trillium* would eventually undergo a $1-million restoration program that would see the proud old vessel returned to Toronto Bay in the spring of 1976.

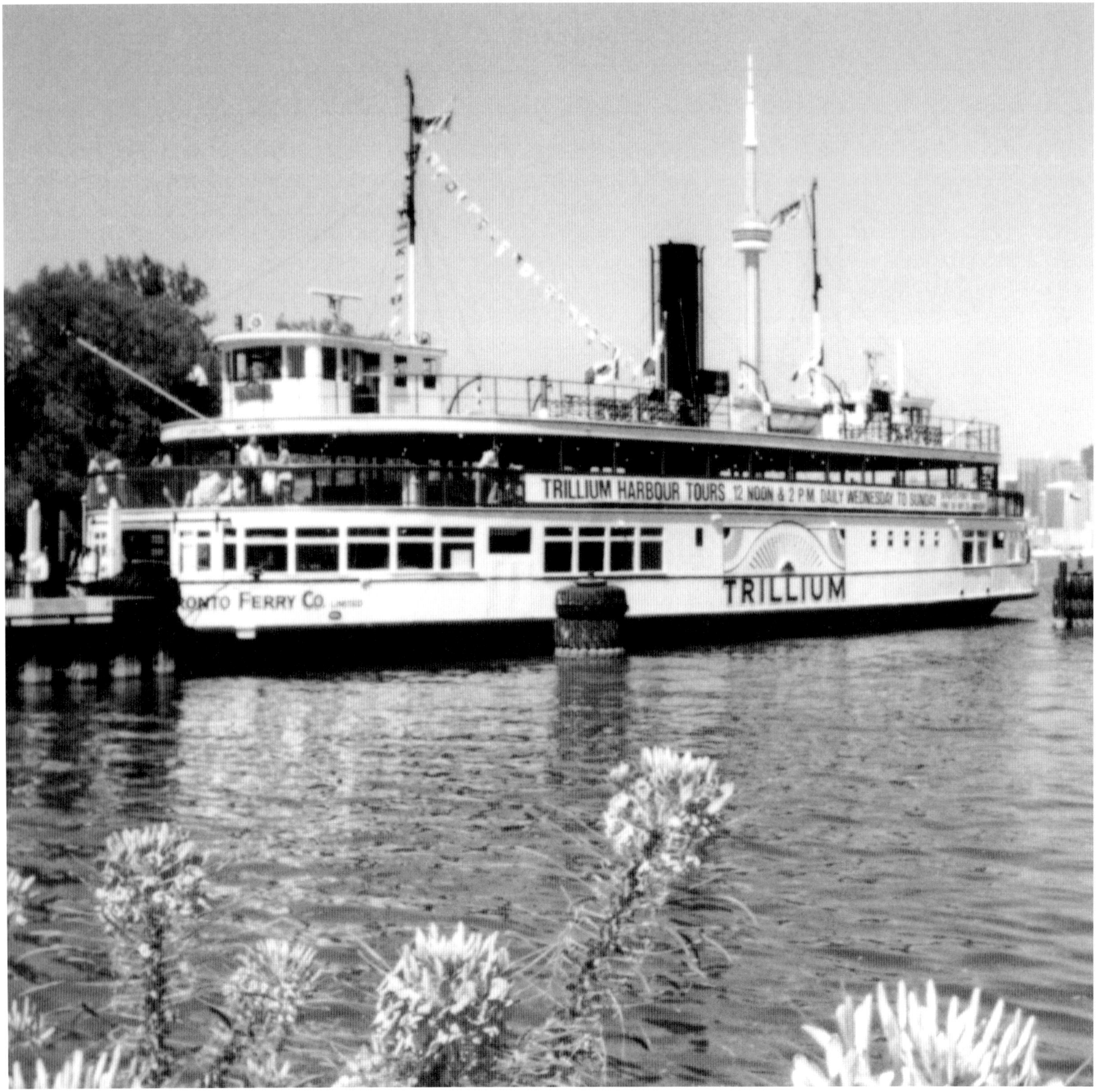

103 Trillium, *the pride of the Toronto Island ferry fleet, as she looked in 1990.*

Horse-drawn delivery wagons in Toronto days of old.

Today, horses are a rare site on Toronto's busy streets and are usually only seen in passing parades (the twenty-five handsome steeds of the Toronto Police Service Mounted Unit are always crowd pleasers) or in horse shows such as those held during the Canadian National Exhibition or Royal Winter Fair. But there was a time when horses were as common on the streets of Toronto as cars are today. There were horses pulling dairy wagons, coal wagons, bread wagons, delivery store wagons, street cleaning wagons, and, until 1931, fire wagons. Even the local junk man had a horse straining in front of his beaten-up old junk wagon. In fact, as recently as 1947, it was reported that Toronto was still a 6,500-horse town. The following photographs are proof horses were once a common sight around our city.

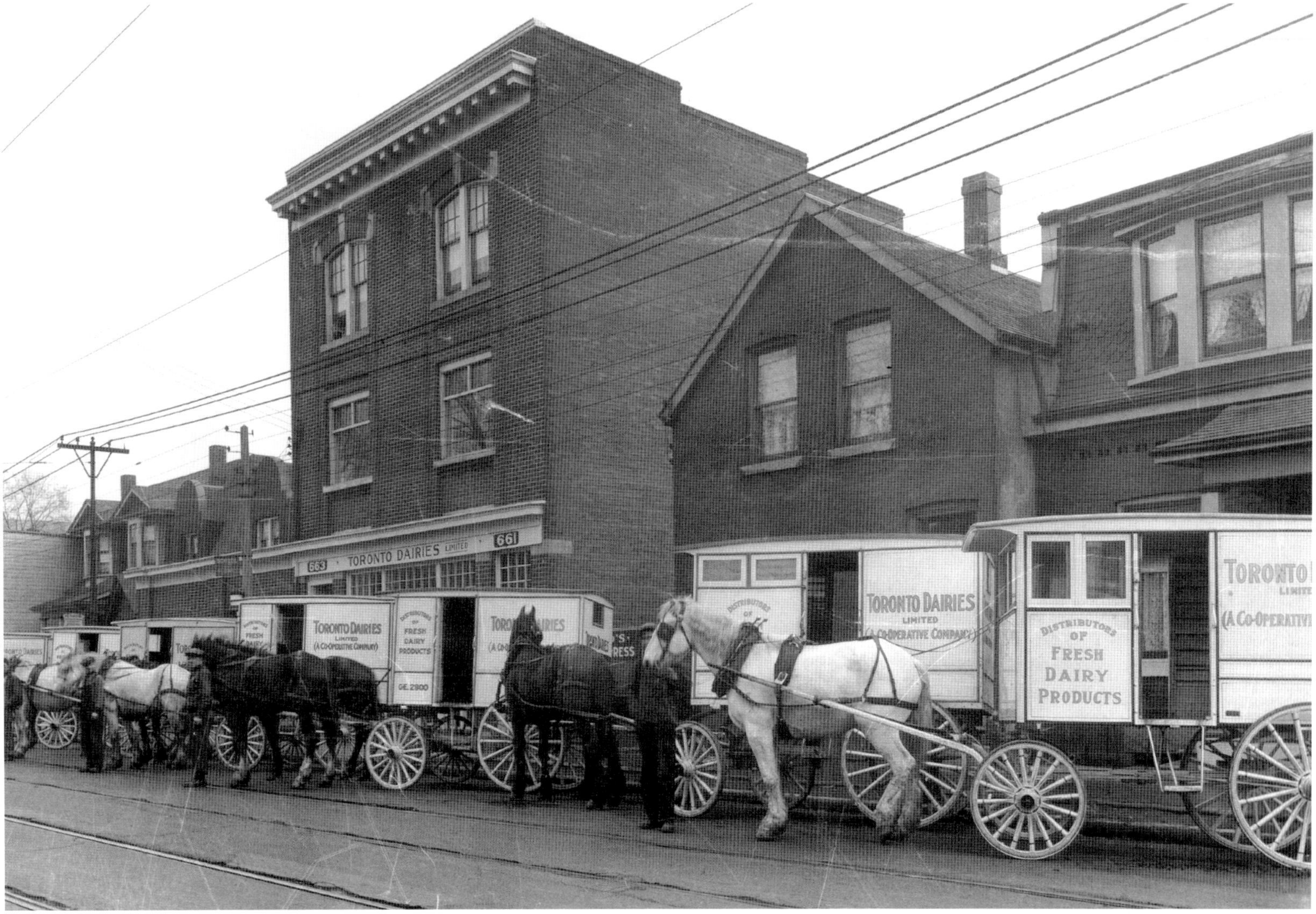

104 Getting ready for the day's deliveries at the Toronto Dairies plant, 661 Gerrard Street East, circa 1940.

This company, which was established in 1932 and operated until 1949, was one of more than one hundred local dairies that served the citizens of Toronto, until mergers and buy-outs eventually reduced that number to a mere handful. Some of the best-known dairies from the past include Acme Farmers, City, Roselawn Farms, Upland, Donlands, and Vita-Milk.

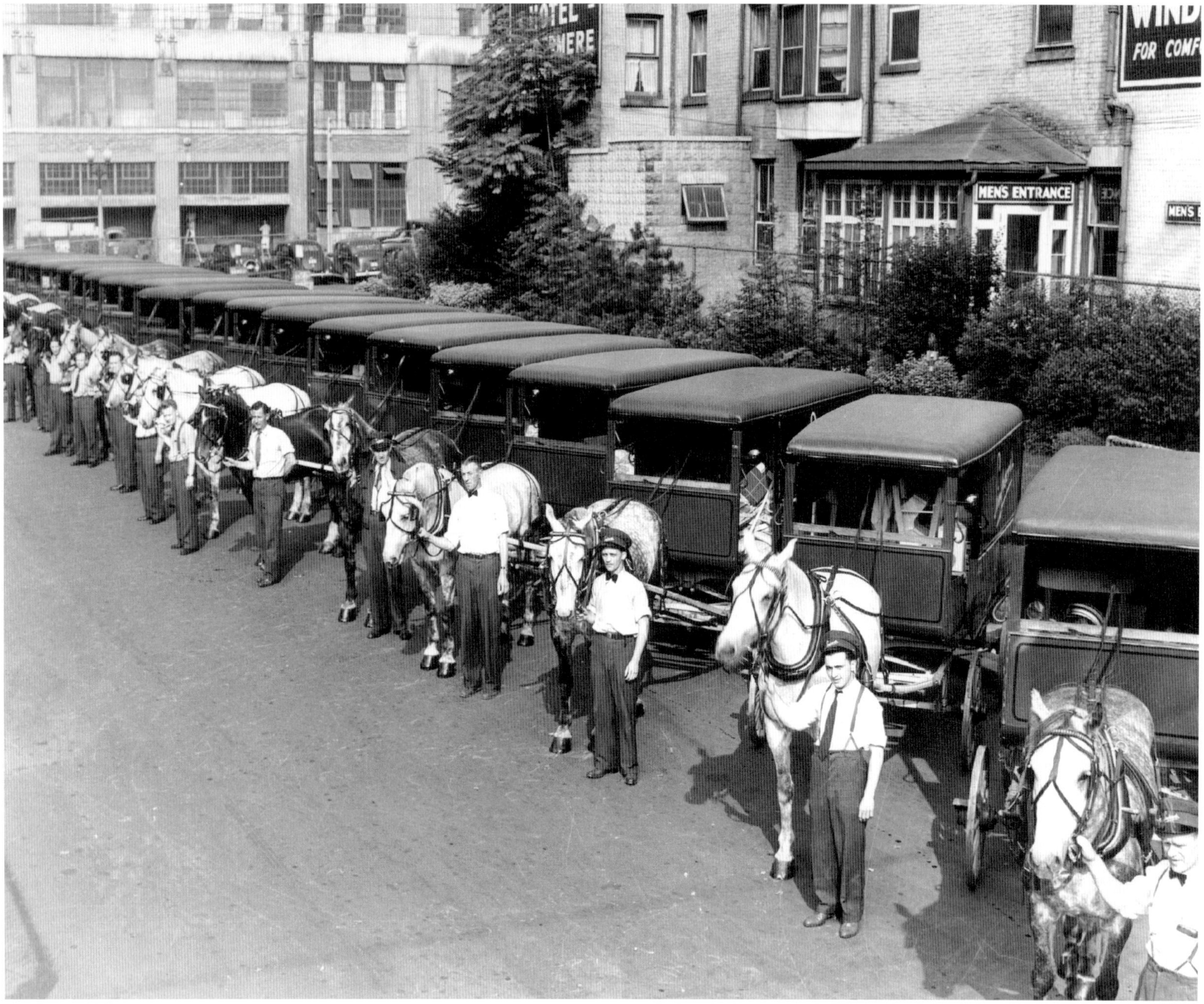

105 The Robert Simpson Company delivery wagons and their drivers outside the Simpson stables on Dalhousie Street, circa 1942.

Simpson's originally did away with its horse-drawn delivery wagons in 1928, but with the start of the Second World War and the resulting gasoline and tire rationing, seventy-five horses were reinstated on forty downtown routes. At war's end the "fleet" was auctioned off, with most of the horses finding new jobs with various Toronto dairies. Eaton's, who once had over four hundred delivery horses, auctioned off its last sixty in 1937. The building in the background of this photograph was built in 1916 as the Simpson Mail Order Building and has recently been converted into a condominium. To the right of the view is the Hotel Windermere, one of several inexpensive apartment hotels on Jarvis Street.

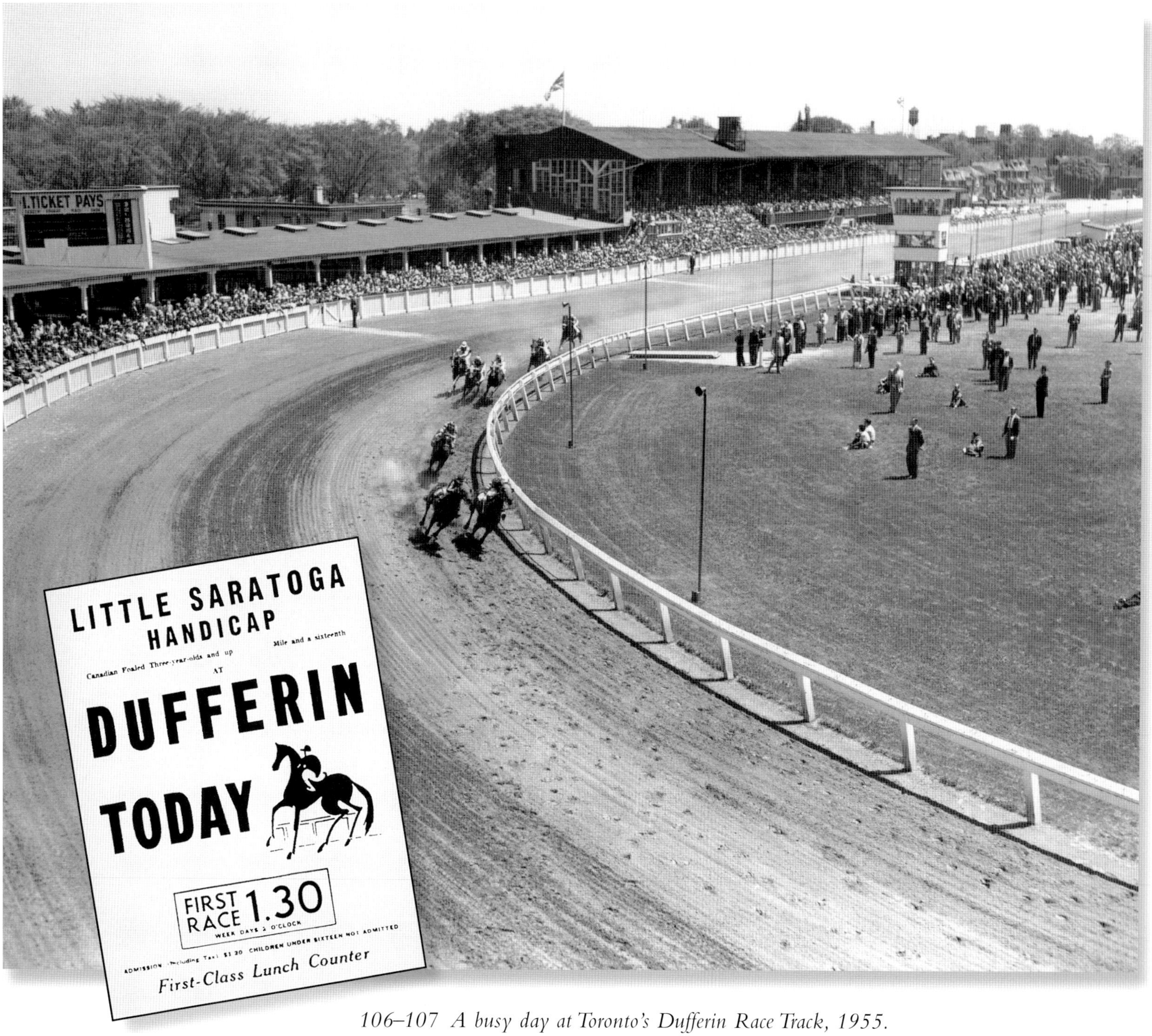

106–107 A busy day at Toronto's Dufferin Race Track, 1955.

Known by those who frequented the city's tracks as "Little Saratoga," a reference to the famous Saratoga track in New York State, Dufferin opened in 1907 and operated until 1955. Several years later, a sprawling shopping centre was built on the site. Other popular city tracks of the day were Woodbine, later Greenwood (1875–1993), Hillcrest (1912–1917), Long Branch (1924–1957), and Thorncliffe (1917–1952). Today, only the new Woodbine, which opened on the northwestern outskirts of Toronto in 1956, still operates.

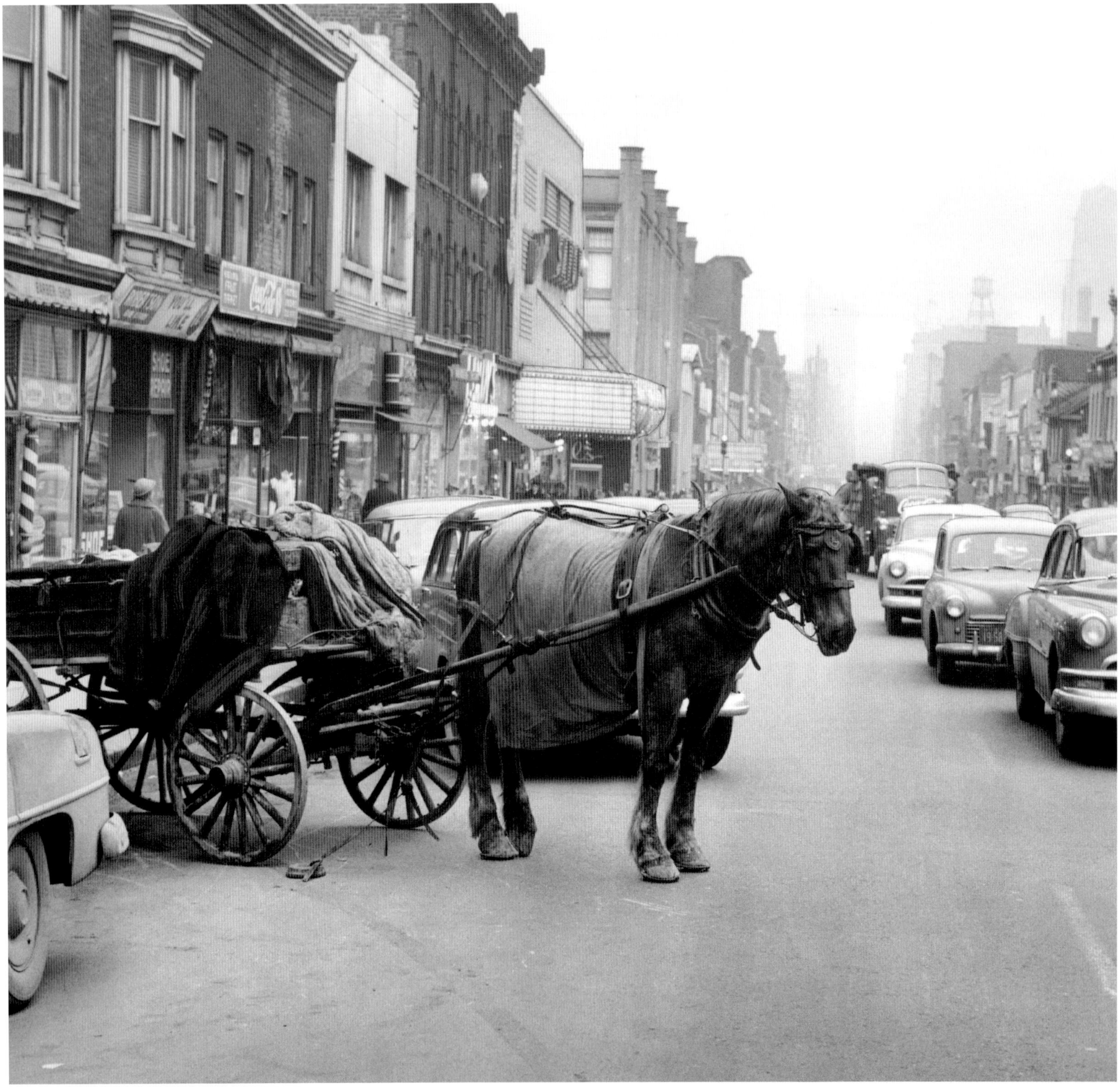

108 This forlorn steed doesn't much care that he (or is it she?) is impeding traffic on Yonge Street north of Gerrard, 1955.

Toronto's rail lines in days of old

From the first train to steam out of the city in 1853, a little locomotive pulling four cars of the newly established Ontario, Simcoe and Huron Railway, to the modern diesels powering mile-long freight trains or the green and white bi-level commuter coaches of GO Transit, trains, both passenger and freight, have been important factors in the successful and ongoing growth of Toronto. And the sights, sounds, and smells of trains continue to be a part of our city.

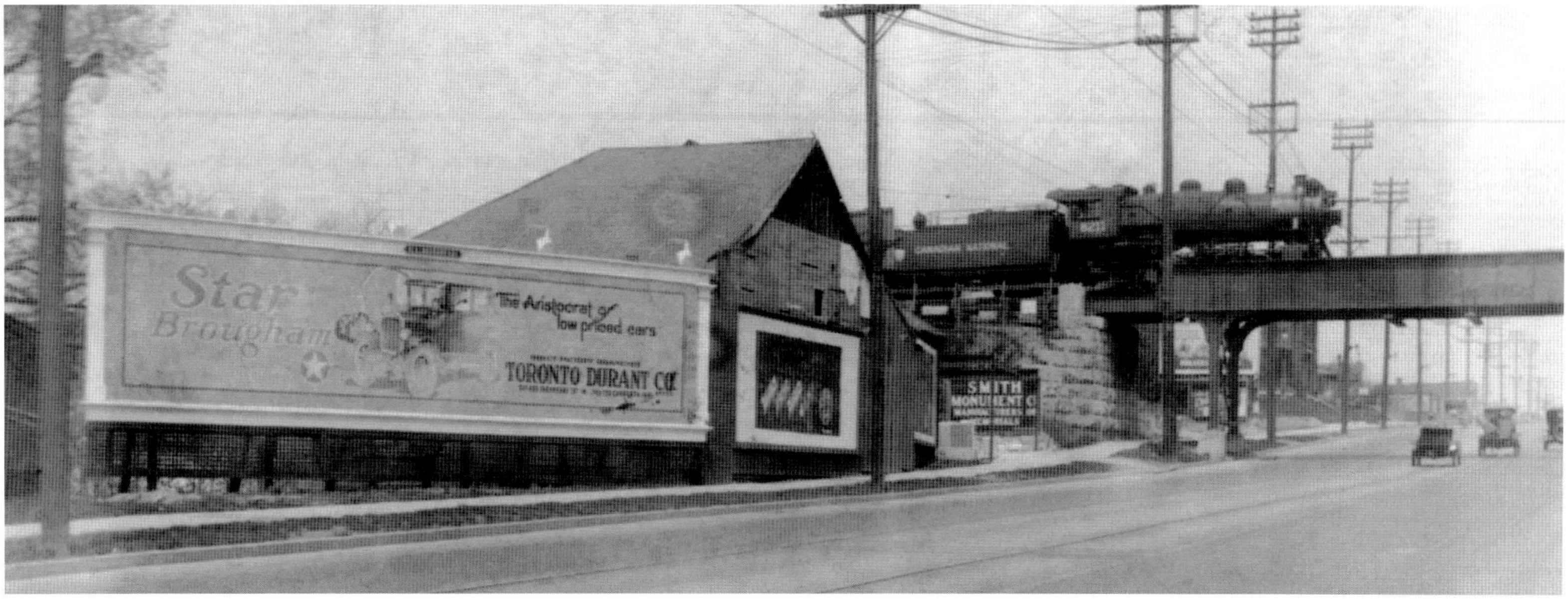

109 A Canadian National freight train on the old Belt Line bridge over Yonge Street north of St. Clair Avenue, circa 1925.

The Belt Line Railway was an 1892 creation of a group of land speculators who had purchased acres of land on the northern outskirts of the young city. Their railway was to be a key component in the successful marketing of their property as future suburban housing sites for prospective customers living in the city. The Belt Line would have two separate segments. The more easterly was called the Don Loop and would serve clients who bought land north of the city and east of Caledonia Road. The other was the Humber Loop, which was destined to serve industrial properties in the hinterland north and west of the city. The Don Loop, which was key to the success of the suburban housing scheme, was advertised as the perfect way for prospective buyers to commute between their downtown workplaces and their new homes in what the developers called "the Highlands of Toronto." Unfortunately, the land boom was in decline even as the first Belt Line passenger train chugged out of the old Union Station on July 30, 1892. Within sixteen short months the owner of the railway, the Belt Land Company, was forced to declare bankruptcy. Toronto's first commuter line was out of business. The tracks, right-of-way, and equipment were soon turned over to the government-owned Grand Trunk Railway. For years the GTR (and, after 1919, the CNR) operated steam trains on a section of the old route hauling goods to companies that had been established along the right-of-way. Eventually, the rails were removed, and today the Belt Line remains as a "linear park," a favourite of walkers, joggers, and cyclists. Incidentally, the Star automobile shown on the advertising billboard to the left of this photograph was manufactured in the Durant factory on Laird Drive in suburban Leaside. This company had been started by William Durant, who had established the General Motors Company south of the border in 1908 only to be ousted as its president a couple of years later. After a second stint with GM, during which he introduced the Chevrolet to a car-hungry nation, Durant was again dismissed. In 1920 he started up another car company, this time under his own name. Durant's Canadian branch plant opened in 1921 and built the Star and other models until all manufacturing ended in 1935.

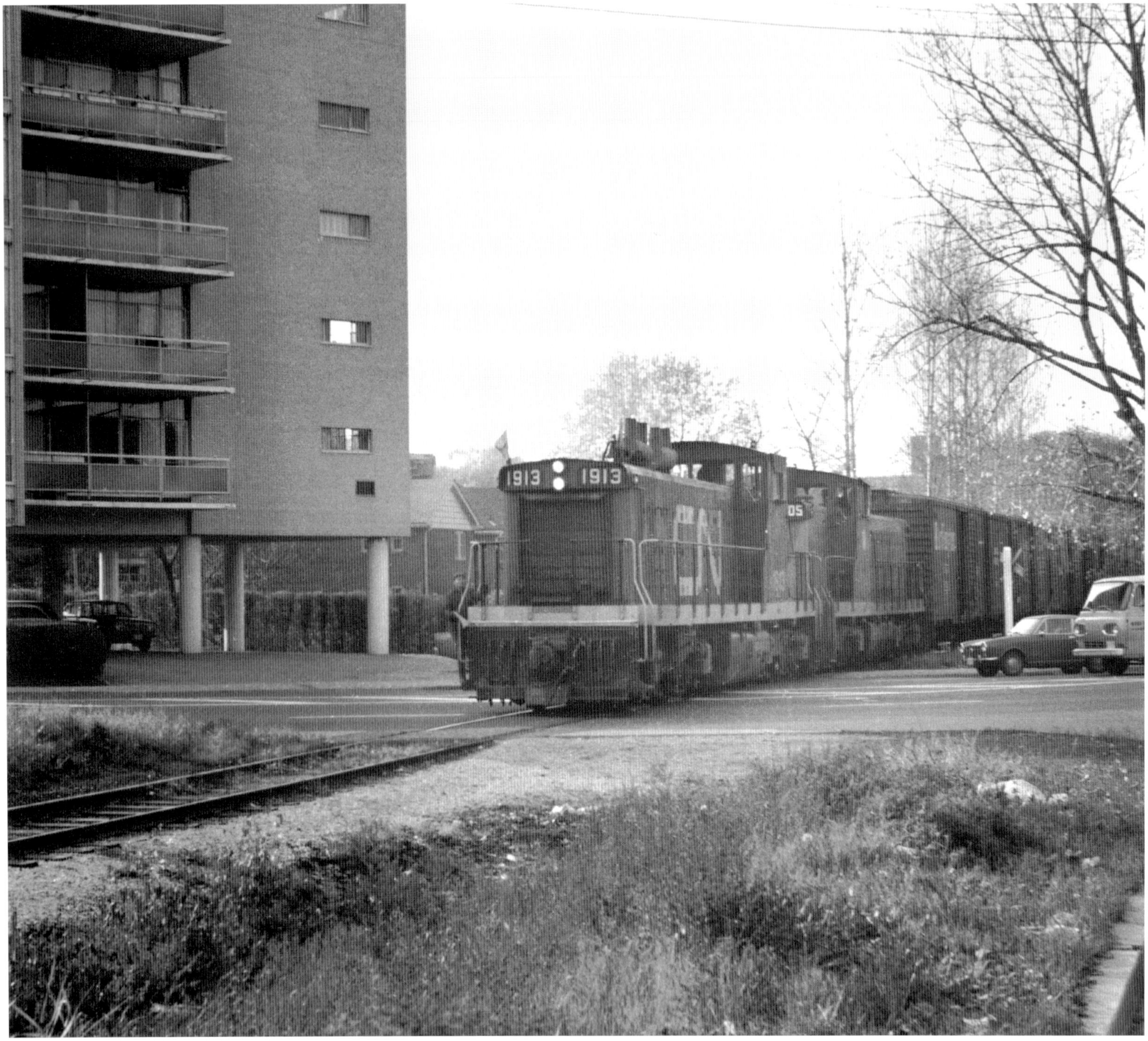

110 Even as late as the 1970s freight trains continued to operate on portions of the Belt Line's Don Loop.

Here we see an unscheduled CN freight train at the Oriole Parkway crossing.

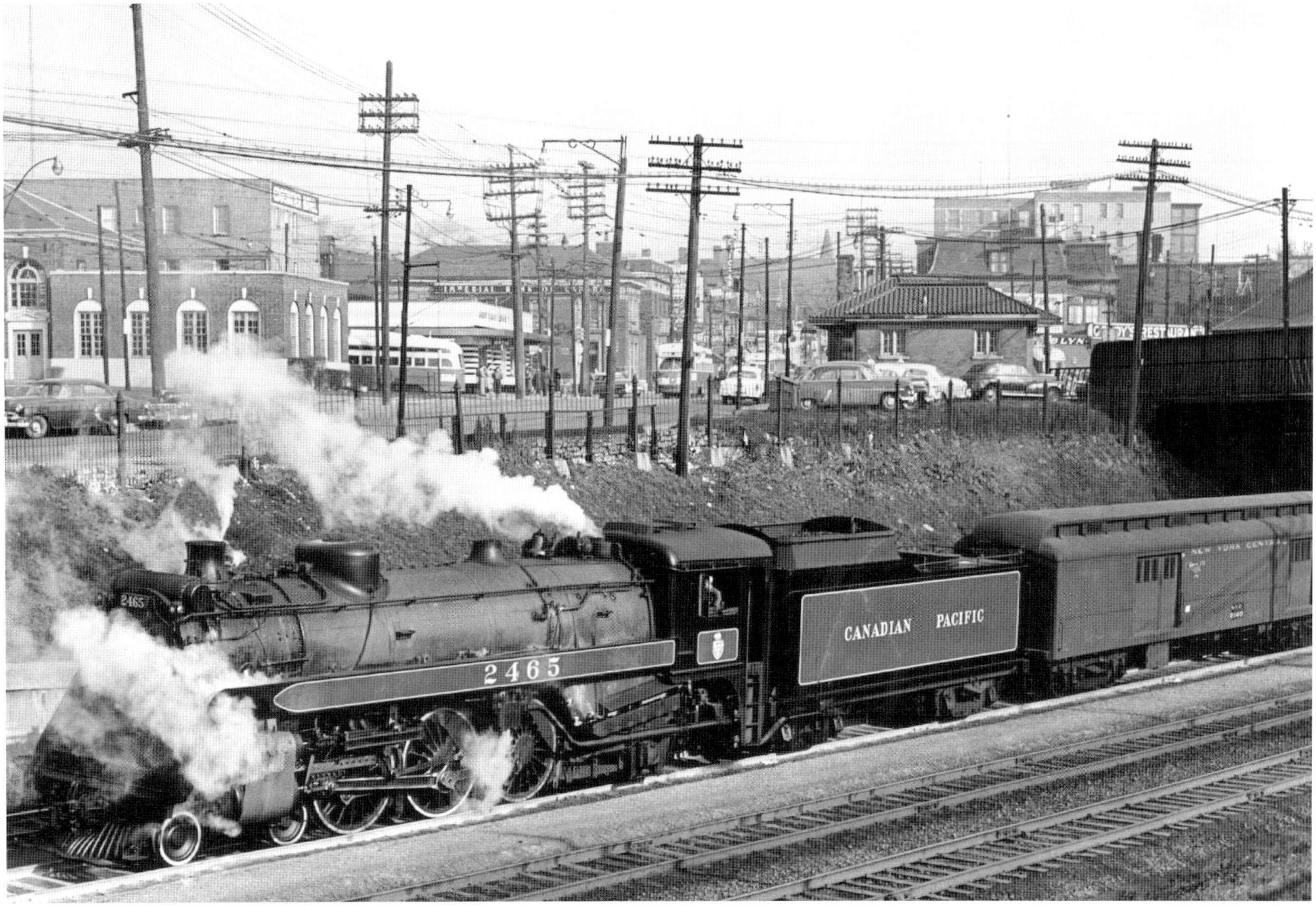

111 Steam trains and streetcars at Sunnyside, circa 1954.

To the extreme left of the view is the TTC's Roncesvalles carhouse. Streetcars have been stored at Roncesvalles Division ever since the privately owned Toronto Railway Company opened the first carhouse on this site in 1895. The present structure, with its many improvements, dates from 1923. Other prominent buildings visible in this view of the busy King, Queen, Roncesvalles, Queensway, and Lakeshore Road intersection are the Gray Coach bus terminal (now a fast food restaurant), a branch of the Imperial Bank of Canada (now a variety store), the former Scholes' Ocean Hotel (still standing), and the Sunnyside railway station with waiting and baggage rooms (both demolished). To the extreme right of the photograph is a portion of the old steel bridge that, before its demolition, connected this intersection with Lakeshore Road. The train in the foreground is a CPR Toronto–Buffalo–New York City passenger train (note the New York Central baggage car) and is powered by a "Pacific" 4-6-2 steam engine that was built by the Montreal Locomotive Works in June 1948. This engine was serviced at Toronto's historic John Street roundhouse (now the home of Steam Whistle Brewery) for almost all of its busy, but unusually short, operating career. Locomotive #2465 was scrapped in 1956 as a result of a major mechanical failure. The engine's demise was a sign of the future; within six years all Canadian main line steam engines had been replaced by diesels.

The city deals with increasing traffic problems

Cars and trucks have also had a major impact on the development of our city. In fact, one of the first things that the city had to do in order to accommodate the growing number of motorized vehicles was to round off the corners at street intersections. Originally, streets met at sharp angles. While buggies and wagons could negotiate the turns, right-turning cars and trucks would frequently mount the curb, resulting in near misses with unsuspecting pedestrians. Over time this led to the development of new verbal phraseology and demonstrative hand signals that are still recognizable today.

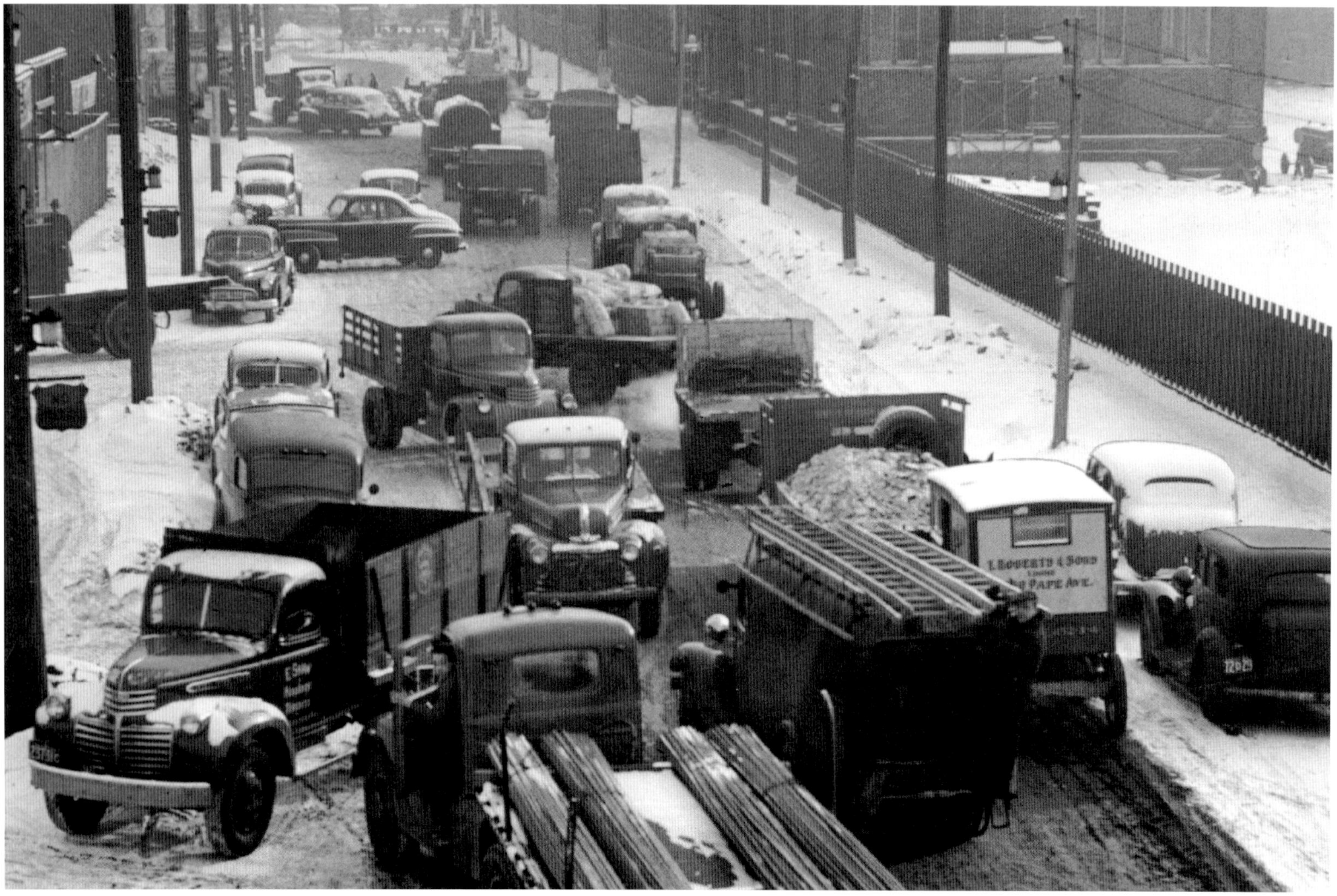

112 An assortment of coal trucks, lumber vans, private cars, and one lonely milk wagon clog Eastern Avenue in this view that looks east towards Booth Avenue, 1948.

To the extreme right of the photograph is the Consumers' Gas Company (now Enbridge Consumers' Gas) Station B, where "illuminating gas" had been manufactured by burning coal since the plant's opening in 1904. Station B was the site of the company's worst industrial accident when, on February 8, 1923, four workers were overcome by carbon monoxide fumes while doing maintenance work in the station's Valve House. Other employees rushed to their aid, and six of them were also overcome. In total, ten Consumers' Gas employees died at Station B that terrible winter day.

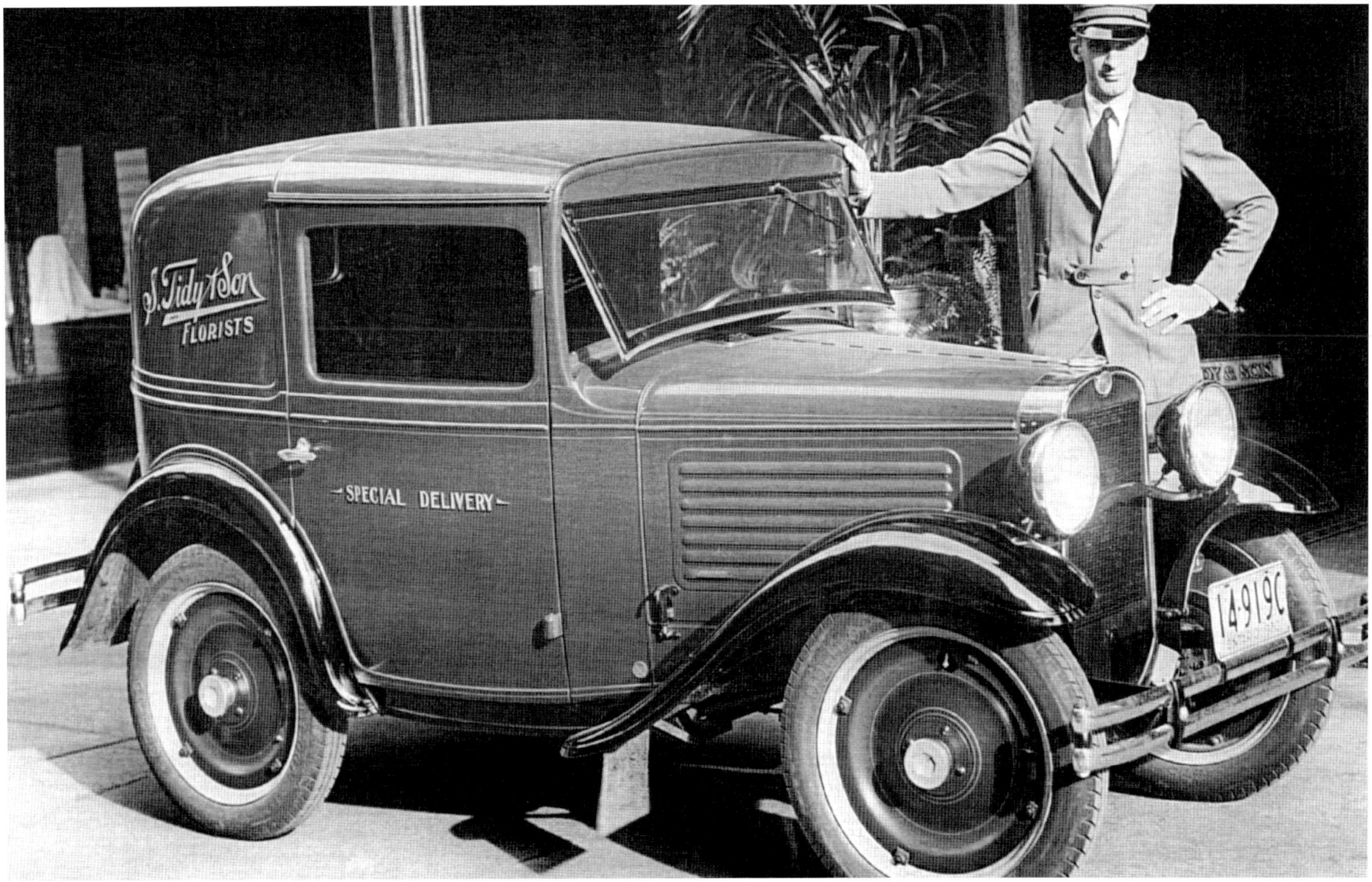

113 S. Tidy and Son deliveryman and his American Austin van, 1930. — *Courtesy Tidy's Flowers*

Many experts on the subject claim that the first motorized delivery wagon appeared on the streets of Toronto just before the start of the twentieth century. Built by the Still Motor Company in their factory on Yonge Street just south of Bloor, the unique vehicle was purchased for $1,000 by Parker's Dye Works (an enterprise that continues in business today as Parkers Cleaners). The contraption was battery-powered and looked very much like a horse-drawn buggy without the horse. One of the most unusual-looking delivery vehicles ever seen on the streets of Toronto was this American Austin Series 138 business coupe, owned by long-time city florist S. Tidy and Son. Stephen Tidy, a skilled gardener in the old country, immigrated to Toronto in 1873 and built a greenhouse on Ontario Street. So much in demand were his flowers and shrubs that within four years Tidy was operating a flower shop on King Street West, right where the T-D Centre now stands. After the founder's death in 1896, his three sons kept the business growing. In 1930, in an effort to expedite deliveries, the boys purchased an American Austin van from the factory in Butler, Pennsylvania. This odd-looking vehicle, which cost the boys about $600, was based on the British Austin basic design; it was left-hand drive, underhood clearances were different, and it was powered by a mirror image of the British Austin Seven 750cc four-cylinder engine. Its exterior design was selected to make it appear more "North American." Most automotive historians agree that the American Austin, with sales of twenty thousand vehicles over a period of only five years, was the first American compact car in history to sell in quantity. Like Parkers Dye Works, S. Tidy and Son is still in business as Tidy's Flowers. Both are among Toronto's oldest companies.

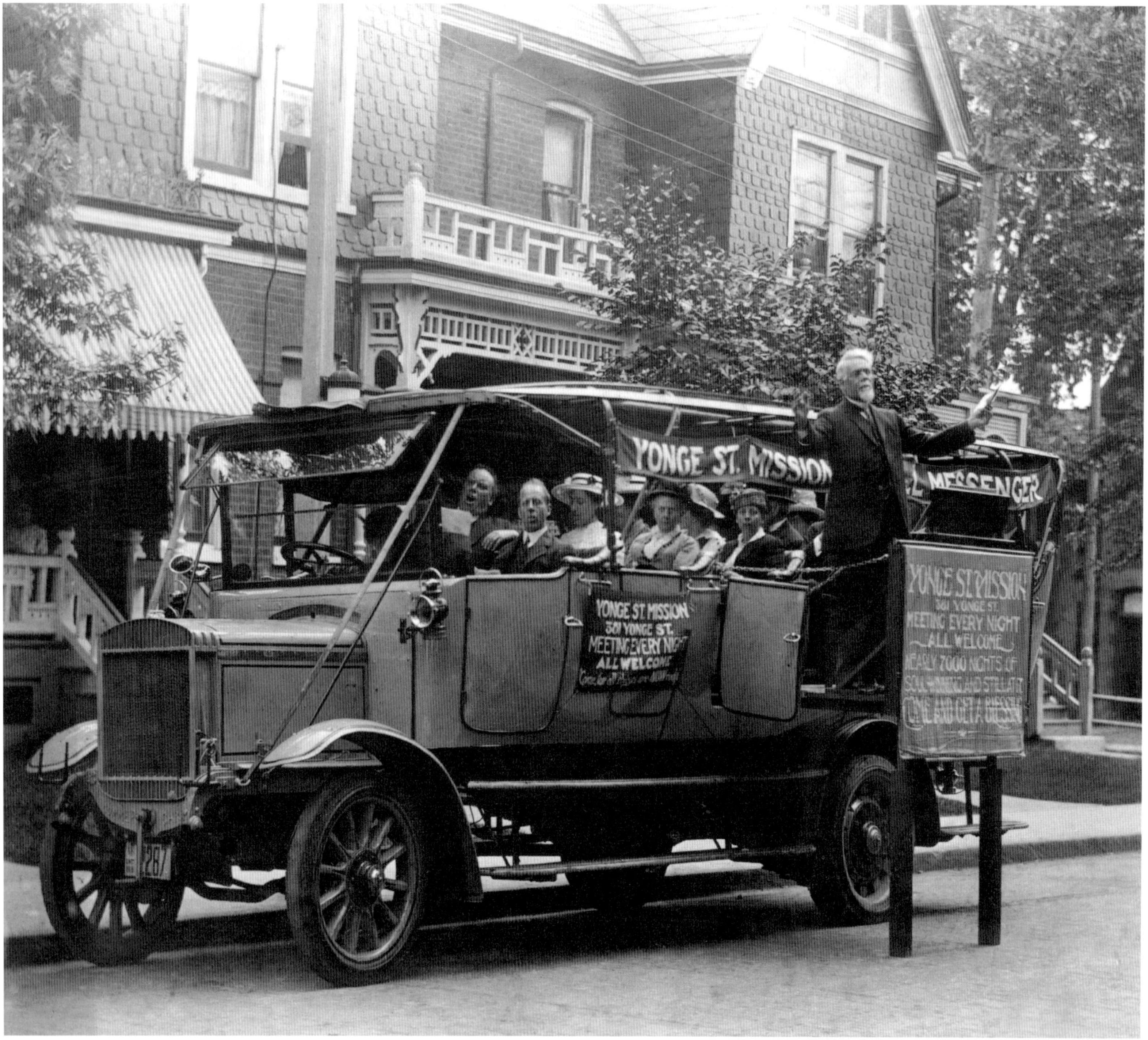

114 John "Hallelujah" Davis, who was born near Boston, Massachusetts in 1844 and emigrated to Toronto at the age of 28, established his Yonge Street Mission in 1896.

Here, taking advantage of the newest wonder of the age, the "horseless carriage," he preaches from his "Gospel Messenger" charabanc, c1920. The Mission, at 381 Yonge Street, continues as one of Toronto's most active social safety nets.

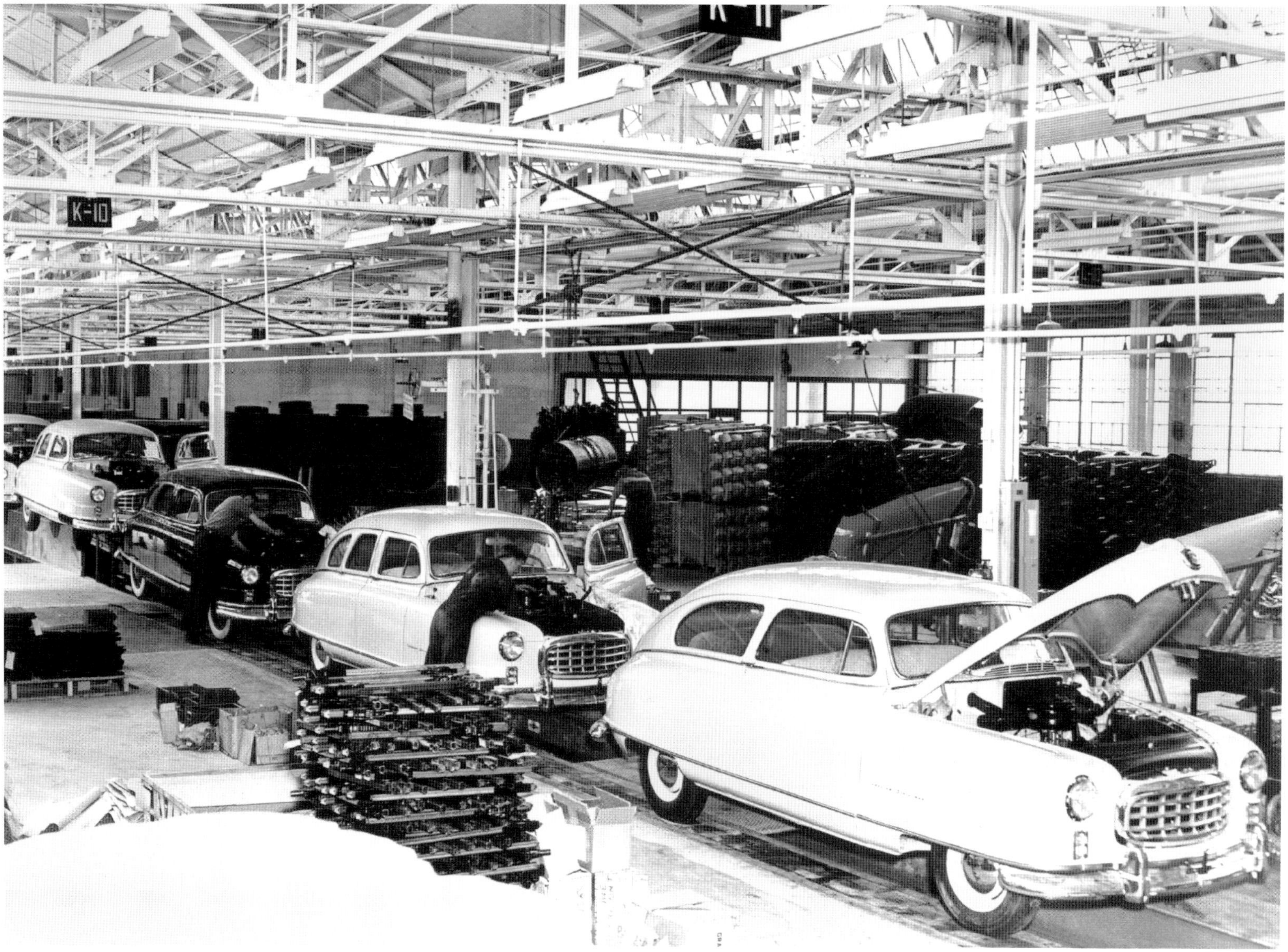

115 Nash Canadian Statesman automobiles begin rolling off the company's new assembly plant at 2951 Danforth Avenue in east Toronto, May 1950.

This factory was originally built in 1923–24 as a Ford assembly plant where the celebrated Model A was produced for many years. In 1946, once Ford had decided to move operations to Oakville, where it would open a modern factory in 1953, Nash Motors of Canada purchased the building, initially using it as a warehouse. The company then decided to build cars in Canada and soon installed an assembly line. The first car, a Nash Canadian Statesman, rolled off the new assembly line on May 11, 1950. While that particular car took two weeks to build, once more workers were hired and initial production problems corrected, cars began rolling off the line at the rate of two an hour. In 1954 Nash became part of the American Motors Corp. and the assembly of Ambassador and Rambler models continued at the Danforth Avenue factory until it was closed in 1957. Four years later AMC was back in business in a new factory in a place called Peel Village, not far from Brampton, Ontario. In 1962 a new Eaton's store opened in the former car plant. Today, the old factory building forms part of the Shoppers World shopping centre.

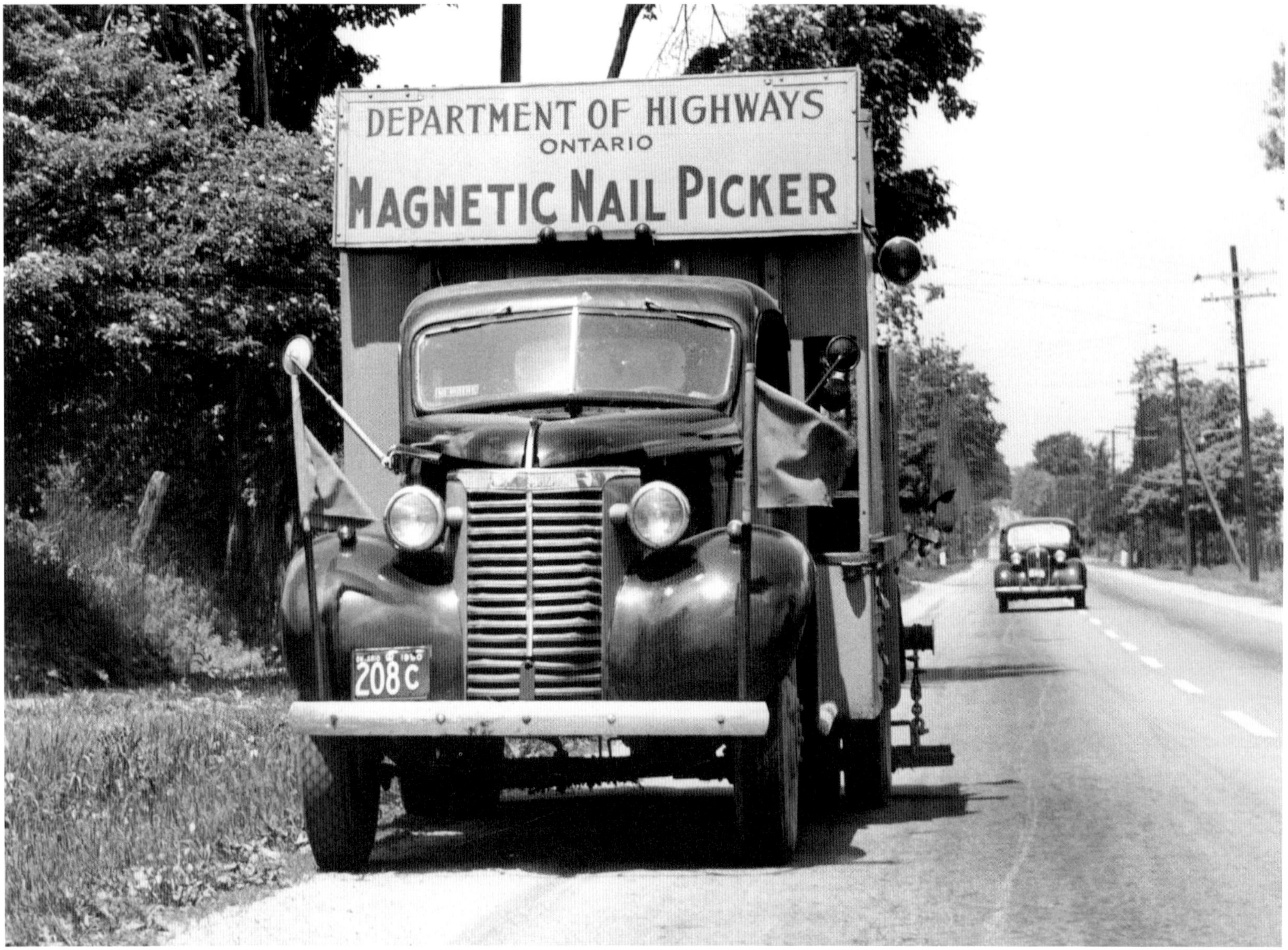

116 The Ontario Department of Highways' "Magnetic Nail Picker," 1950.

Recycling is not a new phenomenon. During the chaotic years of the Second World War, government rationing of rubber tires made these items precious commodities. In an effort to protect car and truck tires from a shortened life span or even destruction as a result of punctures by nails or other metal objects littering highways and byways throughout the province, staff of the Ontario Department of Highways concocted this special vehicle. A powerful magnet was devised using a second-hand generator, a used electric motor, and a large hand-wound coil of copper wire. As the truck cruised highways around the province, the homemade magnet would skim the road surface, picking up tons of stray metal pieces that would then be separated, melted down, and recycled into a variety of new products. After the war, Toronto city officials requested that the truck sweep the parking lots and lakeside areas at Sunnyside Beach, where barefooted bathers constantly complained of cut feet. When the former RCAF Equipment Depot at the foot of Yonge Street (a site now occupied by the Toronto Star building) was being dismantled, this same truck, reported to be the only one of its kind on the continent, swept the area and picked up more than two thousand pounds of stray nails.

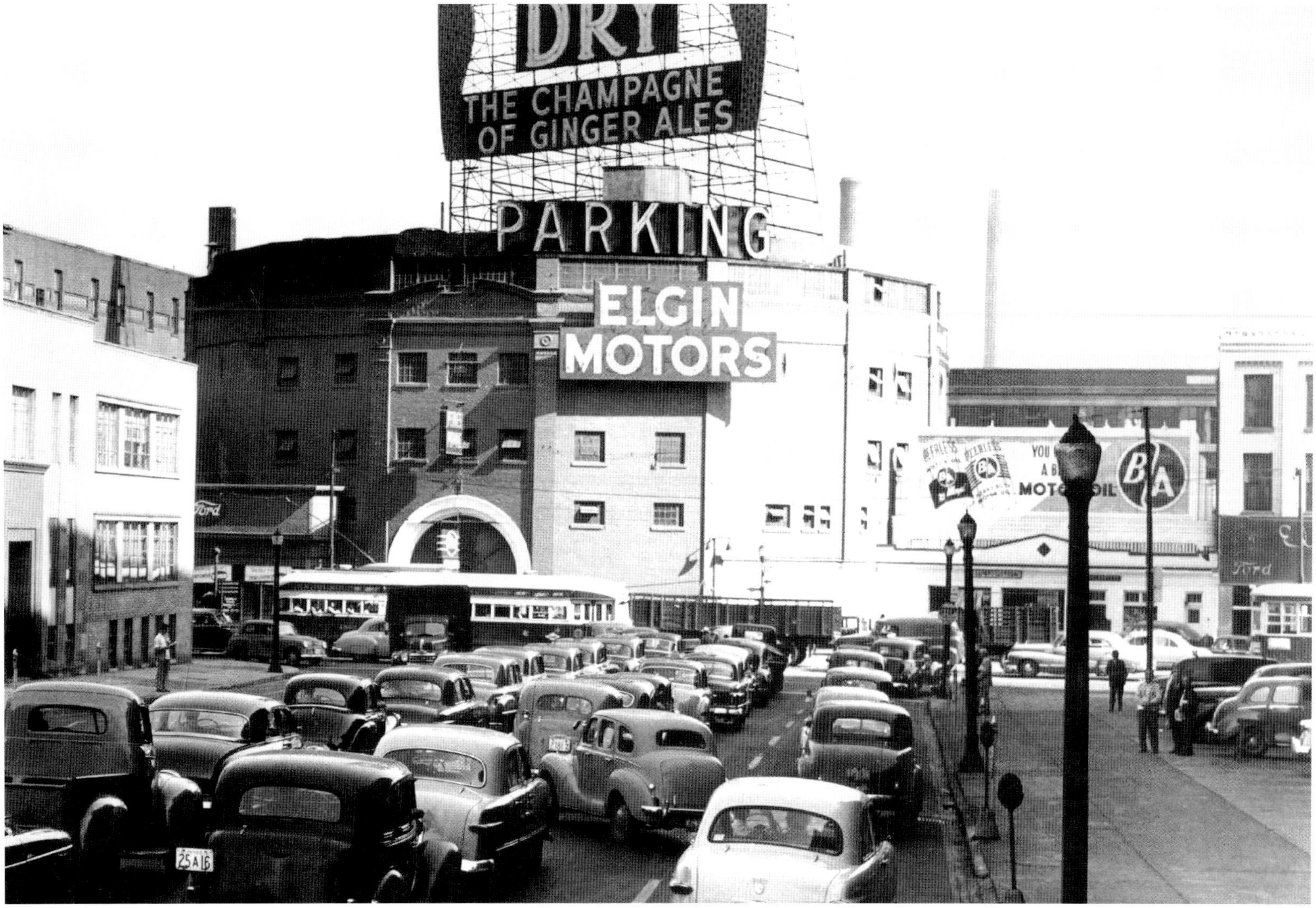

117 University Avenue looking south to Front Street, 1951.

When this photograph was taken in 1951, the Front and University intersection, one of the busiest in the city, was still void of electric traffic signals. All southbound traffic was controlled by the single stop sign visible in the photo. It wasn't until a few years later, when University Avenue had been extended diagonally to intersect with Front Street at York (a project that necessitated demolition of the buildings at the extreme left of the view), that electric traffic lights were finally installed. The circular building in the background, originally known as the Cyclorama, was built in the 1880s as a type of art gallery, where huge paintings depicting historic events, such as the Crucifixion and the Battle of Gettysburg, were viewed by paying customers. In this photograph the building is the home of Elgin Motors, a long-time Ford dealer. Also visible is a westbound PCC streetcar on the Bathurst "Tripper" route, a special rush hour service that operated to and from downtown from a loop at St. Clair Avenue via Bathurst and Front streets. This special service was cancelled in late March 1954, at the same time as the opening of Toronto's new Yonge Street subway. Another feature of Toronto's transportation past is shown on the large billboard that advertises B-A motor oil. Peerless oil and B-A 88 gasolines were produced by the British-American Oil Company, a Canadian operation that was established in Toronto in 1906. This long-time Canadian company was acquired by the American petroleum giant Gulf in 1966.

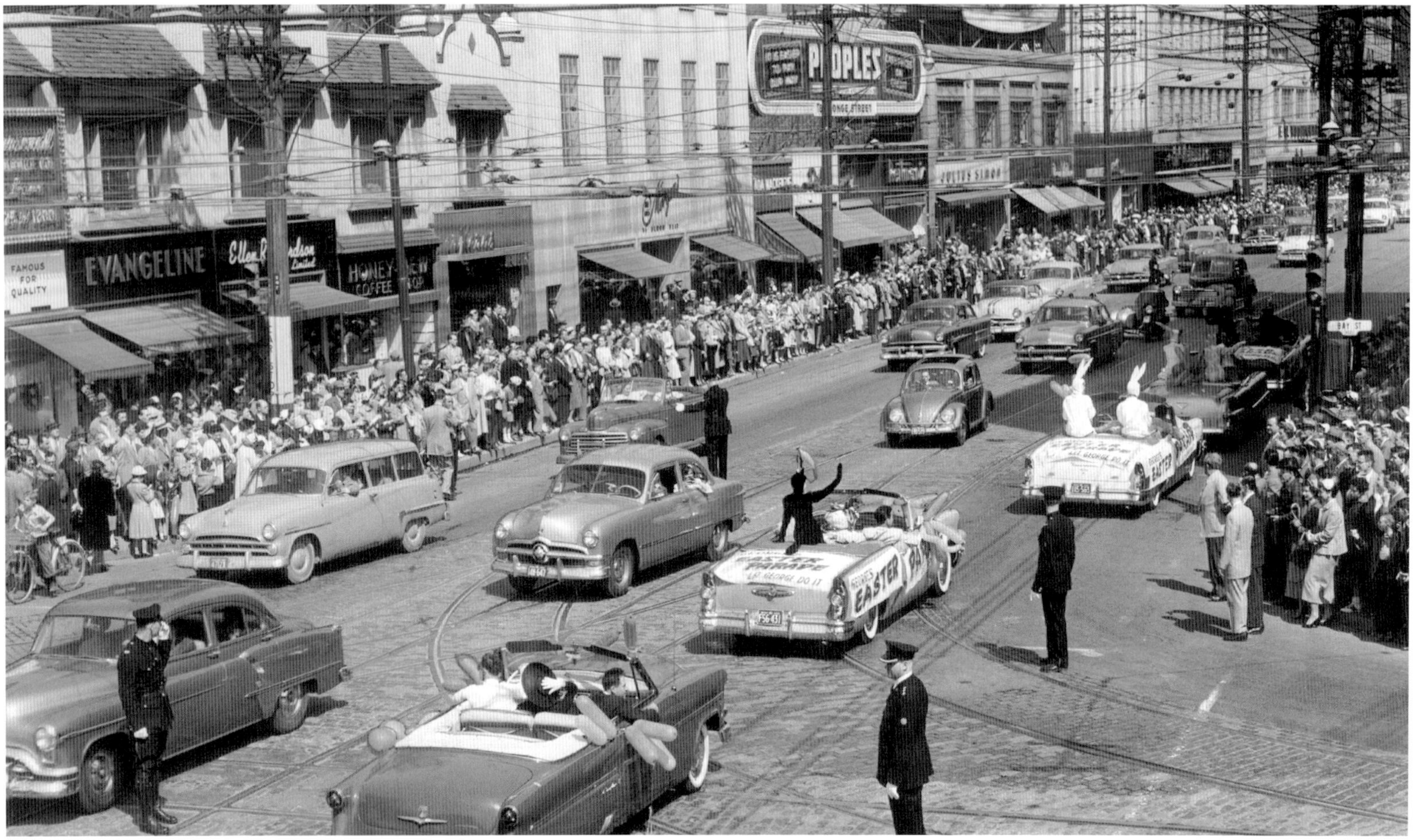

118 Everybody loves a parade, especially the annual Bloor Street Easter Parade, 1955.

One of the oldest traditions in Toronto's history is the Easter Parade, a chance for winter-weary citizens to promenade in their new spring finery for all to see. The first parades began to appear spontaneously in the early 1900s along the waterfront at Sunnyside. With the opening of the amusement park in 1922, these became more structured events, complete with sponsors and prizes. In the early 1950s rumours abounded that the demise of the amusement park was imminent, and before long the once famous Sunnyside Easter Parade was dead. However, it wasn't long before the parade was reborn on a stretch of trendy Bloor Street between Avenue Road and Yonge Street. Then, in Centennial Year, a new Easter Parade appeared on the boardwalk in the Beach area of the city. In 1973, under the sponsorship of the Beaches Lions Club, it moved to Queen Street East, where it remains an early spring feature. Around the same time this photograph was taken, this part of Bloor Street West had taken on the title of "Toronto's 5th Avenue," an interesting turn of events for a street that just a century before was nothing more than a dirt trail carved through the woods. It eventually took on the surname of a pioneer local businessman, brewer Joe Bloore (the final "e" appears on his headstone in the Necropolis). For the car buffs, some of the classics strung out along the street include three 1955 Buicks, a 1953 Dodge convertible, a 1953 Volkswagen, a 1942 Mercury, and the oldest, a 1941 Chevrolet. Some of the stores in the background will be recognizable to an earlier generation of Torontonians: Evangeline, Honey-Dew, Woolworth's, Morgan's, and Zeller's. Morgan's, which opened in Montreal in 1843, expanded into this, its first Toronto store, in 1950. The company was acquired by the Hudson's Bay Company in 1960. Zeller's, which was started in 1931 by Walter P. Zeller with stores in the Kitchener-Waterloo area, also came to Bloor Street in Toronto in 1950. Zeller's became part of The Bay in 1978.

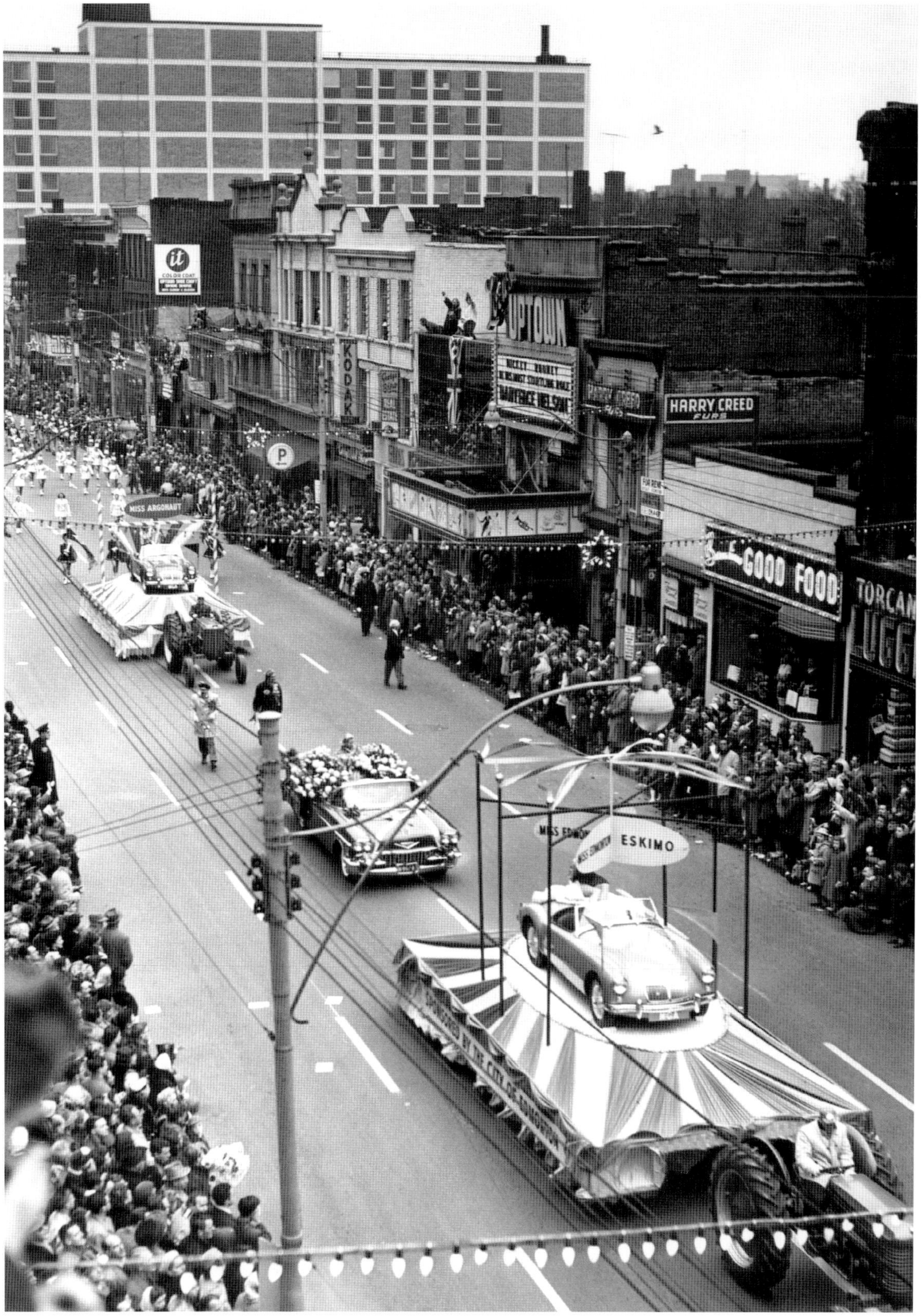

119 Grey Cup Parade on Yonge Street south of Bloor, 1957.

This parade, which was seen by a half million people (or so it was reported), was held on November 30, 1957, and was a run up to that afternoon's Grey Cup game at the University of Toronto's Varsity Stadium. (This facility has been closed and is now in the process of being redeveloped). The Hamilton Tiger Cats were victorious over the Winnipeg Blue Bombers, 32 to 7. The parade itself consisted of seventeen marching bands and dozens of floats, two of which featured representations of the first manmade earth satellites, the Russian-built Sputnik I and Sputnik II. The free world suddenly found itself second in the new, and very menacing, "space race." In the background, on the west side of Yonge Street, is the Uptown Theatre, which was opened by Marcus Loew in 1920 and which, with more than 2,700 seats, was one of Canada's largest movie houses. While still in business, it has an uncertain future. Incidentally, Carol Lucas, Miss B.C. Lions, was Miss Grey Cup 1957.

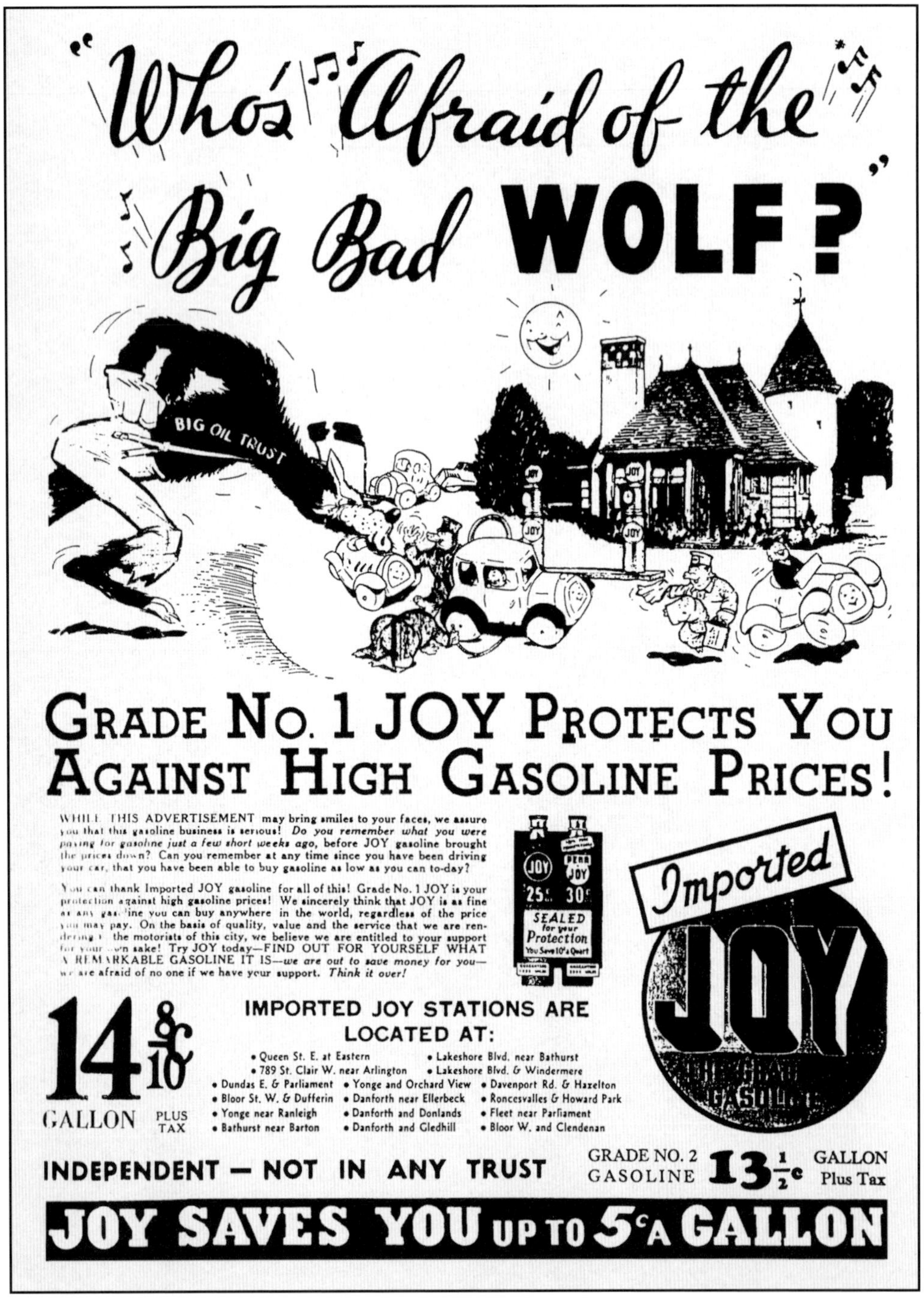

120 Newspaper advertisement for Joy Gasoline, 1938.

To see the impact that the automobile was having on the way the city looked and worked in the early years of the last century, compare the number of listings under "Automobile Garages" in the city directory published at the end of the Great War with that in the directory two decades later. In 1919, the directory lists approximately fifty such garages; in 1938 there are over a thousand garages and another two hundred or so "Automobile Dealers." And of course, as the number of cars on the streets increased, so too did the number of companies selling fuel to power them. Here are just a few of the branded service stations found around town in 1938: B & A, Canadian Oil (White Rose gasoline), Cities Service, Crown Dominion, Good Rich, Imperial, Joy, Lion, McColl-Frontenac, Perfection, Red Indian, Shell, Sun Oil, Supertest, and Vacuum Oil. The Joy Oil Company was a newcomer to the scene, having entered the service station business in Detroit in 1928. Their first station in Toronto opened in 1936, and eventually there were sixteen. Joy stations, designed to look like miniature castles, were unique to the city landscape. The owner of the company was Margaret Austin, a feisty American who, with her husband, owned Sunny Service south of the border. Entering the Toronto market was difficult; both the city and most of the other petroleum companies fought them at every turn, the former ostensibly due to safety concerns with the construction of an oil tank farm near Cherry Street, the latter fearing the outbreak of gasoline price wars. Joy gas was several cents cheaper per gallon, because Joy brought cheaper crude oil into Canada from Texas (and later Romania) by tanker and had the oil refined in its Montreal refinery, resulting in lower production costs. Joy eventually vanished from the Toronto scene (for reasons best left to the imagination) and today only one of their little stations, on Lake Shore Boulevard West at Windermere, remains. Its future remains undecided.

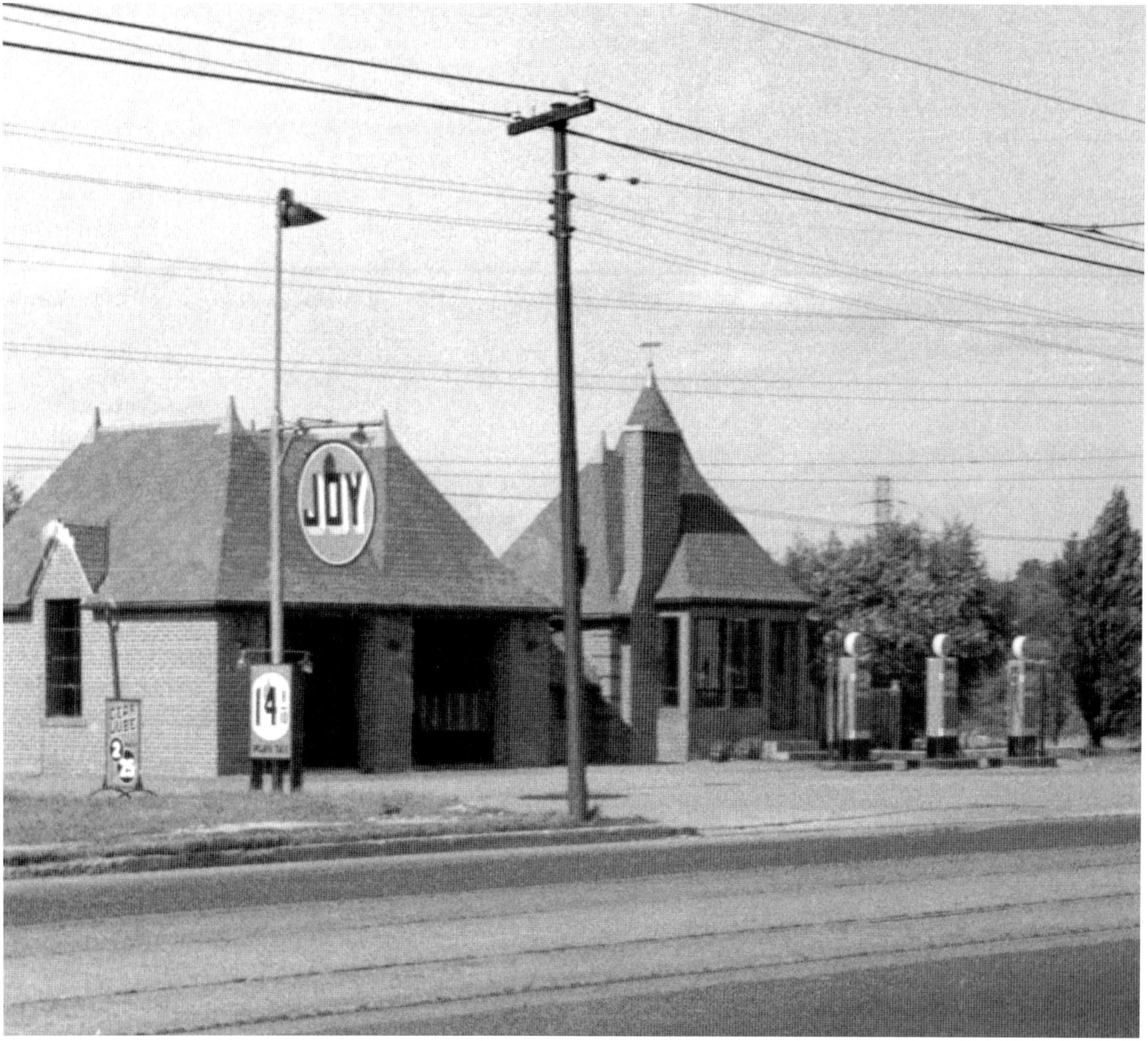

121 A former Joy Oil station still stands at the northwest corner of Lake Shore Boulevard West and Windermere Avenue.

Now abandoned, the little gem, a reminder of an earlier, car-crazed Toronto, is seen here in the 1940s.

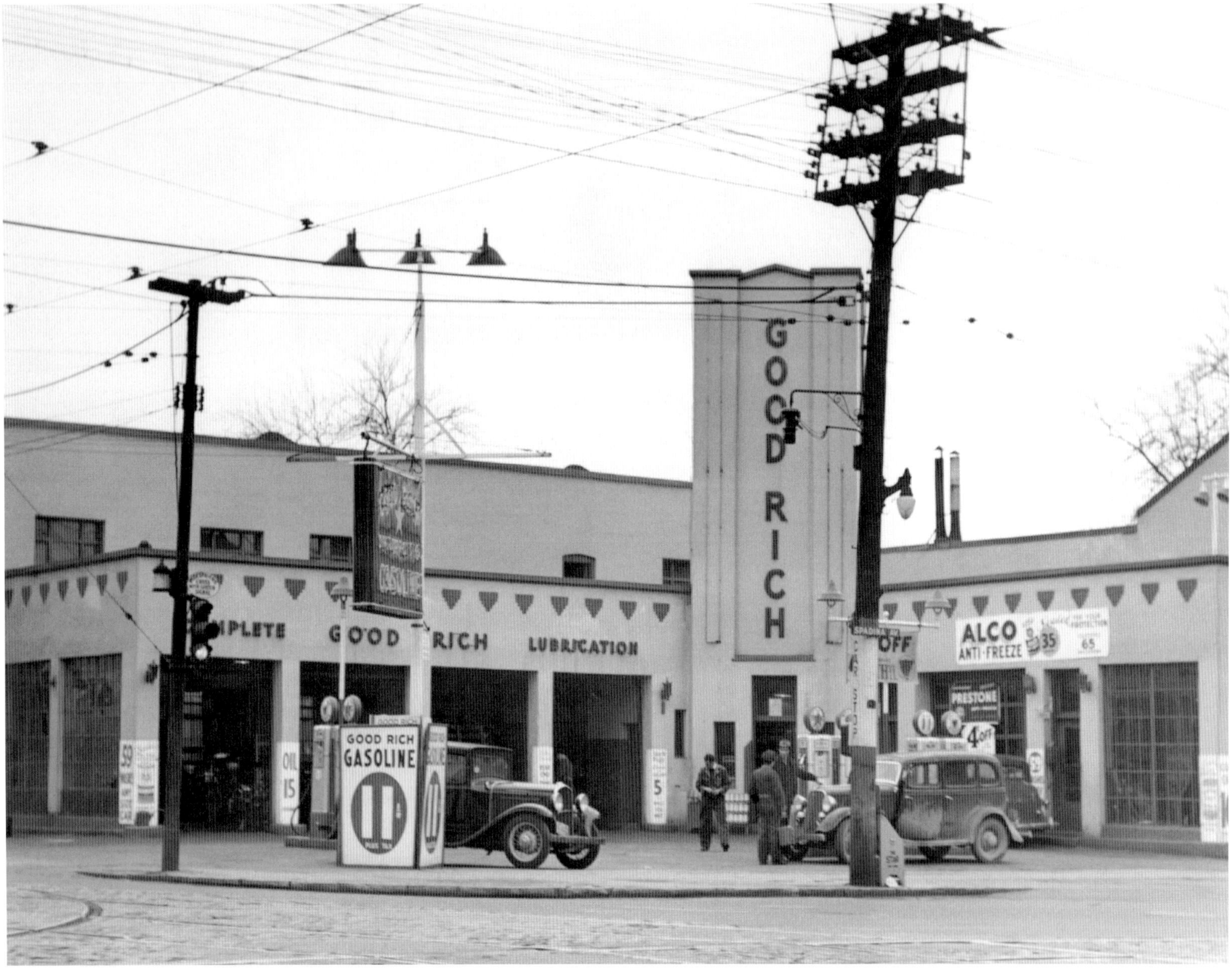

122 Good Rich service station at the southeast corner of Spadina Avenue and Dundas Street W., circa 1937.

Note the price of a gallon (!) of gasoline, 11.9 cents, "plus tax." This tax was introduced in 1925 (initially 3 cents per gallon) to help finance road building throughout the province. Good Rich was a wholly Canadian company that commenced operations in 1935, having purchased the three-year-old Lloyd's Refinery located on the Lake Ontario waterfront in Port Credit. Good Rich enlarged the refinery and began advertising it as the "largest independent refinery in Canada." Good Rich had about a dozen stations in Toronto, with others in smaller Ontario cities. The one shown in the photograph was considered one of the most modern gas stations anywhere in the nation. In 1947, Good Rich was purchased by Trinidad Leaseholds, and this particular station remained in business for the next few years under the Regent banner. Trinidad was purchased by Texaco in 1957, and its Canadian operations ended in 1995.

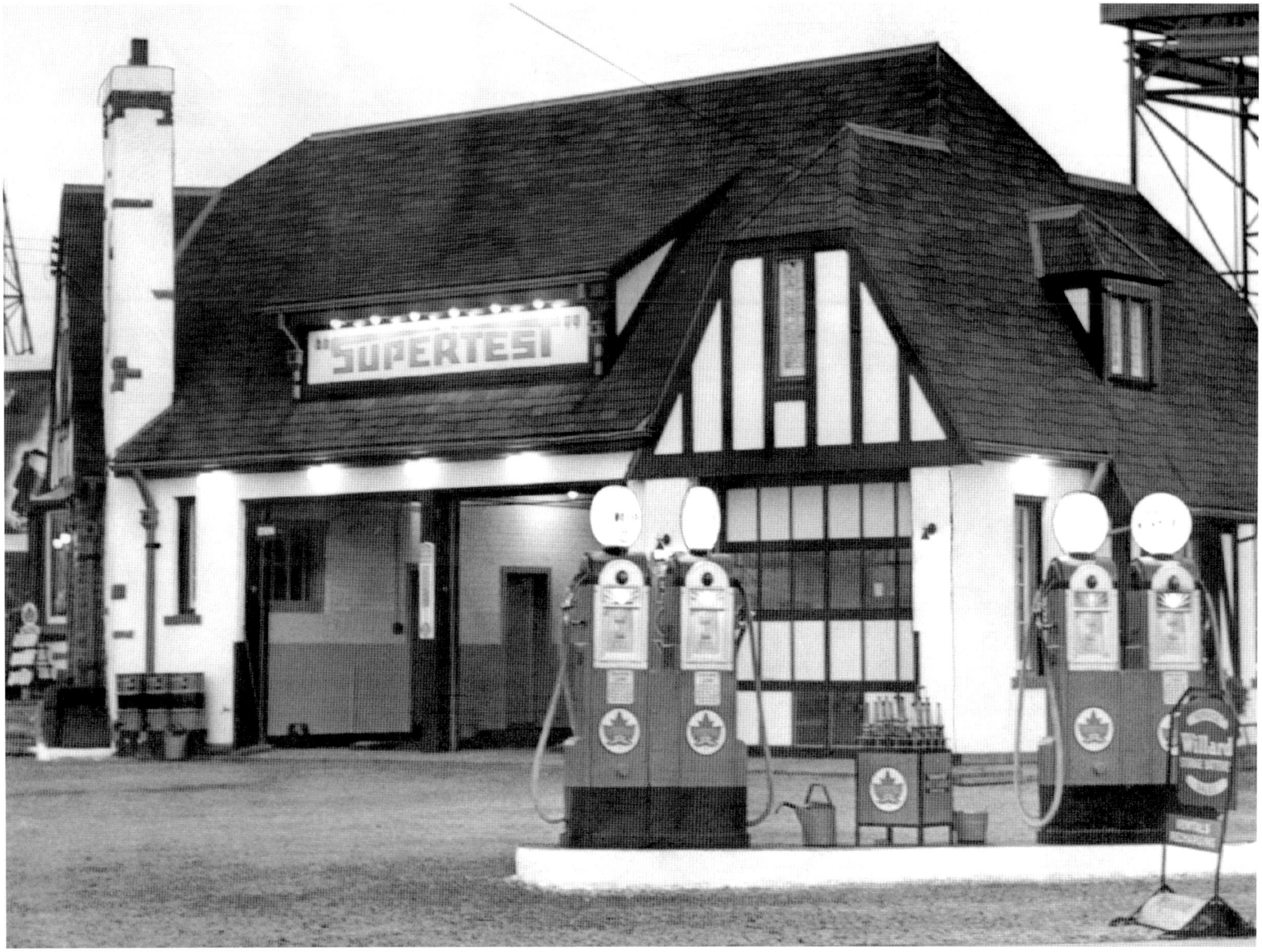

123 Supertest service station, Lake Shore Boulevard West, east of the Humber River bridge, 1939.

Supertest was another Canadian-born petroleum company, begun in London, Ontario in 1923. The first Supertest station opened in Toronto five years later. One reason for the amazing success of this company was the requirement that attendants wash the customer's windshield, check the battery and radiator, and ensure that the tires were properly inflated. All this extra service was free. Like many other Canadian petroleum companies, Supertest couldn't survive the domination of the industry by the multinationals and was sold to British Petroleum (BP) in 1971. A dozen years later, BP's Canadian assets were acquired by Petro-Canada.

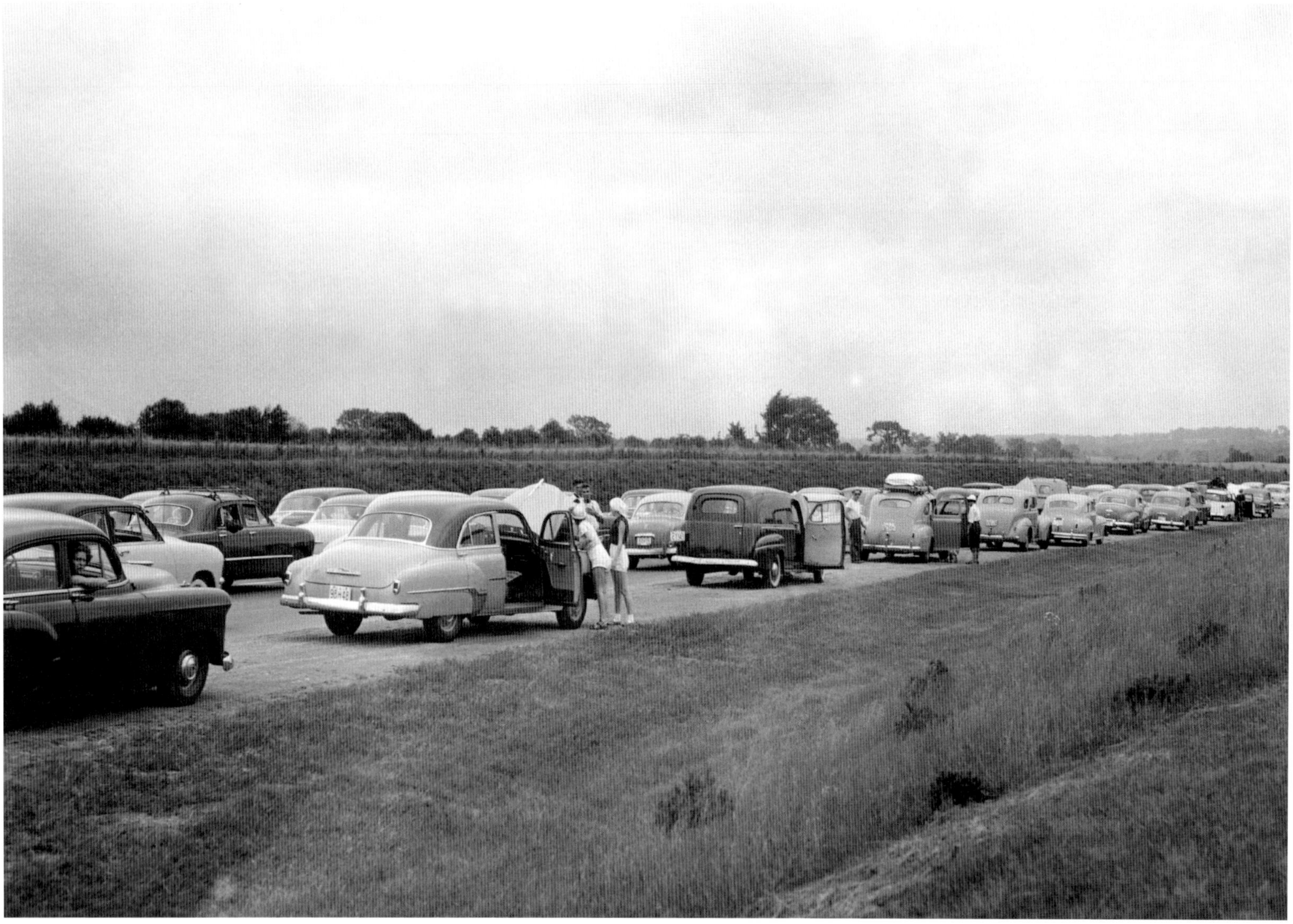

124 Cottage-bound on Highway 400, summer 1954.

Planning for what was originally called the Toronto–Barrie Highway began shortly after the end of the Second World War. By 1947, the necessary surveying, soil testing, and grading operations were complete. Throughout the following year numerous contracts were let, and by December 1, 1951, one lane in each direction was open to traffic. It took another year before two lanes each way were ready. In the summer of that same year government officials decided to rename the highway Number 400, the first in what would be a planned series of major four-lane superhighways throughout the province. But that rather nondescript identification wasn't good enough for the Barrie Junior Chamber of Commerce, which then campaigned to have the new highway renamed the Huronia Highway instead. In fact, members even erected several signs with that proclamation, but it was to no avail. The Department of Highways removed the signs, and in October of 1952 the Toronto–Barrie Highway became known as simply Highway 400. The Highway 400 to Dufferin Street portion of what was originally called the Toronto Bypass, then Highway 401, and now the Macdonald-Cartier Freeway opened to four lanes of traffic in the summer of 1952. The full 11.6-kilometre (7.2-mile) stretch of the Bypass (Weston Road to Yonge Street) was ready by the end of that same year.

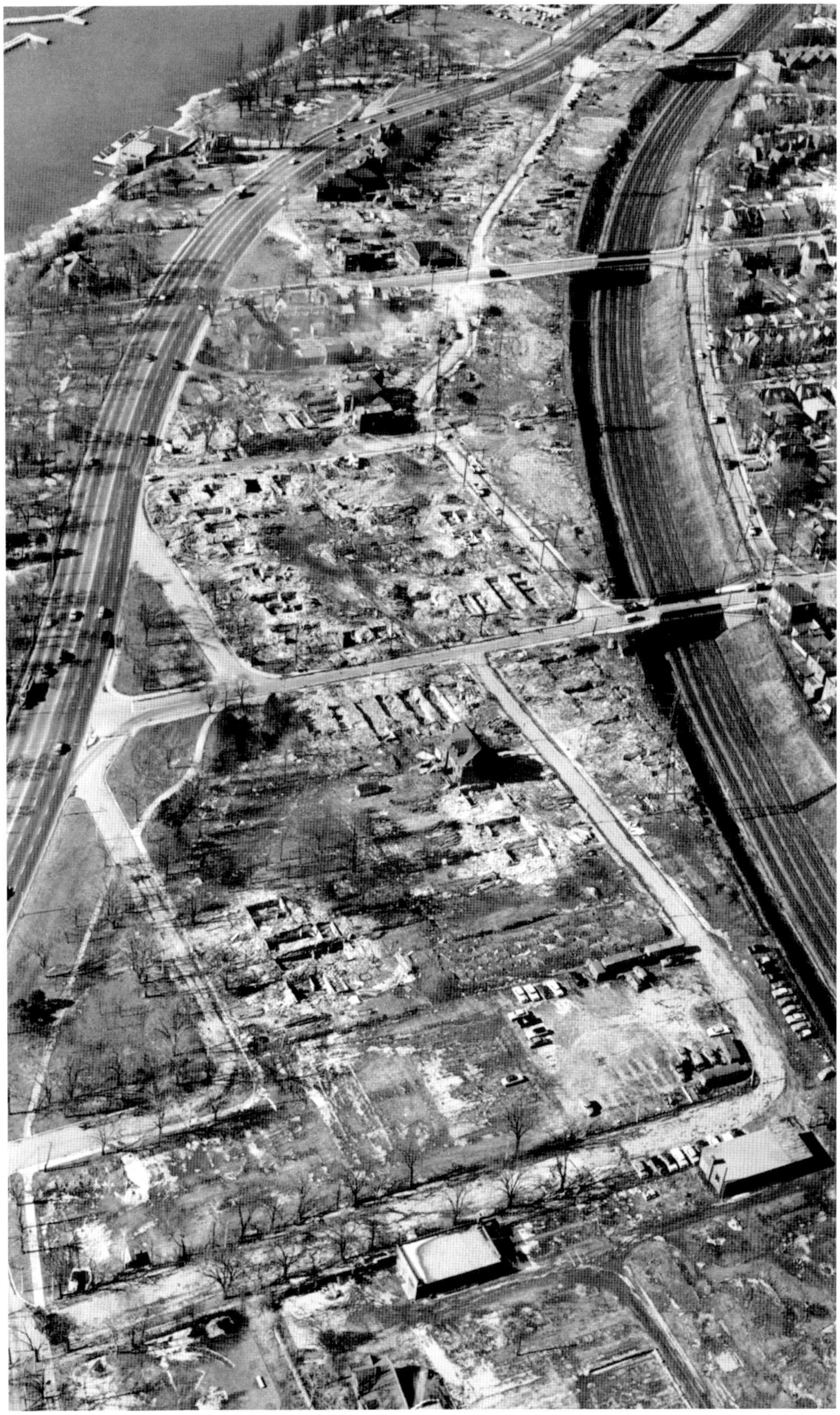

125 Clearing out South Parkdale for the new Gardiner Expressway, circa 1956.

When the announcement of Toronto's new cross-waterfront expressway was made in the *Toronto Telegram* on May 3, 1954, the story was prefaced by the words "How would you like to drive through Toronto during rush-hour at 50 miles an hour and without a billboard in sight?" The possibilities of this new 15.3-kilometre (9.5-mile) superhighway stretching from the Queen Elizabeth Highway in the west to Woodbine Race track in the east were mind-boggling for the beleaguered car and truck drivers of half a century ago. With virtually all of the western routes into and out of the city overflowing with traffic, the new highway, which had been first proposed in the mid-1940s, was truly a godsend — and it might even be ready within four years. There were even plans to have a portion of the highway built out over the lake and a provision for a two-level parking lot for fifteen hundred cars under the Yonge-to-Parliament elevated section. One minor problem associated with building the new highway was the need to demolish approximately 150 houses in the south Parkdale part of town — oh well. A few other interesting proposals for the new highway would have made it a toll road, incorporated a provision for public transit, and taken it through Scarborough to hook up with the new Highway 401. This latter possibility would require the demolition of another 650 or so homes and businesses. Political posturing as to where the expressway should end in the eastern part of Toronto resulted in the massive project staggering to a start, with the first section (the Humber River to Jameson Avenue) ready in 1958. Other sections opened as follows: Jameson to Spadina Avenue in 1962, Spadina to York in 1963, and York to the new Don Valley Parkway and the DVP to Bloor Street in late 1964.

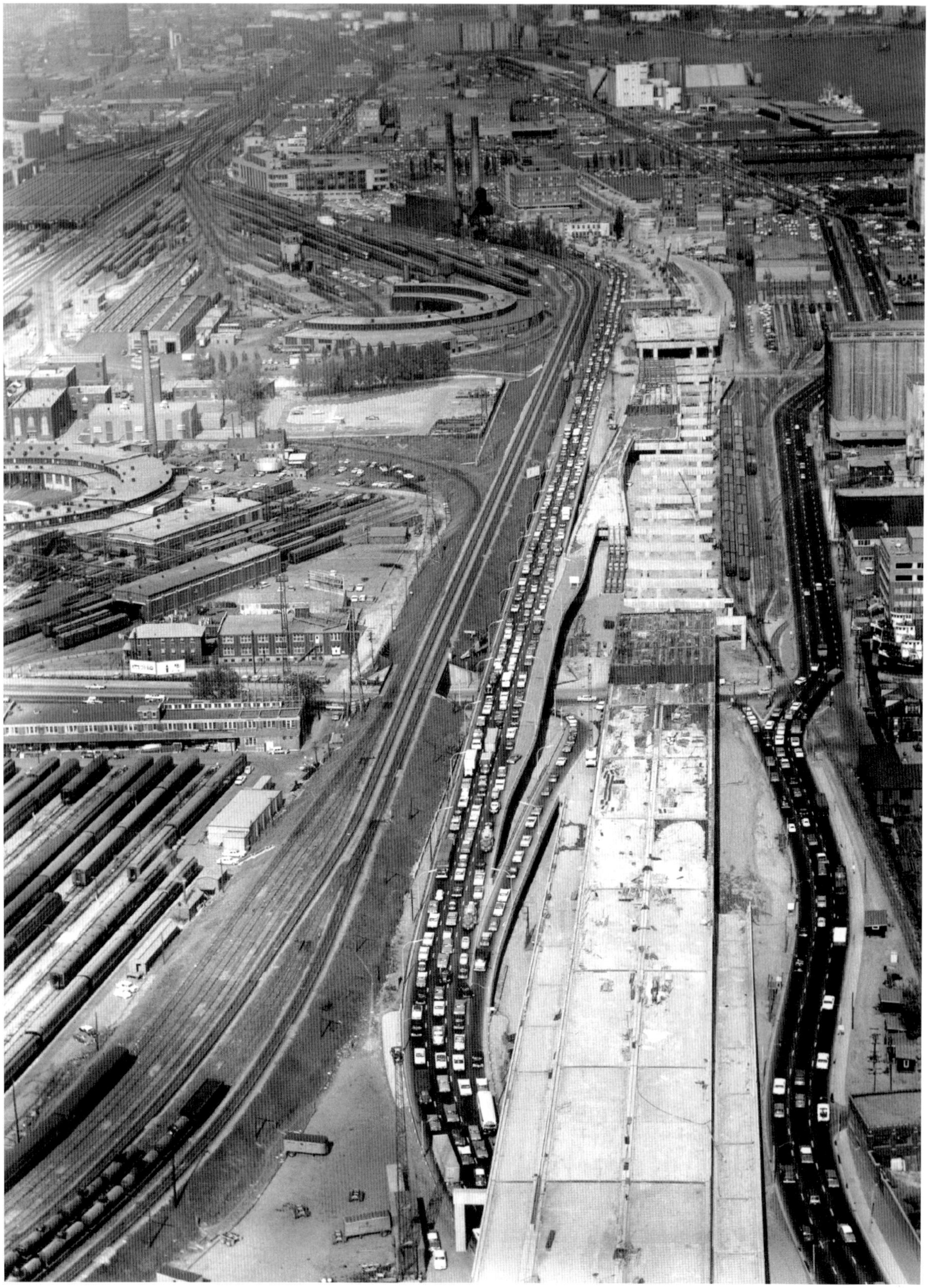

126 Construction of the Spadina Avenue to York Street portion of the Gardiner Expressway caused traffic chaos in the spring of 1962.

Note the two railway roundhouses to the left of the view. The CN facility (left) was demolished and SkyDome now stands on the site; the CP structure still stands, though hopes of it ever becoming a museum devoted to Canadian-born transportation innovations fade daily.

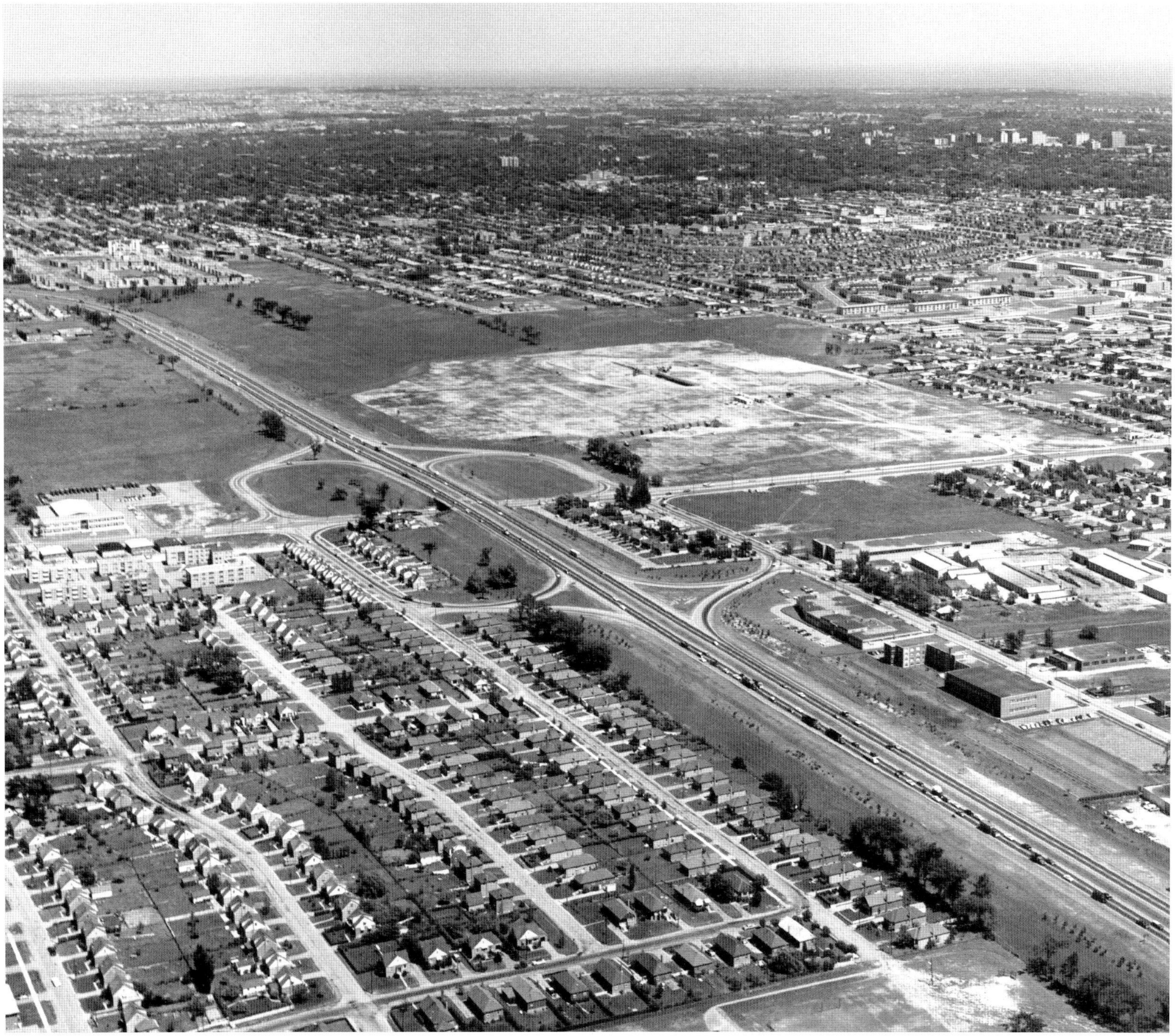

127 Highway 401 looking southeast towards the Dufferin Street interchange and the future site of Yorkdale Shopping Centre, spring 1962.

Yorkdale, the city's first regional shopping centre, boasted 125 stores and parking for 6,736 automobiles when it was officially opened on February 1, 1964.

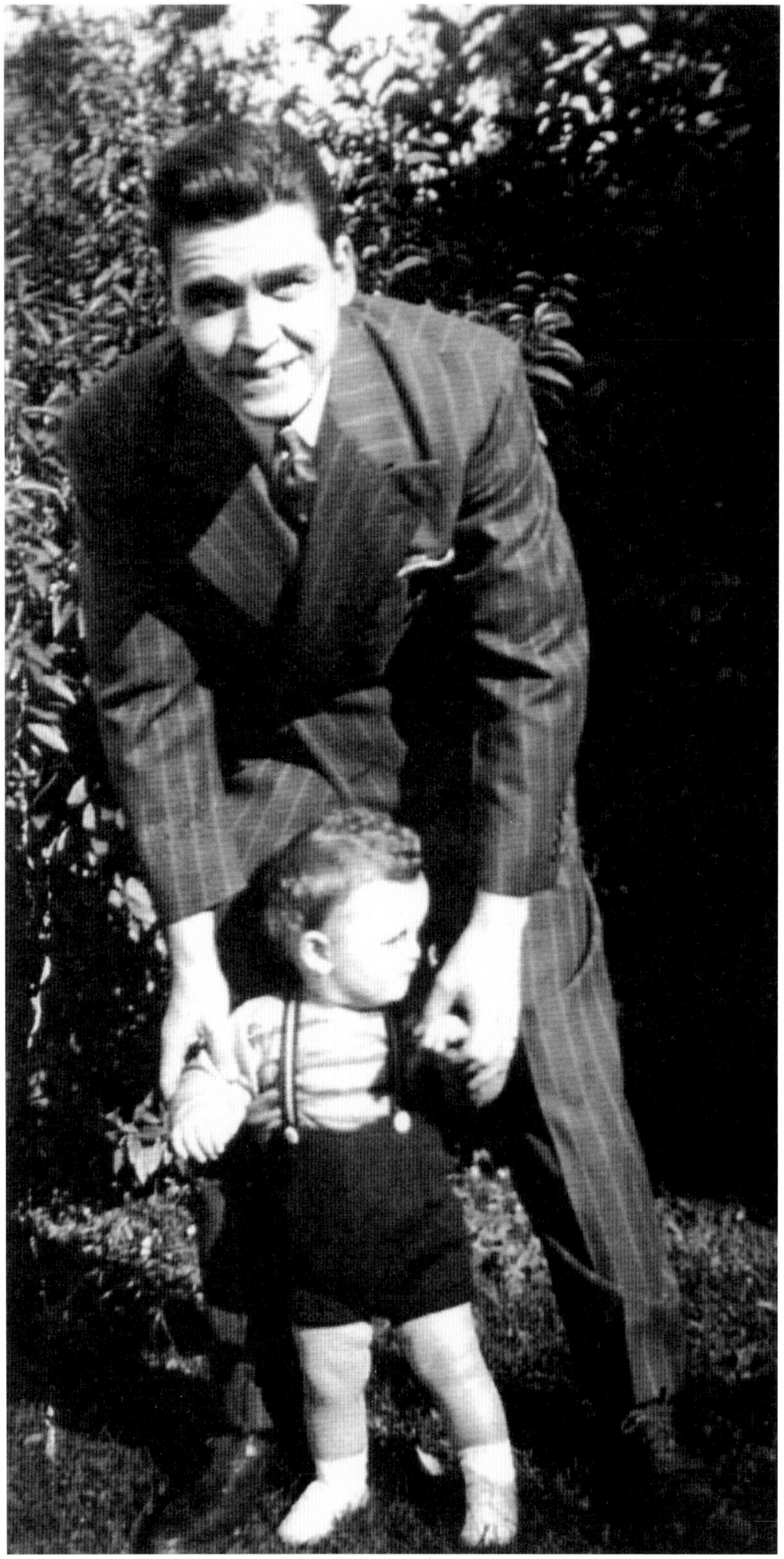

128 "The Way I Was" with my father in 1943.